The Acquisition of Business Assets

To Dibble

The Acquisition of Business Assets

Jonathan Myers, *Solicitor,*
Lovell White Durrant

© Longman Group UK Ltd

ISBN 0 85121 8733

Published by
Longman Group UK Limited
21–27 Lamb's Conduit Street, London WC1N 3NJ

Associated offices

Australia, Hong Kong, Malaysia, Singapore, USA

The right of Jonathan Myers to be identified as the Author of this Work has been asserted by him in accordance with the Copyright, Designs and Patents Act 1988

A CIP catalogue record for this book is available from the British Library.

Typeset by Servis Filmsetting Ltd, Manchester
Printed in Great Britain by Biddles of Guildford Ltd.

Contents

Preface

The aim of this book is to provide a concise, practical guide for practitioners involved in the acquisition of business assets. This book does not expand upon academic points which are better dealt with by numerous text books. Naturally, the book is not a solution to all issues but does explain the difficult areas and suggest possible solutions.

I would like to acknowledge my gratitude to my colleagues at Lovell White Durrant who have provided helpful commentary. In particular my thanks are due to Dele Oguntimoju (Taxation), Michael Ryley (Employment), Steve Ito (Pensions), Tim Jones (Competition), Patrick Wheeler (Intellectual Property), Mark Frewin (Property) and also to Lauressa Bowyer for her many hours of typing and retyping.

The law stated is that in force in England on 1 June 1993.

J D Myers
London
October 1993

Table of Cases

XV

Table of Statutes

Table of Statutory Instruments

Chapter 1

General Considerations

INTRODUCTION

This book covers the legal aspects of buying a business by acquiring its assets and undertaking rather than by acquiring the shares of the company that operates the target business. It is a guide for practitioners and does not attempt to expound academic points which are better dealt with by numerous text books.

This book deals mainly with the purchase of business assets from a corporate vendor by a corporate purchaser. However, the points covered are also relevant for sales by sole traders and by partnerships. Indeed, for sole traders and partnerships a disposal of their business will, by its nature, inevitably involve the sale of business assets. The acquisition by the corporate purchaser may be the purchase of the vendor's entire assets and undertaking. More often it involves the purchase of an operational division or the purchase of one business owned and operated by a multitude of different companies within a group.

It is envisaged that the legal practitioner will first be instructed once the client believes he has struck a deal. The client may feel the deal has been negotiated and merely wants the lawyer to tie up the loose ends. Alternatively he may consider that the transaction has only been agreed in outline and requires the lawyer to negotiate the details. Whatever the circumstances the lawyer should resist either his own temptation or the client's instructions to prepare a contract at this early stage. If the job is to be done well then the drafting and negotiating of the sale agreement should involve the least time in the entire exercise. At this stage the most important step, assuming it is practical, is for the lawyer to meet the client. The purpose of the initial meeting is for the lawyer to:

    (a) understand why the business is being bought and sold;

    (b) understand what is being sold;

    (c) identify who is involved; and

1

(d) discuss the structure for the sale, namely whether the purchaser should buy assets or shares.

Purpose of the sale

A brief discussion with the vendor or purchaser of the reasons for the sale should bring out the main commercial objectives of the transaction including specific concerns. Identification of key issues at an early stage should make the whole negotiation process easier and will enable the lawyer to co-ordinate an appropriate team of specialist advisers (if necessary) from the outset. The reasons for selling can vary enormously and will affect what the vendor sees as the key issues. Examples of different reasons for selling include sales by individual vendors who are retiring, sales by individuals who have inherited a family business, management buy-outs, group reorganisations, unbundling or demergers as defence mechanisms against a hostile bid, group rationalisations and sales by receivers and liquidators.

The timing of the transaction may be connected with the purpose of the sale and be critical to the transaction as a whole. For example, if the sale is a demerger or unbundling process used to counter a hostile bid, timing will be critical. If the bidder's aim is to separate a target into its component parts, it has failed if the target does this itself. Similarly timing is important in group rationalisations either because the transaction must be completed within the current financial year or because overheads must be reduced rapidly if the core business is to survive.

Identify the business being sold

As obvious as it may sound, it is essential to understand and identify the business being sold and the use to which the purchaser will put the assets. This cannot be overstressed. Share sales tend to be rather less complex structurally than asset sales in that through buying the shares the purchaser acquires all the assets and liabilities of the target. Consequently due diligence forms a larger and more important part of share sales than of asset sales and in terms of legal costs can be an expensive process. With asset sales the purchaser does not assume the liabilities except as regards employees, unless this is specifically agreed. With an asset sale the purchaser selects the assets he wishes to buy and leaves behind all other assets. The key to selecting the appropriate assets is as follows:

(1) First, understand what the business is that the purchaser wishes to buy. The Standard Sale Agreement (see Appendix III) includes a definition of the business and this in turn is used to

identify the assets and undertaking the purchaser will buy. It is important to consider each individual element of the business. For example if the business primarily sells paperclips does it include the design, manufacture, packing and sale of the paperclips or is it simply a sales outlet?

(2) Second, understand what assets the vendor uses in order to conduct the business being sold, where these assets are located and who owns them. In the example of the paperclip business it is important to know whether the vendor has its own or an external design team. If it is external, who owns the designs? Equally, it is important to know where the manufacturing and design processes take place and whether the vendor packages the paperclips itself or sub-contracts this service externally.

If the vendor is part of a group it is also necessary to determine which companies in the group own the assets used in the business. For example the leases of the factories may be owned by one service company whereas the long term supply or customer contracts are held by a different company. Care must be taken to ensure that these assets are included in the sale if they are needed by the purchaser for operating the business.

(3) Third, and most important, understand which of the assets used by the vendor are required by the purchaser and which are to be excluded and retained by the vendor. In the example of the paperclip business the purchaser may already have its own metal foundry and surplus premises and will not wish to acquire the long term supply contracts or factory premises. Equally the purchaser may consider that the in-house design team and intellectual property is fundamental to the business and will not be prepared to enter into any transaction unless the key employees are transferred. Conversely, if the design team designs other products for the vendor's group, the vendor may not be willing to agree to the transfer.

(4) Fourth, although it is unusual the purchaser may have agreed to take over some liabilities such as payments under leasing arrangements or after sales repairs. Considerable care must be taken to ensure that the precise nature and scope of these liabilities is identified and that the purchaser does not acquire more than he bargained for.

Identify who is involved

Asset sales are complex transactions. Both the vendor and purchaser will require specialist advisers in various fields. Once the nature of the business has been discussed and key concerns identified it is necessary to consider in what areas specialist advice should be sought. Lawyers will be willing to advise in areas such as employment, pensions, intellectual property, taxation and property. In addition the purchaser will need to specify other advisers such as accountants (particularly if a report or completion accounts are to be prepared), actuaries, insurance brokers and bankers.

The important point is then to establish a clear line of communication. The lawyer should, in accordance with Law Society Rule 15(2), write naming the partner in charge and the members of the team. At this stage it is also necessary to specify the individuals in the purchaser's or vendor's organisation who are authorised to give instructions.

Assets or shares?

One of the first issues the parties will face is the decision of whether to buy assets or shares. This section discusses some of the many separate factors that affect the decision. It cannot be overstressed that in any particular circumstance most of the factors will be irrelevant and that one factor will tend to dominate the decision and determine the form of any particular sale. Which factor predominates will depend largely on the relative negotiating strengths of the vendor and the purchaser and on the specific circumstances of the parties, their objectives and the business being sold. For this reason the list of factors is neither exhaustive, nor set out in order of importance. Many of the factors, particularly relating to taxation are discussed in more detail later in this book.

Double tax charge

If the vendor's business has been successful he will normally wish to sell the shares in the company that operates the business. The classic reason is to avoid a double tax charge. This really applies only where the vendor is a company owned by individuals. A double tax charge may arise if the company sells its assets and the vendor wishes to extract the realised profit from the company. In such a case the company may face corporation tax arising from the disposal of its chargeable assets. If the vendor then extracts from the company what profit is left, either by way of dividend or a return of capital, this will also be taxed.

The concept of double tax is not always as drastic as it first sounds, particularly in the current economic climate where trading and capital losses are perhaps more common than profits and gains. The vendor's company may be able to carry earlier losses forward to set off against the gain or if the capital assets were bought by the company only within the past few years, it is possible that there may be a loss rather than a gain. Also it should not be assumed that the vendor will wish solely to extract the profit from the company. In any event a vendor should always be required to quantify the potential tax charge. There is a prevailing tendency to discuss the theory of the double tax charge without quantifying it. The vendor should be encouraged to consider the practical consequences or even the many reliefs that may be available.

Liabilities

The main reason a purchaser will insist on buying assets, and may perhaps refuse to deal with the vendor on any other basis, is that the purchaser can then select which of the vendor's liabilities he will assume and more importantly which he will leave behind for the vendor to deal with. If, however, the purchaser buys shares, he buys the company as a separate living entity together with its entire history, which of course includes all its liabilities both actual and contingent. Alternatively, if the purchaser buys assets he does not take over any of the vendor's liabilities (except employees) unless expressly agreed.

The purchaser will insist on an asset sale either because he has identified significant liabilities which he cannot risk or because he is simply nervous as to the general state of the business and the risk of unforeseen liabilities. Specific liabilities often relate to actual or potential litigation or to unprofitable contracts. The following are other more general concerns as to the extent of the liabilities:

(1) If the purchaser's finance for the transaction is limited he will probably need to know the precise amount of the liabilities he is taking over. In such a situation the purchaser will normally be willing to take over the vendor's liabilities up to a specified maximum or as specifically itemised in completion accounts.

(2) The purchaser may have no confidence in either the vendor's ability or the vendor's intention to fully and properly disclose the liabilities of the company.

(3) The purchaser may consider that given the financial standing of the vendor there would be little prospect of recovery from the vendor for undisclosed liabilities of the company even if the purchaser were to succeed with a warranty claim against the vendor.

Receivership sale

Receivers nearly always sell assets. To a large extent this is merely one example of the preceding factor, namely that the purchaser is not willing to take over all the liabilities of the company. Also a receiver is only appointed over the assets of a company and does not control the shares in that company unless he has been appointed receiver over the assets of its holding company. Hence, the receiver may not be in a position to sell the shares.

Due diligence

With an asset sale, the purchaser's due diligence exercise should be quicker and therefore cheaper and it will probably be safer. The distinction in the due diligence exercise is that, with an asset sale, the purchaser is verifying the existence and ownership of specified assets and liabilities, but with the share sale the purchaser's exercise is to check the non-existence of certain matters. It is nearly always quicker to check what exists than to check that nothing extra is included in the assets and liabilities of the company.

Warranties and measure of damages

As with due diligence, the warranties in an asset sale are likely to be far shorter and hence quicker and cheaper to negotiate than in a share sale. Further, in a share sale a purchaser will also wish to negotiate a tax indemnity. This is not needed in an asset sale.

The purchaser may consider that if there is a warranty claim the measure of damages will be more generous in an asset sale than in a share sale. In a share sale, unless the warranties are on an indemnity basis, the purchaser will claim for the reduction in value of the shares. This is not necessarily as great as the increase in the liabilities of the target company related to the breach of warranty, particularly if the purchaser has only paid a nominal price for the shares in the first place.

Consents and minority shareholdings

As a general rule the number of third party consents that a vendor (or perhaps purchaser) must obtain are normally greater if it is an asset as opposed to a share sale. The main consents required are discussed later, but include landlord's consent to assign leases and major customer's or supplier's consents to assign contracts. In the current economic climate, however, consents are usually quite easy to obtain if the purchaser appears financially sound particularly in comparison with the vendor. As a result, consents have tended to be easier and quicker to obtain in recent years.

It should also be borne in mind that in some circumstances, there may well be extensive consent requirements even on a share sale. These may arise if there are minority shareholders in a company and pre-emption rules apply either under the Articles of Association or under a shareholders' agreement. Shareholder consents can be particularly difficult and time-consuming to obtain if some of the shares are held in a trust either for the families of other shareholders or for employees or as part of the company's pension fund. A purchaser of shares may need to resort to petitioning the court to buy out minority shareholders.

Change of control provisions

Contracts with the company's major suppliers or customers may have change of control provisions. These would entitle the customers or suppliers to terminate their contracts with the company if some or all of the shares in the company are sold and may therefore deprive the purchaser of the company's main assets. These place the parties in a similar position to an asset sale, namely needing the consent of a third party. Examples of change of control provision are commonly found in software licences and contracts to supply Government departments such as the Ministry of Defence. It is therefore by no means certain that share sales would be quicker to complete.

Financial assistance

The Companies Act (CA) 1985, s 151 will prevent the purchaser from using the assets of the company or a subsidiary as security for a loan made to enable the purchaser to buy the shares in that company. There are no such restrictions on an asset sale. The purchaser can therefore grant a charge over the assets purchased as security for financing the transaction. This can be particularly important in highly geared transactions such as management buy-outs.

Vendor's group organisation

The purchaser may discover either at the outset of negotiations or from its due diligence exercise that the ownership of the assets it wishes to buy is distributed amongst various companies in the vendor's group. By buying one company in the group the purchaser will not necessarily acquire all the assets necessary to conduct that company's business. For example, the vendor may have used separate management companies within its group for owning properties, employing staff and maintaining insurance. Alternatively, the business may be run as divisions of separate group companies. Such a purchaser may choose to buy selected assets from selected companies. In any event the purchaser will want to know that he is buying the right assets from the right companies. This may be dealt with by each company selling to the purchaser such assets as it owns. Alternatively, the vendor may either set up a new company and transfer assets into the company from all over its group before selling the shares in the new company, or transfer the assets into its main trading company which will in turn transfer the assets to the purchaser. A multiple transfer of assets may be time consuming if consents are required and may give rise to unnecessary stamp duty. When dealing with a sale from a group, there will be important tax considerations which are addressed later in the book (see Chapter 7).

Divisions—hiving assets

Sometimes the business being sold is operated as a division of the vendor rather than as a separate subsidiary. Either the purchaser will buy the relevant assets of the division direct from the vendor or the vendor will transfer its assets into a new company before selling the shares in that company. This concept is often referred to as a 'hiving' of assets. Alternatively the vendor may wish to transfer out to a new company all the assets and liabilities not being sold or assumed and then sell the shares in the original company. Again there are tax considerations which are discussed later.

Stamp duty

The purchaser of shares will pay stamp duty at a half of one per cent on the total consideration paid or payable on the shares. The purchaser of assets will pay stamp duty at double this rate but on only part of the consideration. Therefore, it is quite possible that the actual amount of stamp duty paid may be considerably less than that on a share sale. For example, the purchaser of assets will only pay stamp duty on that part of the total consideration which is attributable to assets transferred by the documents. Such assets include property, intellectual property, goodwill, debtors and fixed plant. Stamp duty is not necessarily paid on assets transferred by delivery and the purchaser may wish to apportion a significant part of the price to these assets, subject to other tax considerations.

Furthermore, if documents of transfer for certain assets are executed outside the United Kingdom stamp duty will not be payable until the documents are brought back into the United Kingdom. By executing and keeping such documents outside the United Kingdom the purchaser can significantly reduce the stamp duty it must pay. Stamp duty cannot be avoided on a share sale as the stock transfer forms will need to be stamped before the purchaser can be registered as the owner of the shares.

Capital allowances

The purchaser of assets can claim capital allowances on certain items such as plant and machinery (see Chapter 7, page 122). The risk for the vendor of assets is the possibility of balancing charges if the assets are sold for more than their written-down value.

Base cost

For the purpose of its own capital gains base cost the purchaser of assets buys those assets at the value attributed to them at the time of purchase. If the purchaser buys shares, the company will continue to be considered as having bought those assets at the original base cost to the company. If the purchaser himself intends to dispose subsequently of these assets he will prefer to have acquired them at the higher base cost to minimise capital gains or corporation tax on a subsequent disposal.

Tax losses

The tax losses of a company may be available to the purchaser of the shares in the company but are not available to the purchaser of the assets unless the hive across procedure is followed (see Chapter 7, page 127). Under the Income and Corporation Taxes Act (TA) 1988, s 343, if certain conditions are satisfied, the tax losses of a trade can be transferred to a new company and set off against future profits of the same trade if conducted by the receiving company. Such an arrangement is subject to attack by the Inland Revenue under the principle in *Furniss v Dawson* [1984] 1 All ER 530 whereby the Inland Revenue are entitled to ignore each of the individual steps and consider the substance of the transaction as a whole.

In any event most vendors recognise the value that the tax losses represent to the purchaser and negotiate some payment for these. However, a purchaser should not pay for tax losses until such time as it has been able to use them.

Roll-over relief

The purchaser may defer tax payable on the sale of other qualifying assets by rolling over the gain made on disposal into the acquisition cost under the Taxation of Chargeable Gains Act (TCGA) 1992, s 152. This is discussed in Chapter 7, page 119.

Trading stock and work in progress

The purchaser will be able to deduct before tax the acquisition cost of trading stock and work in progress. The acquisition cost of shares, on the other hand, is not deductible.

EARLY STEPS

Heads of terms

The purchaser and vendor should consider whether or not they wish to sign heads of terms before proceeding to due diligence and negotiating the sale agreement. The heads of terms, which should be a brief document, will summarise in general terms the basis of the transaction that has been agreed in principle. Most importantly the heads of terms must state that they are 'subject to contract'. This is a hallowed statement signifying that the terms set out are nothing more than an intention and will not become binding on any party until a formal contract has been negotiated, executed and exchanged. The concept goes back at least as far as 1877 when Jessel MR stated in *Winn v Bull* [1877] 7 Ch 29 that 'where you have a proposal or agreement made in writing expressed to be subject to a formal contract being prepared, it means what it says; it is subject to and is dependent upon a formal contract being prepared.' The danger of not including a statement of subject to contract is that one party may subsequently argue that the heads are a binding agreement either as the main contract or as a collateral contract. In deciding whether a contract exists it was stressed in *Kleinwort Benson Ltd v Malaysian Mining Corp* [1987] 1 WLR 799 and *Edwards v Skyways Limited* [1964] 1 All ER 494 that a court will seek to ascertain what common intentions should be ascribed to the parties from the terms of the documents in question and the surrounding circumstances. Even if the words 'subject to contract' are used the purchaser should be wary of creating an ancillary contract. Disputes that arise when a sale is not completed often centre around allegations by the vendor that it has incurred costs such as commissioning an accountant's report on the express understanding that the purchaser would reimburse the cost if the transaction failed.

The execution of heads of terms is not an essential part of the transaction and will not be appropriate in all instances. The various disadvantages and advantages in using heads of terms are listed below.

Disadvantages

The parties may try to negotiate specific parts of the transaction in detail. This takes time and the heads are not the appropriate forum for protracted negotiations. Rather, the time spent negotiating detailed heads of terms is usually better spent on starting due diligence or negotiating the main agreement. The lawyer's time will add to costs and is unlikely to result in time savings at a later stage. Furthermore, the time frame for completing the transaction may not allow the luxury of negotiating heads.

The purchaser will be negotiating the heads from a position of weakness in that it will know far more about the vendor's business once the due diligence has been completed. The purchaser may be tempted to take a stance it might not have chosen if the same negotiations had taken place at a later stage.

One party may seek to reject a point in the sale agreement because it was not covered in the heads of terms. For example, a vendor may refuse to undertake restrictive covenants as these were not mentioned in the heads of terms. Alternatively, a purchaser may refuse to provide a parent company guarantee if this was not covered in the heads.

Advantages

If the heads are restricted to general terms they are a useful means of outlining the transaction and identifying the main areas the parties want to see included in the sale agreement. For the purchaser's lawyer, it is a useful basis from which to start preparing the draft sale agreement.

It is also a useful means of identifying difficult points without which either party will not complete the transaction. For example, it may be essential to the purchaser that particular plant and equipment is transferred. If the vendor is adamant that it be retained, it is better for all concerned that the deadlock be established early.

Most importantly the heads can contain terms that are binding on the vendor and purchaser. This is normally dealt with by specifying in the heads that all its contents are subject to contract except for specified paragraphs. The main areas that the parties will wish to be binding are:

(a) confidentiality;
(b) costs;
(c) exclusivity period.

CONFIDENTIALITY

If a separate confidentiality agreement has not been signed an appropriate undertaking can be embodied in the heads. Confidentiality agreements are discussed in more detail later.

COSTS

It is normal practice for the heads to specify that each party will be responsible for the costs of its own advisers. However, if one party is to bear the costs of the other it is important to specify this in the heads and ensure it is binding on all parties.

EXCLUSIVITY PERIOD—LOCK OUT CLAUSES

Once the purchaser has started due diligence, it will be incurring both the costs of professional advisers and dedicating considerable internal management time to the project. Ideally the purchaser would wish to have the vendor negotiate actively with the purchaser on an exclusive basis during an initial period. However, the purchaser should be aware that the effect of the decision by the House of Lords

in the recent case of *Walford v Miles* [1992] 1 All ER 453 is that the
purchaser can achieve exclusivity only in the sense that the vendor
undertakes not to negotiate with a third party for a fixed period. The
vendor cannot be forced to negotiate with the purchaser.

In *Walford v Miles* the House of Lords maintained the long
established principle that a mere agreement to negotiate is unenforceable because it lacks the certainty necessary for a binding contract and
held that any concept of a duty to carry on negotiations in good faith
is inherently repugnant to the adversarial position of the parties when
involved in negotiations. However, the House of Lords approved the
concept of exclusivity (lock-out) clauses. Indeed the clause in dispute
in *Walford v Miles* was a lock-out clause in that it represented an
undertaking by the vendor not to negotiate with anyone other than
the purchaser. The clause was not framed as an obligation on the
vendor to negotiate with the purchaser in good faith. However,
despite being framed as a negative provision, the House of Lords held
that the clause was unenforceable as it lacked certainty in that it was
not for a fixed period of duration. The House of Lords believed that a
period of exclusivity would be valid and binding on the vendor
provided that consideration passed between the parties, that the
terms of the period were certain and the parties intended to be bound.
Lord Ackner stated that:

There is clearly no reason in English contract law why A, for good
consideration, should not achieve an enforceable agreement whereby B,
agrees for a specified period of time not to negotiate with anyone except A in
relation to the sale of his property.... But I stress that this is a negative
agreement—B by agreeing not to negotiate for this fixed period with a third
party, locks himself out of such negotiations. He has in no legal sense locked
himself *into* negotiations with A.

An exclusivity clause, therefore, requires careful drafting. The
duration of the exclusivity period should first be clearly defined. It
should then identify the consideration passing. This is normally the
purchaser proceeding with due diligence and thereby incurring the
costs of its professional advisers or, alternatively, a vendor may
demand a cash payment in return for the exclusivity period. Whether
or not this is a deposit towards the purchase price is a matter for
negotiation. A cash payment is unusual and either reflects the
bargaining strength of the vendor, or, in recent times, may be
demanded by receivers and liquidators in recognition of the duty they
owe to the creditors.

It is questionable whether lock out clauses are worthwhile. They
may give the purchaser some assurance before incurring professional
costs but the courts will not order the vendor to negotiate. The main

remedy for an aggrieved purchaser would be to seek an injunction within the exclusivity period and compensation for the costs it incurred. If an *ex parte* injunction is to be sought the purchaser should ensure that the exclusivity clause is clear and precise. In particular the purchaser should not grant exceptions to the exclusivity as the court will then require the attendance of the vendor before granting the injunction.

Set out below is the form of a lock-out clause which could be used in a heads of agreement. The introduction to the heads will specify that the clause is binding on both parties and is not subject to contract.

In consideration of the purchaser incurring the costs of its professional advisers in commencing due diligence and negotiating the binding agreement the vendor hereby undertakes to the purchaser that during the period from today until midnight on [   ] 19[   ] it shall not negotiate the sale of the business with any person (either directly or indirectly) other than the purchaser

Common provisions in heads of terms

The only essential content of the heads of terms is to specify that they are subject to contract except for one or two specific clauses. Apart from that, there are no rules regarding the contents. In fact the heads should outline the transaction in as general terms as possible. Normally both the purchaser and vendor will wish to identify the business being sold and the price paid, together with the method and timing of payment. The purchaser should specify any key assumptions made in reaching the price such as net asset position or profitability of the business and alert the vendor to the fact that the price may change if the assumptions are not correct.

It is advisable for the purchaser to draw attention to any points which may cause difficulties if they are not raised until a later stage. The main areas are the fact that the purchaser will require the vendor to give warranties and perhaps indemnities, enter restrictive covenants and perhaps provide a parent company guarantee or some form of security.

Information questionnaire

At an early stage the purchaser's solicitors will prepare an information questionnaire raising detailed questions as part of the due diligence process in relation to the business. Early responses to the information questionnaire will assist the purchaser's solicitors in tailoring a standard sale agreement to the vendor's business. A standard form is set out in Appendix II. The questionnaire is very much in a standard form and should always be amended to reflect the business being sold. For example, if the business is a retail operation the purchaser will be particularly concerned about the level and quality of stocks. If the business is a service industry, the purchaser will be more interested in the staff and existing contracts than the state of the plant and machinery if any.

Before issuing the questionnaire the purchaser's solicitors should first collect and review all information that the vendor has already given the purchaser. (It can be embarrassing to discover that the information requested was in fact supplied to the purchaser six weeks before the date of the request.) However, the purchaser should bear in mind that some of the information supplied previously is historic and revised updates should be requested.

The purchaser should avoid asking for superfluous information. Generally the more information requested the longer it will take for the purchaser and its solicitors to review. This increases not only professional costs but also the risk that important information embedded in the general mass becomes overlooked. Although there is a school of thought that, if the vendor is besieged with questions, its management will be too occupied to negotiate with anyone other than the purchaser, it is important to consider who is operating the business if the full time attention of senior management is taken up with demands for information. The area is of particular significance in management buy-outs where there is the risk that an unwilling vendor will demand that management devote the whole of their time and attention to managing the business or otherwise risk breaching their terms of employment.

As and when the information is supplied, it is in both the vendor's and purchaser's interests to ensure that the documents and complete copies are carefully indexed. The documents will normally be referred to by the vendor in its disclosures against the warranties. It is fair for the purchaser to resist disclosure of any documents referred to in the disclosure documents and care should be taken to ensure complete copies are supplied.

Confidentiality agreements

The vendor should consider with its lawyer whether a confidentiality agreement is necessary. It may be that the purchaser signed a confidentiality agreement at the outset of negotiations. If no agreement has been signed, the vendor may want an appropriate agreement before revealing any confidential information as part of the due diligence.

It is not essential to have a written agreement. As a matter of common law, if the purchaser receives information relating to the vendor's business which he knows or ought to know is confidential, the purchaser is under a duty to maintain the confidence and not to use the information. However, from the point of view of enforcement and for the sake of certainty, the vendor should provide a draft confidentiality agreement to the purchaser as early as possible. A standard form of agreement is set out in Appendix I. The essential elements of a confidentiality agreement are an acknowledgment by the purchaser that:

    (a) the existence of the negotiations and all information received relating to the vendor's business is confidential;

    (b) the purchaser will maintain the confidentiality and ensure that all persons receiving the information maintain the confidentiality;

    (c) the purchaser will only use information for assessing its acquisition of the business and for no other purpose;

    (d) the purchaser will return all the information and either return or destroy all copies if the transaction does not complete.

A further level of protection sought by some vendors is an undertaking by the purchaser not to solicit the vendor's employees if the transaction fails.

When presented with the draft confidentiality agreement, the purchaser should ensure that there are adequate exemptions to the confidentiality obligation. For example, the purchaser may be required to make disclosures either under the rules of a stock exchange or pursuant to a court order. On the other hand, the vendor should seek to restrict the number of exemptions. In order to ensure an injunction will be available the vendor will wish to restrict the number of exemptions to the confidentiality obligation and hence minimise the risk of the injunction being overturned.

Property issues

Subject to the importance of the property assets as part of the business acquisition, it is advisable that the purchaser's solicitors carry out a full investigation of title to establish that the purchaser will acquire the property assets free from any adverse encumbrances, obligations or restrictions.

A full investigation of title is time consuming and should be started as early in the negotiation process as possible. However, assuming the properties are significant assets, a full investigation of title is to be preferred to either reliance upon a certificate from the vendor's solicitors that the vendor has a good and marketable title (since certificates of title are qualified and their benefit depends upon the status of the firm of solicitors providing them) or reliance upon warranties and indemnities alone since the purchaser would rather have problems disclosed before the purchase than have to rely upon a right to sue under warranties which will be subject to general limitations. The purchaser will seek extensive property warranties in addition to investigating title.

Investigations

The main investigations that a purchaser should carry out are:
(1) General enquiries of the vendor's solicitors.
(2) Searches and enquiries of the public registers.
(3) Investigation of title to the properties.

GENERAL ENQUIRIES

The purchaser's solicitors will raise preliminary enquiries with the vendor's solicitors to obtain general information about the property. Replies to enquiries should be reinforced by a specific warranty that all written replies to enquiries in respect of the property (whether on behalf of the vendor and/or themselves) by the vendor's solicitors are true and accurate in all respects *and* there is no fact not disclosed which would render any such information insecure or misleading.

The matters to be covered by enquiries are as follows:

Title details—whether the property is freehold or leasehold; ownership of boundary walls and fences; details of any disputes affecting the property; details of any disputes with owners of adjoining properties; details of notices received; details of services available to the property; details of access and shared facilities; details of encumbrances, covenants or restrictions affecting the property; planning/rating.

In addition where the property is leasehold the following further information is required:
Lease details—confirmation of compliance with landlord's and tenant's covenants in the lease; service charges; insurance; the need to obtain any consents to the assignment of the lease.

SEARCHES AND ENQUIRIES

A number of searches and enquiries should be made in respect of each property. The searches are listed below and should be submitted by the purchaser's solicitors at the earliest opportunity. The results of these searches (other than the local land charges search) are normally supplied within two to three working days after the date of their submission. The time it takes to receive local land charge search results varies greatly depending upon the particular local authority and can take between one and four weeks to obtain. Likewise the cost varies depending upon the local authority.

Search	*Information provided*
Local land charges search and additional enquiries (Forms LLC1 and Con 29)	Details of development plans, drainage, maintenance of roads, road schemes, statutory or informal notices under public health acts, housing acts, highways acts and under building regulations, planning decisions and controls, orders revoking or modifying planning consents, resolutions made under a compulsory purchase order, listed building details and tree preservation orders.
Index map search (LR Form 96)	Whether the freehold or leasehold title is registered, the title number if the land is registered, and, if not registered any cautions against first registration, or priority notices affecting the property.
Central Land Charges Search (Form K15)	Where title is unregistered, any encumbrances registered against the estate owner(s) specified in the search in respect of its period of ownership.
Land registry search (Form 109)	Details of any entries on the vendor's title subsequent to the date of the office copy entries supplied.
Commons Search (Form CR21)	Whether the land is registered as common land or as a town or village green.

In addition, depending upon the location of the property, enquiries may need to be raised with British Rail, National Rivers Authority, British Coal, the British Waterways Board or London Regional Transport. Replies are normally obtained within five working days of making the enquiries.

TITLE INVESTIGATION

The vendor should be required to deduce its title to any properties included in the business sale at the earliest possible stage to reduce the possibility of the vendor not disclosing unacceptable encumbrances on the title.

Pre-completion searches

Following exchange and prior to completion of the business acquisition, the purchaser's solicitors should submit a further search to establish the right to have the transfer of the property registered in priority to any other person dealing with the property or to have the property conveyed in priority to matters affecting the estate. In the case of registered land, this involves a search at HM Land Registry against the title number to the land and in the case of unregistered land, a search against the vendor and previous estate owners for the length of period of each estate owner's ownership. Either search affords to the purchaser a priority period during which either the transfer of registered land must be completed and an application made to HM Land Registry for its registration or the conveyance of unregistered land must be completed.

CONSENTS AND APPROVALS

In many transactions it is either necessary or thought by one of the parties to be commercially worthwhile to obtain consent for or approval of certain items before the business transfer is completed. Areas in which consents or approvals are often needed are described below and relate to:

(1) Articles of association.
(2) Shareholder agreements.
(3) Banking finance arrangements.
(4) Industry consent.
(5) Property.
(6) Contracts.
(7) Stock Exchange class consents.
(8) Consideration shares.
(9) Substantial transactions with directors.
(10) Non-UK purchasers.
(11) Competition approvals or clearances.

It is normal practice, subject to negotiation, for contracts to be executed on the basis that completion will only take place once the relevant consents have been obtained or approvals given. In the interim period the business will still be managed by the vendor. The vendor will be unwilling to allow the purchaser to manage the business in case completion never takes place. The purchaser will not wish to manage the business for fear of becoming a shadow director of the vendor under CA 1985, s 741. Rather, it is normal for the vendor to undertake in the sale agreement to carry on managing the business in its ordinary course and not to enter into transactions outside the ordinary course of trading without the purchaser's prior consent. An appropriate provision is contained in Clause 5.1 of the standard sale agreement (Appendix III). Subject to the relative negotiating strengths the vendor may agree not to undertake specific matters in relation to the business without the purchaser's prior consent.

Articles of association

It is common for the articles of association of a company that is a management buy-out vehicle, a joint venture company, or which is owned by multiple shareholders to provide that the sale of the assets and undertaking of the company requires the consent of specified individuals. The articles are on public record and the purchaser runs the risk of a disgruntled shareholder seeking to have the sale set aside if its consent was not obtained. The vendor is likely to have disclosed its articles as part of its disclosures against the warranties.

The relevant consent requirement is normally contained as a class right in the articles or sometimes as a restriction on the powers of the directors. In any event, if the vendor's shares are divided into more than one class, the purchaser should check the vendor's articles of association. Equally, if the vendor is part of a group, the purchaser should check the articles of association of each parent company and the ultimate holding company. Often the articles of the holding company will provide that consent is required for the sale of the assets of the holding company and of any of its subsidiaries.

Sometimes the restriction is drafted so that consent is only required on the sale or disposal of a 'material' part of the assets and undertaking. If in doubt the purchaser should insist that the vendor obtains from its shareholders either a consent or an acknowledgment that their consent is not required.

As a result of the House of Lords' decision in *Russell v Northern Bank* [1992] 1 WLR 588, it is likely that the next few years will see the return in popularity of 'golden shares'. These are single shares in a company containing special rights which effectively grant the shareholder, normally an institution, the right to veto certain actions of the company. One right would be that a sale of the business will require the consent of the holder of the golden share. Alternatively the sale of assets requires shareholder approval and the voting rights of the golden share will outweigh the rights of all other shares (*Foss v Harbottle* (1843) Hare 461).

Shareholder agreements *— could explain a little more*

It is common for a shareholders' agreement to provide that the sale of the assets and undertaking of the company requires the approval of the shareholders. Similar restrictions will often be contained in the articles of association of the relevant company (see page 18). Traditionally the vendor would be a party to the shareholders' agreement and will give an appropriate undertaking to each of the shareholders. However, as a result of *Russell v Northern Bank* it is less likely that companies will be parties to such agreements lest any provision in the agreement is considered a fetter of the vendor's statutory powers and the agreement is declared invalid.

Unlike the articles of association, the shareholders' agreement is not normally a matter of public record. The purchaser should ask the vendor for a copy of the shareholders' agreement, assuming that the vendor is a party. Before disclosing the agreement the vendor should ensure that he is not in breach of any confidentiality undertakings contained in the agreement and if necessary first obtain the consent of the other parties before disclosing the agreement to the purchaser.

Banking and finance arrangements

If the vendor has granted any fixed or floating charges over any of the assets, the purchaser will insist that it acquires these assets free of all such charges. The existence of the charge will normally have been revealed to the purchaser either by the results of its initial company search against the vendor or through the disclosure exercise. In relation to a fixed charge, the purchaser should insist that completion will only take place if a deed of release in terms satisfactory to the purchaser is delivered at or before completion. The chargee is unlikely to provide the release before completion and therefore this is invariably the last condition precedent to be satisfied. Difficulties over timing are normally resolved by the respective lawyers giving appropriate undertakings, particularly if the chargee will not release the charge until it has received part of the sale proceeds. As regards the floating charge, if the sale of the vendor's assets is an event of crystallisation, the purchaser should insist on a similar deed of release. If the sale does not crystallise the charge, the purchaser should insist on receiving a certificate of non-crystallisation in terms which are to its satisfaction. It is of course a fact of life that the bankers may seek to renegotiate the vendor's finance arrangements, particularly if the purchase price will be a significant realisation for the vendor.

Further consents to the sale may also be needed under the terms and conditions of the vendor's loan stock, loan agreements and other finance arrangements including leasing contracts. Similar consent provisions may be contained in the financing arrangements of the vendor's shareholders and ultimate holding company. For example, a loan agreement may provide that a disposal of the assets of the holding company or of any of its subsidiaries requires the prior written consent of the lender. Similarly, considerable thought must be given to cross default provisions if the vendor is part of a group of companies. A purchaser will have no knowledge of such agreements and will insist on a warranty by the vendors that no consents are required (see standard sale agreement, warranty Q6—Appendix III).

The vendor should take care to check that the sale of the assets will not put it or its parent companies in breach of covenants given in any loan agreements. In particular the vendor should check for cross default provisions which would affect the other companies in the vendor's group.

Industry consents

For certain businesses the purchaser may require the prior consent or approval of an industry regulator before it can commence the new business or amalgamate it into its existing business. The precise nature and requirements for such approvals are beyond the scope of this book but common examples are in the fields of insurance (see the Insurance Companies Act 1982 and the Financial Services Act 1986), banking (see the Banking Act 1979), newspapers (see the Fair Trading Act 1973), telecommunications, building societies, Ministry of Defence contractors and bars, hotels, restaurants and off-licences (see the Licensing Act 1964 and the Hotel Proprietors Act 1956).

Property

There are three areas relating to the vendor's property where the purchaser may require the consent or approval of a third party before proceeding to completion. These are landlord's consent, survey and environmental audit.

(1) Landlord's consent

Nearly all leases contain restrictions against alienation restricting the circumstances in which the lessee (the vendor) may assign, sub-let or share occupation of the property. It will be necessary to comply with these provisions where the business is being sold, rather than where the company holding the tenancy is being sold. However, change in control restrictions may also apply on a share sale. Generally, there will be a requirement that the landlord's consent is obtained before the lease can be assigned. Provided that there is no absolute bar against assignment, it will be implied at law (if not expressly) that the landlord's consent is not to be unreasonably withheld—Landlord and Tenant Act 1927, s 19(1).

Traditionally some vendors oppose asset sales on the basis that it takes too long to obtain the landlord's consent and the long delay between exchange and completion causes uncertainty for the business. The effect of the Landlord and Tenant Act 1988, however, is to impose a statutory duty on the landlord to consider an application for consent to assign 'within a reasonable time'. The landlord may be liable to the vendor in damages if the vendor suffers loss through the landlord's unreasonable delay in considering the application. Whilst pursuant to the Landlord and Tenant Act 1988 the burden is now on the landlord to show that it acted reasonably in withholding consent or in imposing conditions upon its consent, the landlord is entitled to require references, accounts and other relevant financial information. If the purchaser is setting up a new company to take over the business of the vendor, since that new company will have no track record, the landlord may well be entitled to look for additional security, such as a parent company or bank guarantee or a rent deposit.

If consent is required pursuant to the lease not only for the assignment of that lease but for sharing occupation or parting with possession of the property, the vendor who allows the purchaser into occupation pending consent to the assignment will breach the provisions of the lease. The landlord would be entitled to sue for damages for breach of covenant and/or endeavour to forfeit the lease (although the risk of forfeiture is extremely unlikely in the current market). If the vendor does allow such occupation pending landlord's consent, the agreement should include appropriate indemnities from the purchaser and oblige the purchaser to vacate immediately on notice.

Occasionally leases do not require consent for sub-letting and this may be a more suitable structure. This is less satisfactory for the vendor, however, as it will remain liable as tenant of the landlord and there is a risk that in years to come the purchaser may be unable to pay the rent. The vendor will then be in a similar position as if it were still the original tenant under the lease and it will remain liable if an assignee defaults unless the landlord releases to vendor in the licence to assign.

(2) Survey

The purchaser will sometimes make completion conditional on receiving a satisfactory surveyor's report in relation to the property. It is normal practice for the purchaser to order a survey for two reasons. Firstly, as with any property, a purchaser wants an assessment of the physical state of the property and an assessment of whether it will be suitable for its business. Secondly, the purchaser will require the surveyor to assess potential liabilities under repairing obligations in the lease and in particular for dilapidations. This is very important if the lease has nearly expired.

The purchaser should resist allowing the vendor to impose a condition drafted in general terms that the purchaser must be satisfied with the result of a survey. Inevitably there is always *something* wrong with a property and the vendor will not wish to let the purchaser use a minor problem as an excuse for not completing the transaction. A suitable compromise, however, is to incorporate a degree of materiality. For example, the condition will not be satisfied if the results of the survey estimate that the cost of 'essential' repairs will exceed a specified amount or that the property is unfit for the purchaser's proposed use.

(3) Environmental audit

Purchasers, particularly American corporations, are becoming increasingly sensitive as to the potential environmental liabilities in properties they acquire. Often difficulty arises if the purchaser insists not only on extensive environmental warranties and indemnities but also on applying different liability limitation compared to that negotiated on the other warranties. This may be unacceptable to the vendor. A suitable compromise is for completion to be conditional on the results of an environmental audit. As with the surveyor's report (see (2) above) it is advisable to define a level of materiality to prevent the purchaser using the results as an excuse not to complete. At the time of writing, costs for an initial investigation are in the region of £3,000 to £5,000 + VAT. Bore samples will increase these costs.

If an audit is to be undertaken, the vendor should agree the letter of instruction with the purchaser. The vendor will not wish to authorise any work which would require the landlord's consent such as taking samples from the foundations, walls or roof of the property.

Contracts

Often on a business transfer, parties to contracts with the vendor will need to consent to or agree to the contract being assigned or novated to the purchaser. This is discussed in more detail in Chapter 4.

If there are contracts which are essential to the conduct of the business, the purchaser should make obtaining consent to assign or novate these a condition precedent. For example, the business may be the sole distributor of certain products within the United Kingdom. Alternatively the business may have three long-term customer contracts essential to its operations.

If the price paid for the business has been calculated on turnover it is important to the purchaser that he benefits from all existing contracts. If these contracts require consent to assign or novate the purchaser may insist that completion only takes place once a specified number of consents have been given or, in particular, consents in relation to the most important contracts comprising a specified percentage of annual turnover. In addition, the purchaser will normally base the price on the assignment or novation of all contracts and provide that the price reduces on an agreed formula if any consents are not obtained within a specified period.

Stock Exchange class consents

Procedures laid down by the International Stock Exchange of the United Kingdom and Republic of Ireland Limited ('the Stock Exchange') may be relevant if either the vendor or purchaser are quoted companies or are subsidiaries of quoted companies. If the transaction falls within one of four relevant classes full compliance with the relevant procedure will be a condition precedent to the completion of the transaction. The procedures are set out in the *Admission of Securities to Listing* (the Yellow Book) and the requirements are contained in Section 6 of Chapter 1 of the Yellow Book. The Yellow Book is currently being revised and the existing edition is due to be entirely replaced. At the date of going to press the class tests have not been significantly revised, but there are a number of proposed detail changes and clarifications. However, since those changes were not finalised at the date of going to press and further revisions are possible in the light of comments it is not appropriate to review them here.

The comments below are a summary of the provisions of the current Yellow Book. Purchasers and vendors who are listed companies should seek guidance from their solicitors and other professional advisers concerning Stock Exchange requirements at a very early stage in any transaction. The Stock Exchange may, as discussed below, require the publication of announcements or listing particulars. Listing particulars are technical documents which must be drafted by professionals and approved by the Stock Exchange and any transaction timetable must be adjusted accordingly. The Yellow Book also requires the approval of shareholders for certain transactions and it may be necessary for the contract to have a gap between exchange and completion. It is possible to obtain derogation from certain Stock Exchange requirements but this must be applied for in the early stages of a transaction. The precise procedure is dictated by the relevant Class of the transaction.

(A) SUPER CLASS 1

A Super Class 1 transaction will require an announcement to be made to the Company Announcements Office of the Stock Exchange and to the press and will require a circular to be sent to shareholders. Unlike the other Classes, a Super Class 1 transaction will also require the prior approval of shareholders in a general meeting.

(B) CLASS 1

A Class 1 transaction will require an announcement to be made to the Company Announcements Office of the Stock Exchange and to the press and will require a circular to be sent to shareholders. However, a Class 1 transaction is not sufficiently important to require shareholder approval.

(C) CLASS 2

A Class 2 transaction will require an announcement to be made to the Company Announcements Office of the Stock Exchange and to the Press. They do not require a circular to be issued or prior shareholders' approval.

(D) CLASS 3

A Class 3 transaction will require an announcement to the Company Announcements office and the press and for a circular to be issued, but only if some or all of the consideration is to be satisfied by the issue of securities for which a listing is to be sought.

(E) CLASS 4

A Class 4 transaction will normally require the prior consent of the company in a general meeting.

Class tests

The tests for Super Class 1, Class 1 and Class 2 transactions relate to the size of the transaction. The test for a Class 3 transaction relates to the form in which the consideration is to be satisfied. The test for a Class 4 transaction depends on the relationship between the parties involved.

In testing for Super Class 1, Class 1 and Class 2 transactions it is necessary to make three comparisons between the listed company and the business it is disposing of or acquiring. The comparisons relate to net assets, net profits, the consideration and, where shares are issued as consideration, the shares to be issued compared with those previously in issue. If any of the comparisons produces a value of 25 per cent or more then it is a Super Class 1 transaction. If the value is 15 per cent or more but less than 25 per cent it is a Class 1 transaction. If the value is 5 per cent or more but less than 15 per cent then it is a Class 2 transaction.

The assets comparison operates by comparing the value of the assets being sold to the value of the assets of the acquiring or disposing company, whichever is listed. The assets means the book value of the net assets (excluding intangibles and after deducting loan capital and tax provisions) taken from the most recent published consolidated accounts adjusted to take account of the subsequent transactions which have already been notified to shareholders. The Stock Exchange Quotations Committee may be willing to relax the test if a significant element of the assets sold comprise intangible assets such as goodwill.

The profits comparison operates by comparing the net profits before tax and excluding extraordinary items attributable to the assets being sold compared to either the vendor as a whole or the purchaser.

The consideration comparison operates by comparing the aggregate value of the consideration received with the assets or gross capital of the vendor or purchaser as appropriate. If part or all of the consideration is to be determined after completion, such as an earn-out or completion accounts (see pages 43–47), the parties should seek guidance from the Stock Exchange who in turn will wish to ask the parties' financial advisers to elaborate on the expected consideration.

The equity comparison operates by comparing the equity capital issued as consideration by the purchaser to that previously in issue.

There is a further comparison in the case of an acquisition by a listed purchaser. This compares the value of the purchaser's market capitalisation and various assets and liabilities (including debt securities) with the value of the consideration payable and various assets and liabilities of the target.

The test for a Class 4 transaction depends on the relationship between the parties involved in the transaction including their respective officers and associates. A Class 4 transaction is one where a company enters into a transaction with or for the benefit of a 'Class 4 party'. A Class 4 party is a director or substantial shareholder of the company or an associate of such party. It includes any people who, within the year before the transaction, were directors of the vendor or purchaser or any other company which is within its group of companies (including subsidiaries of its ultimate holding company) and includes shadow directors as defined by CA 1985, s 741. A substantial shareholder means any person who is or was within the preceding year a holder of 10 per cent or more of the nominal value of any class of capital of the vendor or any other company within its group, including subsidiaries of its ultimate holding company having rights to vote in all circumstances at general meetings of the relevant company. A wide definition of associate is contained in Section 6 of Chapter 1, paragraph 1.2 of the Yellow Book.

Finally, for very large acquisitions (which may constitute reverse takeovers) the Stock Exchange may require shareholder approval. The purchaser will also normally be treated as a new applicant for listing, its securities will be suspended and it will be required to publish listing particulars. The acquisition will be a reverse takeover if the purchaser, being a listed company, issues to the vendor as consideration for the asset sale, shares in the purchaser which are equal to or greater than 30 per cent of the issued share capital of the purchaser. Under rule 9 of the City Code on Takeovers and Mergers the vendor will be under an obligation to make an offer for the entire issued share capital of the purchaser unless a whitewash procedure is granted by the Takeover Panel.

The class tests are summarised below.

Summary

Class	Test	Announcement to Stock Exchange and Press	Requirements circular	Shareholder approval
Super Class 1	25% or more	Yes	Yes	Yes
Class 1	15% or more	Yes	Yes	No
Class 2	5% or more	Yes	No	No
Class 3		Yes	No	No
Class 4	Relationship with director or substantial shareholder or associate	Yes	Yes	Yes at Stock Exchange's discretion

Consideration shares

If part or all of the purchase price comprises shares in the purchaser, the purchaser must check whether it has sufficient authorised and issued share capital and whether the directors have existing authority to allot and issue new shares under CA 1985, s 80. If the authorised share capital is not adequate it will be necessary to convene a shareholders' meeting to pass an ordinary resolution increasing the authorised capital. Likewise if the authority to allot and issue has expired or is insufficient a further ordinary resolution of the shareholders will be needed.

If the purchaser is a listed company it is likely that it will need to apply for a listing of the consideration shares. Under the rules of the Stock Exchange if the shares of a particular class are listed all shares issued in that class must be listed. The purchaser will need to prepare listing particulars unless the consideration shares will comprise less than 10 per cent of the issued listed shares after they have been issued. If listing particulars have been issued during the previous year some of the contents requirements for the new listing particulars are relaxed.

The purchaser should consider whether the business being bought needs to be valued for the purpose of CA 1985, s 103 (exemptions). The purchaser should identify the need for an independent valuation as early as possible to avoid subsequent delay nearer completion.

It should be noted that substantial acquisitions of public company shares as well as takeovers are governed by the City Code on Takeovers and Mergers ('the Code'). The Code applies to offers for all listed *and unlisted* public companies considered by the Takeover Panel to be resident in the United Kingdom, the Channel Islands or the Isle of Man. The Takeover Panel may be asked for advice by telephone and responds very quickly to enquiries. It is also generally flexible about giving exemptions to Code requirements where appropriate.

Substantial transactions with directors

The asset sale may need the prior approval of shareholders of a relevant company if the vendor is a director or a person connected (as defined in CA 1985, s 346) with a director of the purchaser or its holding company or the purchaser is a director or a person connected with a director of the vendor or its holding company (see CA 1985, s 320). The relationship does not extend to directors of subsidiaries. The transaction must involve the acquisition of non-cash assets (as defined in CA 1985, s 739(1)) of more than £100,000 or 10 per cent of the company's net asset value as determined by the audited accounts for the preceding financial year. CA 1985, s 321 contains various exceptions to the requirement of shareholder approval including the transfer of assets within a group of companies. Under CA 1985, s 317 a director of a company who is in any way, whether directly or indirectly, interested in a contract or proposed contract with his company is required to declare his interest at the meeting of the board. Furthermore, a disclosure of the transaction may need to be made in the company's annual accounts as a result of CA 1985, s 232.

Finally, where directors or associated persons are involved, the purchaser and vendor should both take care to ensure that there is no

breach of CA 1985, s 330 which imposes restrictions on several classes
of transactions for the benefit of directors including loans, guarantees, quasi-loans and credit transactions.

Non-UK purchasers

It is rarely necessary to obtain government consent before selling a
business to a non-UK purchaser. Historically it was necessary to
obtain the prior consent of the Treasury before transferring all or part
of a business to a company outside the United Kingdom. Failure to
obtain approval was a criminal offence under the Income and
Corporation Taxes Act 1970 (TA), s 482 as re-enacted in the Income
and Corporation Taxes Act (TA) 1988, ss 765–767.
The general offence was abolished by the Finance Act (FA) 1988,
s 105(6). However there is one important exception that remains.
Under TA 1988, s 765(1)(*d*) it still continues to be an offence for a
company resident in the United Kingdom for tax purposes to transfer
shares in a non-resident subsidiary to a non-resident purchaser.
Therefore in an asset sale, if the purchaser is non-resident and the
assets include shares in a non-resident company, the vendor should
consider the need to obtain prior Treasury approval.

Competition approvals and clearances

Introduction

Merger control and competition law are becoming increasingly
important factors in business acquisitions. At an early stage the
parties should consider whether any prior approvals or clearances to
the transaction are required under both domestic and EC law. It
cannot be overstressed that the purchaser and vendor should
continue to consider the need for approvals and clearances throughout the course of negotiations as a change in the terms of the
transaction may trigger the relevant legislation which regulates anti-
competitive practices, mergers and the creation or expansion of
monopolies.
The five main areas in which approvals may be needed and which
are discussed below are:
(1) The Restrictive Trade Practices Act (RTPA) 1976.
(2) The Fair Trading Act (FTA) 1973.
(3) Article 85 of the EEC Treaty 1957 (Article 85) dealing with
anti-competitive agreements.
(4) Article 86 of the EEC Treaty 1957 (Article 86) dealing with
abuse of a dominant position.

(5) EC Council Regulation (EEC No 4064/89) regulating concentrations between undertakings (the Merger Regulation).

RTPA 1976 is the area to which most attention has been given in this section as this is likely to be the most relevant area for readers of this book. The main criticism of RTPA 1976 is that the tests for registration are rigid and complicated and, unlike Article 85, do not consider the likely effect of the relevant restrictions on competition. The wide scope of the tests imposes a heavy administrative burden on the Office of Fair Trading (OFT) as, although many agreements are registrable, few of these may have any real adverse effect on competition. The future of RTPA 1976 and FTA 1973 is somewhat uncertain. The form of RTPA 1976 has been considered in the Government's Green and White Papers of 1988 and 1989 (*Review of Restrictive Trade Practices Policy* Cmnd 331, 1988 and *Opening Markets: New Policy on Restrictive Trade Practices* Cmnd 727, 1989). Both propose legislation aimed at dealing with anti-competitive effects rather than the form of an agreement. The White Paper suggests the prohibition of anti-competitive agreements together with much wider powers of investigation. Substantial fines would be imposable under the new legislation. Third parties harmed by anti-competitive agreements may bring proceedings for damages. In 1992, the Government confirmed its intention to introduce new legislation giving stronger powers to deal with cartels when the legislative timetable permits. The Government reiterated its intention to introduce a prohibition on anti-competitive agreements and concerted practices. The Government's Green Paper on the Abuse of Market Power published in November 1992 considered the case for parallel changes to UK competition law (namely the monopoly provisions of FTA 1973 and the Competition Act 1980) to prohibit the abuse of market power by individual companies along the lines of Article 86.

The Green Paper suggested three possibilities for change including a proposal to adopt a general prohibition on abuse of market power in place of existing legislation similar to the Article 86 approach and supported by strong investigatory powers for the OFT, financial penalties for breach and the possibility of third party actions. It was reported in the press in April 1993 that the Government had backed down on its proposals under industry pressure and was merely proposing to strengthen existing legislation by giving wider investigatory powers to the OFT and by granting power to the Director General of Fair Trading to grant interim orders prohibiting abuses of market power.

The Restrictive Trade Practices Act (RTPA) 1976

Written details of any restrictive agreement (whether written or oral) which amounts to a 'registrable agreement' as defined in RTPA 1976 and which does not fall within an exemption must be sent to the OFT for registration. Registration has two particularly important consequences for purchasers. First, through registration, the terms and conditions of the asset sale agreement and all related agreements can be inspected by a third party as they appear on the public register. Related agreements may include the vendor's disclosure letter and any bundles of documents including existing customer contracts, patent applications and litigation summaries which are integral parts of the overall transaction. Second, if there are significant restrictions in the transaction which some parties are not willing to abandon, the Restrictive Practices Court (see below) may declare the restrictions void and demand appropriate undertakings for the benefit of other parties. Breach of these undertakings would place the parties in contempt of court.

RTPA 1976 applies both to restrictive agreements affecting the supply of goods and those affecting the supply of services. The provisions relating to goods and services are very similar.

WHEN DOES AN AGREEMENT NEED TO BE REGISTERED?

RTPA 1976 applies to agreements or arrangements between two or more persons carrying on business in the United Kingdom in the production or supply of goods or services or in the application of a manufacturing process to goods, being agreements in which two or more of the parties accept restrictions in respect of the matters contained in RTPA 1976, s 6 in relation to goods and those contained in reg 3(2) of statutory instrument (SI) 1976/98 in relation to services. Those restrictions relate to:

(a) prices to be charged for goods or services; or

(b) the terms or conditions on or subject to which goods or services are to be supplied; or

(c) the quantities or descriptions of goods to be produced, supplied or acquired or the extent to which, or the scale on which services are to be made available supplied or obtained; or

(d) the manufacturing process to be used, or the quantities or the description of goods to which such a process is to be applied; or

(e) the form or manner in which services are to be made available, supplied or obtained; or

(f) the persons to, for or from whom or the areas or places in or from which goods or services are to be supplied or acquired.

For an agreement to be registrable under RTPA 1976, restrictions of the type listed in s 6 or art 3(2) of SI 1976/98 must be accepted by two or more parties to it. Careful consideration needs to be given as to how many restrictions are being undertaken and by how many people. One situation commonly overlooked is where the vendor and directors of the vendor or the directors of the vendor's parent company accept restrictions. The vendor and its directors will constitute separate persons each accepting restrictions for the purposes of RTPA 1976. However, 'inter-connected bodies corporate' are treated as a single person. Therefore an agreement solely between a parent company and a subsidiary is not registrable, even if both accept restrictions. Equally if the vendors are two or more companies in the same group, the agreement will not be registrable merely because both vendors undertake restrictions unless the purchaser also undertakes restrictions. However, in *Re Cadbury Schweppes Ltd's Agreement* [1975] 2 All ER 307 a parent company and a subsidiary were not treated as a single person where two companies agreed to accept restrictions on the supply of goods to a third which was a subsidiary of one of them.

COMMON RESTRICTIONS

In an asset sale, the entire transaction, namely the main sale agreement together with all ancillary agreements, must be looked at in the light of RTPA 1976. Account must be taken not only of restrictions in the main sale agreement but also of those contained in other agreements entered into as part of the transaction, such as exclusive licence agreements, side letters, and service contracts. For example, as part of the sale arrangements, the purchaser may grant an exclusive licence to a company in the vendor's group covering intellectual property rights. Part of the licence will be an undertaking by the purchaser not to sell goods covered by an invention. Restrictions will be found in non-competition covenants included in service contracts executed by key employees on completion as part of the transaction.

When there is a delay between exchange of contracts and completion, the asset sale agreement will often contain restrictions on the vendor to protect the purchaser during the interim period. Basic provisions are contained in Clause 5.1 of the Standard Sale Agreement (Appendix III). The vendor will undertake that the company will refrain from doing certain acts or matters pending completion. An example of such a clause which may amount to a restriction is the obligation not to enter into any contract for the acquisition or the sale of goods outside the normal course of business.

provides a road map

EXEMPTIONS

RTPA 1976 expressly excludes from registration agreements of the type described in Sched 3 of the Act. They include exclusive dealing agreements, trademark agreements, patent and registered design agreements, know-how agreements, copyright agreements and agreements as to goods with an overseas operation.

For the purposes of an asset sale, the most important exemption relates to the restrictive covenants sought by a purchaser in order to protect the goodwill of the business being purchased. Clause 15 of the Standard Sale Agreement (see Appendix III) contains common examples. The exemption is contained in the Restrictive Trade Practices (Sale and Purchase and Share Subscription Agreements) (Goods) Order 1989, SI 1989/1081 and the Restrictive Trade Practices (Services) (Amendment) Order 1989, SI 1989/1082. These orders do not contain a blanket exemption for agreements that come within their terms but provide that in deciding whether or not an agreement is registrable no account shall be taken of any restriction:

which limits the extent to which the person accepting the restriction may compete with the acquired enterprise, or may be engaged or interested in, disclose information to, or otherwise assist any business which so competes,

provided that the restriction subsists for no longer than the permitted period. A number of conditions must be satisfied for the exemption to apply:

(1) The vendor must agree to transfer the whole of his interest in a business as a going concern to the purchaser. The exemption will not apply to a mere agreement for the sale of specific assets or where the vendor is disposing of only part of his interest in the business.

(2) The agreement must not contain price restrictions.

(3) Such restrictions as are accepted may only be accepted by the vendors, their associated companies or by individuals.

(4) The restrictions to be disregarded must last for not more than five years from when the agreement becomes operative or for not more than two years beyond the expiry of any relevant employment or services contract, whichever is the later.

CONSEQUENCES OF REGISTRATION

Particulars of the registrable agreement have to be furnished to the OFT before the relevant restrictions the agreement contains take effect and, in any event, within three months of the date of the agreement. That is the date of exchange of contracts, not the date of completion. If a purchaser fears an agreement may be registrable, it should incorporate into it a suspension clause similar to that in Clause

16.11 of the Standard Sale Agreement (see Appendix III). Such a clause does not relieve the parties from the obligation to register a registrable sale agreement, it merely suspends the operation of the relevant restrictions until particulars of the agreement have been furnished to the OFT. Such particulars must be furnished within three months of the agreement being made. Failure to register renders the restrictions void and unenforceable. It will also be unlawful to seek to give effect to, to enforce or purport to enforce restrictions in an unregistered agreement. Any third party suffering damage as a result of such an unlawful act will have a right of action. The Director General of Fair Trading may also apply to the Restrictive Practices Court for an order restraining a party from operating such an agreement. Any person who breaches such an order will be in contempt of court and will be liable to a term of imprisonment or a fine or both.

Once an agreement has been registered in the register of restrictive agreements (which is open to public inspection), the Director General may refer it to the Restrictive Practices Court for a decision on whether the restrictions it contains are contrary to the public interest. Alternatively the Director General may confirm he has decided not to refer the agreement to the Court where:

(a) any directly applicable provision of EC law applies to the agreement;

(b) the agreement has expired or has been terminated;

(c) all the relevant restrictions have been removed;

(d) the Secretary of State for Trade and Industry has discharged the Director General from his duty to take proceedings where he is satisfied that the restrictions are not of such significance as to call for investigation by the Court.

It has to be noted that if one party only removes the restrictions it does not automatically save the agreement unless the remaining restrictions are too insignificant to justify reference.

SUMMARY

In order to establish whether an agreement is registrable the following steps should be followed:

(1) Consider whether you have copies of all the agreements comprising the entire transaction. These may be a mere sale agreement or may include other ancillary agreements such as service contracts, licensing agreements, supply agreements etc.

(2) Consider whether there are two parties carrying on business in the United Kingdom in the supply or production of goods or in the supply of services.

(3) Which part of RTPA 1976 are you considering—goods or services or both?

(4) Establish which parties are accepting restrictions.
(5) Do any of the exemptions apply?
(6) Find out whether there is an information agreement pursuant to the Restrictive Trade Practices (Information Agreements) Order, SI 1969/1842 which brought within RTPA 1976 information agreements relating to the prices, charges or terms and conditions on which goods are to be supplied. This Order does not apply to service agreements.
(7) If registrable, insert a suspension clause.

The Fair Trading Act (FTA) 1973

FTA 1973 governs the control of mergers in the United Kingdom and applies to 'mergers qualifying for investigation'. The sale of business assets above will not give rise to a qualifying merger. However, a sale of business assets often represents the merger of two businesses where it is combined with the transfer of business activities such as goodwill or the benefit of contracts. Under FTA 1973, s 64 the Secretary of State for Trade and Industry, when concerned about the likely impact of a proposed or completed qualifying merger on the public interest, may refer such a merger to the Monopolies and Mergers Commission (MMC) for investigation. In deciding whether to make a reference to the MMC the Secretary of State may ask for advice from the Director General of Fair Trading, as the OFT usually carries out a preliminary examination of the merger. Whatever the outcome of the MMC investigation is, the final decision of whether to allow the merger to go ahead or not will be made by the Secretary of State.

A 'merger qualifying for investigation' occurs where:
(1) Two or more enterprises must cease to be distinct. This will be the case where they are brought under common control or ownership or when one of the enterprises ceases to be carried on as a result of an agreement between the enterprises to prevent competition. There will be a common control when the acquirer becomes able materially to influence the policy of the target or to control the policy of the target or acquires a controlling interest in the target.
(2) At least one of the merging enterprises is carried on in the United Kingdom or by or under the control of a company incorporated in the United Kingdom.
(3) The merger has taken place within the last six months (unless it has taken place in secret).
(4) Either:
    (a) the enterprises are both engaged in supplying or consuming goods or services of the same description and have

between them at least 25 per cent of the market of those goods or services in the United Kingdom or a substantial part of it (the 'market share test'); or

(b) the gross value of the assets acquired exceeds £30,000,000 (the 'assets test').

It remains the policy of the authorities to refer mergers to the MMC primarily on competition grounds. The MMC will analyse the merger to find out whether it falls within FTA 1973 and whether it operates against the public interest (as defined by FTA 1973, s 84). Where a qualifying merger is considered to have a potentially adverse effect on the public interest, the Director General of Fair Trading may, as an alternative to a reference to the MCC, negotiate statutory under-takings with the parties relating to the separation or division of certain parts of the business. These undertakings will be legally binding. If, however, no undertakings can be negotiated and the MMC investigates the merger and finds that it operates or may be expected to operate against the public interest, the Secretary of State has power to order the parties not to proceed with a proposed merger or to order divestment by the purchasing company if the merger has been completed.

If an asset sale is a qualifying merger under FTA 1973, because of the risk of an order for divestment the purchaser should make completion conditional on prior approval by the OFT using a clause similar to that in Clause 4.1(b) of the Standard Sale Agreement (see Appendix III). To obtain prior approval the parties involved must contact the OFT and provide details of the transaction and its expected effects, if any, on competition and on other matters of public interest. For this purpose a new statutory pre-notification procedure was introduced by the Companies Act 1989 and has been in effect since April 1990. The procedure is only available for proposed and not completed mergers and the merger proposal must have been made public. The procedure involves the purchasing party to a proposed qualifying merger completing a prescribed form know as a 'Merger Notice' and submitting it to the OFT. Once such a notice has been accepted by the OFT, the period within which the merger must be evaluated starts to run. If the merger has not been referred by the end of this period it is deemed to be cleared. The initial period lasts for 20 working days. This initial period can be extended by two further extensions of 10 and 15 working days respectively to a maximum of 45 working days. Purchasers seeking clearance and other parties submitting information to the regulatory authorities face prosecution if they supply false or misleading information.

It is important to note that since 1 October 1990 fees have been payable in respect of applications for merger clearance. The fees vary from £5,000 to £15,000 and depend on the value of the assets taken over. If the Secretary of State has considered a proposed merger and made a decision as to clearance or otherwise in respect of it a fee will also be payable even if no application for clearance has been made.

Article 85 of the EEC Treaty 1957—The Control of Anti-Competitive Practices

The parties should consider Article 85 in transactions where either of the parties involved belongs to a corporate group with a turnover in excess of approximately £150 million or the vendor and the purchaser together enjoy 5 per cent or more of the total market for the relevant goods or services in the area of the common market affected by their agreement and one of the parties, normally the vendor, is accepting restrictive covenants. Article 85(1) prohibits agreements which restrict competition. Article 85(2) provides that agreements prohibited by Article 85(1) are automatically void unless exempted under Article 85(3). Furthermore, the Commission has power to impose fines on parties in breach of Article 85(1). Article 85(1) stipulates that:

the following shall be prohibited as incompatible with the common market: all agreements between undertakings, decisions by associations of undertakings and concerted practices which may affect trade between Member States and which have as their object or effect the prevention, restriction or distortion of competition within the common market . . . .

The definition of 'undertaking' is extremely wide and was defined in the *Propylene* case (86/398/EEC) [1988] 4 CMLR 347 as 'any entity engaged in commercial activities. . .' As a general rule Article 85 does not apply to an agreement between a parent and its subsidiary 'which although having separate legal personality, enjoys no economic independence'.

To fall within Article 85 an agreement must have as its effect or object the restriction of competition in the EC or a substantial part of it and there must be effect on trade between Member States. In *La Technique Minière v Maschinenbau Ulm* (Case 56/65 [1966] ECR 935) the European Court of Justice stated that for Article 85 to apply 'it must be possible to foresee with a sufficient degree of probability on the basis of a set of objective factors of law or of fact that the agreement in question may have an influence, direct or indirect, actual or potential, on the pattern of trade between Member States'.

For Article 85(1) to be triggered the impact of the agreement on competition or inter-state trade must be 'appreciable'. The Commission issues guidelines from time to time on its views on appreciability. The main provision of the most recent guidelines issued in 1986 provides that the prohibition in Article 85(1) will not apply to agreements where the parties together do not enjoy more than 5 per cent of the total market for the goods or services in the area of the common market affected by their agreement and the parties do not have a combined annual turnover exceeding 200,000,000 ECU (approximately £140–150m).

Article 85(1) does not apply to total or partial concentrations as such unless they contain clauses giving rise to restrictions on competition. Concentrations are dealt with under Article 86 or the Merger Regulation.

In an asset sale the provisions most likely to restrict competition are non-competition covenants given by the vendor to the purchaser or any arrangement purporting to divide up geographic or product markets. An undertaking not to compete with the business transferred for a specific period within a specific geographical area will commonly be given by the vendor to the purchaser (see Clause 15 of the Standard Sale Agreement—Appendix III). The aim of such covenants is to protect the goodwill of the transferred business and to stop the vendor from using its privileged position to compete with the purchaser in a way likely to damage the value of the business transferred. Such protection must not be excessive if it is not to infringe Article 85.

Where it is only specific individual assets of a business that are transferred, a prohibition on competition on the vendor will not usually be required to protect the purchaser and is likely to infringe Article 85(1). However, where the transfer includes goodwill and/or know-how, a non-competition clause will be permissible provided it goes no further than is necessary to protect the value of the business transferred. In deciding whether a restrictive covenant is permissible under Article 85(1) three questions must be considered. First, is the restraint on the business activities that the vendor may carry on wider than is necessary to protect the value of the business transferred? Second, is the geographic area over which the restraint operates wider than is necessary? Third, does the restraint operate for longer than is necessary? If the answer to any of these three questions is that the restraint goes further than required, the restrictive covenant is likely to infringe Article 85(1). In respect of duration, the EC Commisssion has suggested that, as a general rule, five years will be a reasonable period where both goodwill and know-how are transferred but that two years is more appropriate where goodwill alone is transferred. Of course, the Commission will determine each case in the light of the particular circumstances.

If a non-competition covenant appears likely to infringe Article 85(1) exemption is possible under Article 85(3) although such an exemption is unlikely to be granted in respect of restrictive covenants because of the difficulty of showing that such provisions fulfil the four requirements set out in Article 85(3) that must be satisfied if an exemption is to be available. Exemptions are only available if four requirements, two positive and two negative, are fulfilled. The two positive requirements are that the agreement must first contribute to improving the production or distribution of goods or to promoting technical or economic progress and second allow consumers a fair share of the resulting benefit. The two negative requirements are that the agreement must not impose on the undertakings concerned restrictions which are not indispensable to the attainment of the first two criteria and that it must not afford the undertakings concerned the possibility of eliminating competition in respect of a substantial part of the products in question. If a covenant goes further than necessary to protect the value of the transferred business, it is conceptually very difficult to see how there will be scope for exemption under Article 85(3).

Article 86 of the EEC Treaty 1957—The Control of Dominant Positions

Article 86 provides that:

any abuse by one or more undertakings of a dominant position within the common market or a substantial part of it shall be prohibited as incompatible with the common market insofar as it may affect trade between Member States.

An undertaking which abuses its dominant position on a particular product and geographic market may be fined by the EC Commission or sued in reliance on Article 86 for damages and/or an injunction in a national court by a party that has suffered damage.

In the past it has been held that Article 86 may be infringed where a company holding a dominant position within the EC strengthens that position, by acquiring control of another company or business in the same market, to such an extent that it practically eliminates effective competition in that market. However, since the Merger Regulations (Reg 4064/89/EEC) came into force the Commission no longer has power to apply Article 86 to such transactions although Article 86 remans applicable for the purposes of private motions before national courts.

The Merger Regulation

Since 21 September 1990 mergers having a 'Community Dimension' have been regulated by the Merger Regulation. Mergers have a Community Dimension where:
  (1) The combined aggregate worldwide turnover of all the parties involved is at least 5,000,000,000 (5 billion) ECU. The turnover is not just that of the companies involved but of the groups to

which they belong. For this purpose a group includes both holding companies and subsidiaries.

(2) The aggregate Community turnover of each of at least two of the parties concerned is more than 250,000,000 (two hundred and fifty million) ECU.

As an exception the Merger Regulation does not apply if a merger has its primary impact within one Member State. This is the case where more than two thirds of the Community turnover of each party concerned in the merger is in one and the same Member State. In such circumstances the provisions of national merger control will apply. There are special provisions for banks and other financial institutions, for which turnover is replaced by a calculation based on the ratio of assets to loans and for insurance companies, for which turnover is replaced by gross premiums.

The Merger Regulation is mainly applied to 'concentrations'. A concentration may occur in one of two ways: first, two or more parties that were previously independent may merge so as to become one new independent business or secondly, one or more persons who already control one business may acquire direct or indirect control of another business. A party is regarded as acquiring control if it has the possibility of exercising 'decisive influence' on another party in particular by ownership or the right to use all or part of the assets of the other party, or rights which confer decisive influence on the composition, voting or decisions of the other party's board of directors or of its shareholders' meetings.

The Commission is concerned to assess the impact of a merger on competition in the EC. The Commission will prohibit a merger if it concludes that the merger would create or strengthen a dominant position as a result of which effective competition would be significantly impeded in the common market or in a substantial part of it. The Commission's first step is to identify the relevant product and geographic markets in which the parties might be regarded as dominant. Having identified the relevant markets, the Commission will then consider:

(a) whether either of the parties already enjoys a dominant position in any such market which will be strengthened by the merger; or

(b) whether the concentration will create a dominant position in any such market; and

(c) whether (if a dominant position will be created or strengthened) that will significantly impede effective competition in the common market or a substantial part of it.

It is not clear precisely how the Commission will apply these tests. However, it is suggested that market share is normally the most

important indicator of dominance though not the only factor. The Merger Regulation indicates in its recitals that if the parties' combined market share does not exceed 25 per cent in the EC or in a substantial part of it a merger between them is unlikely to impede effective competition. In examining a merger the Commission is required to take account of the need to maintain and develop effective competition with the EC and of actual or potential competition, whether from inside or outside the EC. It must also take account of: (1) the market position and economic and financial strength of the parties to the merger; (2) the availability of alternative products; (3) barriers to entry; (4) the interests of consumers; and (5) the development of technical and economic progress as long as it is to consumers' advantage and does not form an obstacle to competition.

A transaction to which the Merger Regulation applies must be notified to the Commission on the prescribed form (Form CO) within one week after announcing a bid, reaching an agreement or acquiring control, whichever occurs first. 20 copies of the notification have to be provided. Parties must not give effect to a merger before they notify it to the Commission and for three weeks thereafter. Unless the Commission extends this period, parties may conclude a merger after the three week period has expired. In the case of a public bid, the suspensory requirement does not prevent a bidder from acquiring shares in the target as long as the bidder does not exercise the voting rights attaching to the shares. The Commission has power to waive the suspensory requirement (conditionally or unconditionally) if a party would otherwise suffer serious damage.

Within one month of receiving the notification, the Commission has to decide whether to approve the merger or to open proceedings. The Commission is only likely to open proceedings if it has serious concerns about the impact of the merger on competition in the EC. The one-month period will be extended if the Commission considers that the information supplied with the notification is materially incomplete. Where the Commission opens proceedings, it then has a further four months in which to issue a final decision. During this period the Commission carries out a detailed appraisal of the merger. It has power to request further information from the parties and to inspect documents at the parties' premises and failure by the parties to provide the information required or to co-operate in an inspection may cause the four month period to be extended. The Commission issues a written Statement of Objections to the parties, to which they can provide a written response, and holds oral hearings for the parties and for interested third parties. The Commission liaises with interested Member States throughout the proceedings.

It is open to parties to try to avoid a prohibition decision by offering appropriate undertakings to the Commission. The Commission has power to accept undertakings (and subsequently enforce them) if it is satisfied that they meet its concerns about the merger. An undertaking might involve, for example, modifying the scope of the original agreement or selling off one or more overlapping businesses to a third party.

The Commission can prohibit a merger or order divestiture (or other appropriate action) if a merger has been completed. It can impose substantial fines (of up to 10 per cent of turnover) on parties who give effect to a merger either during the suspensory period or after the Commission has issued a decision prohibiting it; and on parties who fail to divest businesses (or take other action) where the Commission has ordered them to do so. It can also impose smaller fines on parties who fail to comply with certain procedural requirements.

Chapter 2

The Purchase Price

HOW IS THE PRICE ESTABLISHED?

There is no golden rule as to what is the appropriate price to pay for a particular business. It is debatable whether calculating the price is an art or a science. It is often a combination of the two. There are formulae and ratios that purchasers use as guides such as basing the price on a multiple of earnings or net assets. Such formulae only give an indication. The adjustment to the indicative price is an art in that the purchaser takes account of the cost saving benefits it can bring to the vendor's business, potential profit increases arising from market synergies and identified liabilities which may affect future profitability. Ultimately the price is quite simply that which the purchaser is prepared to pay for the particular business and which the vendor is prepared to accept.

The simplest method of valuing the business is to agree a fixed price to be paid in full by the purchaser in cash on completion. Alternatively the purchaser and vendor may agree that some or all of the price is to be based on the net book value of the assets or by reference to earnings. The standard sale agreement (see Appendix III) envisages a price based on a fixed cash sum plus net asset value. Where the price is based on net asset value or on earnings, the appropriate value is normally determined by accounts prepared as at completion or such other effective transfer date as the parties have chosen and subsequently agreed by the purchaser and vendor through their accountants. To simplify preparation of the accounts the parties may agree it appropriate for the completion date to be at the end of a month.

Completion accounts

Completion accounts will usually be needed if the price is to be based on earnings or net asset values. The sale agreement should

43

contain a detailed set of rules governing preparation and agreement of the completion accounts. The purchaser's and the vendor's accountants are normally the people who are asked to agree the completion accounts and their advice must be sought. If the purchaser's and the vendor's accountants are to be involved, and it is strongly recommended that they are, it is imperative that they should be involved as early as possible in negotiating this part of the sale agreement.

The rules in the sale agreement governing the completion accounts should cover the main areas listed below. The list is not definitive and must be adapted to the circumstances:

(1) What is the balance sheet date and, if appropriate, what period is the profit and loss account to cover?

(2) Who is to prepare the first draft of the completion accounts?

(3) On what basis are the accounts to be prepared and what form are they to take?

(4) What is the mechanism for the other party to agree or dispute the draft accounts?

(5) What if the parties cannot agree?

The first two areas are relatively uncontentious. Whether it is the purchaser's accountants or the vendor's accountants who prepare the first draft, the other party's accountants should have access to their working papers if the rules are properly negotiated.

The most difficult area is agreeing the basis on which the completion accounts are to be prepared and the form they are to take. The form may be a simple balance sheet or alternatively it may be necessary to prepare something equivalent to annual statutory accounts including details such as a cash flow statement complying with Financial Reporting Standard No 1 which replaces statements of source and application of funds provided under SSAP No 10. Prices based on a multiple of earnings tend to require more detailed and thorough completion accounts than net asset value based prices.

The rules in the sale agreement need to specify carefully, and in order of priority, the accounting rules and practices to be used in preparing the completion accounts. The rules would normally specify that the completion accounts are to be prepared in accordance with:

(a) generally accepted accounting practices or the statements of standard accounting practice (SSAPs) in order to give a true and fair view;

(b) the same accounting practices as used consistently in previous accounts of the business, normally over a period of several years;

(c) specific accounting rules legislated for in the sale agreement.

In order to avoid disputes, the sale agreement should specify the priority to be given to each of these rules. It has been common practice to prioritise the need to prepare the accounts in accordance with SSAPs. However, accounting practices are changing constantly and SSAPs are in the process of being replaced by Financial Reporting Standards. For the sake of clarity, one possible solution is to provide that the SSAPs to be used are those that applied at a specified date even if changed subsequently between exchange and completion.

For a purchaser there are dangers in relying on accounting practices used in previous accounts of the business unless the purchaser's accountants have a clear and thorough understanding of what these practices were. For example, the purchaser may object to the practices used by the vendor in accounting for work in progress and obsolete stock. It is possible that previous accounting practices, although not objected to by the vendor's auditors, may produce a disadvantageous result for the purchaser in completion accounts. The purchaser will wish to avoid any such disadvantageous practices. To avoid potential disputes the parties should set out in a letter, preferably attached to the sale agreement, any specific adjustments that will need to be made for the purpose of the completion statement. It is also often useful to include in the side letter, by way of illustration only, a worked example of a pro forma completion statement to which both sets of accountants agree and to which they can refer back when the actual accounts are to be prepared.

The greater the thought and attention given by both parties to developing the completion account rules, the less likely that the parties will be unable to agree the actual completion accounts. Again, it must be stressed that the purchaser and vendor should involve their respective accountants in the negotiation of the rules as early as possible.

In any event, the rules should provide a means of resolving any impasse that does arise. Normal practice is to refer the matters in dispute to an independent accountant. This is an additional cost for one or more of the parties and is in itself a reason for ensuring that disputes are resolved wherever possible before referring to a third party for resolution. The vendor should ensure that the sale agreement provides that the purchaser is obliged to pay that part of the price that is not disputed as soon as possible and that interest is paid on the additional amount if any that the purchaser is subsequently required to pay.

It is perhaps worth mentioning the importance of the sale agreement stating that the independent accountant will act as an expert rather than as an arbitrator. The decisions of an arbitrator are subject to rights of appeal to a court on a point of law under the Arbitration Act 1979, whereas there is no right of appeal against the decision of an expert even if the decision was negligent. This was affirmed by the Court of Appeal in *Baber v Kenwood Manufacturing Co Ltd and Whinney Murray & Co* [1978] 1 Lloyd's Rep 175. However, the major disadvantage of an arbitrator is that, unlike an expert, he cannot be sued for negligence in respect of loss or damage arising out of his decisions. As between themselves, the purchaser and the vendor are bound under the terms of the sale agreement by the decisions of the expert, but the provisions in the sale agreement do not prevent the aggrieved party, whether it be the purchaser or the vendor, from attempting to bring a claim against the expert if it can be shown that such party has suffered loss under the normal principles of the law of negligence (see *Arenson v Casson Bechman Rutley & Co* [1977] AC 405).

Earn outs

Earn outs are a means of linking the price to the future performance of the business in the hands of the purchaser after completion. Earn outs were particularly popular in the 1980s especially where the vendor worked as an employee of the purchaser in a service-based business after completion as it is a means of providing an incentive to the vendor where the profits may depend heavily on the skills of the employees. As earn outs are based on future performance and are only payable in the future, they enable the purchaser to agree to a price it may not be able to afford at completion and which it will not be obliged to pay unless profits are generated. All vendors should seek specialist tax advice if considering deferring consideration through an earn out as there may be adverse capital gains tax consequences particularly if the earn out is not achieved.

Earn outs are becoming less and less popular as the disadvantages often outweigh the advantages. The main disadvantages are caused by the fact that the earn out distorts the way in which the business would otherwise be managed. Employees will understandably be more concerned as to short-term profit rather than long-term growth as part of the purchaser's group.

The basis of calculating an earn out is generally the same as for completion accounts. However, the emphasis has shifted in that the business is now controlled by the purchaser rather than the vendor and the earn out will be calculated over a period of perhaps several years following completion. The vendor will wish to protect their ability to maximise payments under the earn out. Ideally the vendor will wish to retain absolute control over the way in which the business is managed. Purchasers, not surprisingly, are unwilling to permit this. Instead, the vendor will normally seek undertakings from the purchaser only to operate the business in the same or a similar manner to the way it was operated before the sale. Such undertakings will normally be unacceptable to the purchaser who may wish to dispose of part of the assets or reduce inherent costs by utilising existing central services such as its own accounts department. Even if at the time of sale the purchaser does not intend such rationalisation, it will not wish to fetter its discretion to do so in the future and to be able to adapt the business as it wishes to changing market circumstances. The vendor will also wish to impose restrictions on the ability of the purchaser to extract dividends or to levy management charges and revalue assets. Furthermore, earn outs encourage the vendor to concentrate on short-term profitability whereas the purchaser's concern is more likely to be the long-term prospects of the business. The purchaser should also consider what is to happen to the business after the earn out period as it will be extremely difficult to motivate the vendor if he is still a key employee.

In summary, earn outs should only be used where the purchaser intends to allow the vendor to operate the business after completion on a very similar basis to the way the vendor operated it previously and as a separate entity. Earn outs are impractical if the business will be operated as a division of the purchaser rather than a stand alone subsidiary. In any event, the vendor will want some assurance guaranteeing the basis on which central charges will be allocated to the business. If an earn out is to be used, it is recommended that it does not form too significant a part of the purchase price as this will distort priorities. The purchaser is likely to impose a cap or limit on the maximum amount payable under the earn out. The limit will be relevant for calculating stamp duty as the Inland Revenue will look to the maximum price payable and how this has been allocated. The vendor should resist assuming that the full earn out will eventually be paid and concentrate instead on the formula and past performance to consider the realistic expectation. The vendor should also take advice on the tax implications of identifying the maximum price payable as the Inland Revenue will at the time of sale assume that the maximum price is payable and tax the vendor accordingly.

APPORTIONMENT OF THE PRICE

The apportionment of the price between the respective assets has complicated tax consequences which are discussed in detail in Chapter 7. The apportionment will affect the corporation tax liabilities of the parties (particularly in relation to chargeable gains and capital allowances) and the stamp duty to be paid by the purchaser. The interests of the vendor and the purchaser are largely opposed and it is sensible for the matter to be resolved by stipulating the apportionment in the sale agreement. This is envisaged in the second column of Schedule 1 of the standard sale agreement (see Appendix III). If completion accounts are required, it is common practice to require the relevant accountants to agree the apportionment at the time they agree the completion statement as the price will not be finalised at the time of contract.

HOW IS THE PRICE TO BE PAID?

The purchaser and vendor need to agree:
   (a) the form of the payment; and
   (b) the timing of the payment.

The form of the payment

The most popular form of payment is cash. It is the simplest form and does not require complicated provisions or professional advice both of which will add to the purchase costs.

Other main forms of payment involve the issue of shares or loan stock by the purchaser. Alternatively assets of one business may themselves be used to buy the assets of another business. This is rare in the United Kingdom but is relatively common in Eastern Europe particularly in joint ventures where one party, normally from part of the old Soviet Union, simply does not have hard currency available but may have valuable commodities. The main concern with cash is to ensure that the method and arrangements for payment are clearly stated in the sale agreement and that the purchaser has adequate notice of whether a banker's draft or telegraphic transfer is required. If some or all of the payment is to be satisfied by the issue of shares, the purchaser must check whether it has sufficient authorised and issued share capital and whether the directors have adequate existing authority under CA 1985, s 80. The purchaser may need to convene an extraordinary general meeting of the shareholders if insufficient share capital or authority exists and consider the need to disapply any pre-emption rights. The purchaser will also need to file a duly stamped copy of the asset sale agreement with the Registrar of Companies within one month of the allotment of the shares (CA 1985, s 88). Furthermore, if the purchaser is a public company, whether or not its shares are quoted, it is prevented by CA 1985, s 102 from allotting the consideration shares to the vendor unless the consideration for the allotment has been independently valued pursuant to CA 1985, s 108 and a report regarding the value has been made to the purchaser by an independent person within the six months preceding the allotment. The preparation of the valuation and report will of course involve the purchaser in further cost and expense and the purchaser will also be required to send a copy of the report to the vendor (see CA 1985, s 103(1)(c)).

In the case of an unquoted company, the vendor is primarily concerned as to the marketability of the shares and this should not be underestimated. Also, the vendor should consider the need for warranties similar to those it would seek on a share purchase. In particular the vendor should seek assurances that the current shareholders have waived any rights of first call they have on the new shares and, if necessary, are prepared to enter into a shareholder's agreement with the vendor. All of these involve cost for the purchaser and may discourage the purchaser from using shares.

If the purchaser is a listed company it may need to apply for a listing of the consideration shares. The purchaser will need to prepare listing particulars unless listing particulars have been issued in the last year or the consideration shares will comprise less than 10 per cent of the listed shares after they have been issued. In the case of a purchaser issuing quoted shares, the difficulties of knowing whether the 10 per cent threshold is exceeded and whether class tests are appropriate are compounded if the total consideration has not been determined and depends on completion accounts or an earn out. Care must also be taken to ensure that, if the price of the consideration shares falls, the total shares to be issued do not exceed 30 per cent of the purchaser's share capital as the vendor may then be obliged to make an offer to purchase the remainder of the purchaser's share capital under rule 9 of the City Code. Perhaps most importantly the vendor should remember that the value of the consideration shares can go down as well as up and the purchaser may require the vendor to agree to restrictions on the manner and timing of subsequent sales of the shares by the vendor.

Where the vendor insists on receiving cash for the consideration, it may still be possible for the purchaser to raise the cash by issuing shares rather than by increasing borrowings. If the purchaser is a listed company, it is likely to prefer to issue shares, as increasing its borrowings will increase its gearing ratios as seen by the market. Alternatively, the purchaser may simply not be prepared to face the cost of borrowing. There are two main methods by which the purchaser can raise the cash: through a share issue namely a rights issue or a cash placing.

Rights issue

In a rights issue the purchaser offers to its existing shareholders the right to subscribe in cash for such number of shares in proportion to their existing holdings as will raise a sum (after deduction of the rights issue costs) equal to the consideration needed for the acquisition. As with any other share issue, the purchaser may need to seek approval of its shareholders to increase the authorised share capital and to authorise the directors to allot the shares pursuant to CA 1985, s 80. A special resolution of the shareholders may also be needed if the statutory pre-emption rights granted by CA 1985, s 89 are to be disapplied. The purchaser will need to remember that a minimum delay of between 14 and 21 clear days may be needed in between exchange and completion if either an ordinary resolution or special resolution of shareholders is needed.

Assuming the purchaser obtains the relevant authorities from its shareholders, it will make the offer to the shareholders to subscribe for shares by issuing a provisional nil paid allotment letter which under Stock Exchange rules must be open for acceptance for a period of at least 21 days. As it is possible for the allotment letters to be dealt with in this 21 day period, rights issues are attractive to institutional shareholders as they may be able to sell the rights to subscribe.

A rights issue is normally underwritten in order to ensure that the purchaser is guaranteed that it will receive the necessary funds. Underwriting can be expensive, representing sometimes up to two per cent of the issue proceeds, and the underwriting costs normally depend on the length of the time period from the date of the announcement of the rights issue until such time as the offer closes. Occasionally, rather than face the underwriting costs, purchasers may make the rights issue at a deep discount. The risk of a deep discount rights issue is that the purchaser cannot guarantee that the proceeds of the issue will be sufficient to meet the acquisition in the asset sale but it does avoid the underwriting costs.

Cash placing

A cash placing is one in which the subscription offer is made to investment clients of the purchaser's merchant bank or broker rather than to its existing shareholders. The merchant bank or broker will charge a commission for procuring the subscribers and may agree to subscribe itself for the balance if it fails to procure sufficient interest from its clients. Cash placings are normally cheaper than rights issues. However, the problem with a cash placing is that existing institutional shareholders may not be willing to consent to the disapplication of pre-emption rights.

The timing of payment

Naturally the vendor will want the price to be paid in full on completion. If part of the price is determined by completion accounts, the vendor will want the price to be paid as soon as it is determined, or as soon as part of it is determined if the balance is disputed. The purchaser will wish to consider the timing of payment in the context of the whole transaction. It may be appropriate for the purchaser to pay only part of the price on completion and make a retention of the balance or defer the balance. A retention will normally be made where the purchaser is concerned about specific liabilities identified in the due diligence or disclosure exercises. Alternatively, the purchaser may simply consider that there is a high probability of claims arising under the warranties and is unsure as to the financial ability of the vendor to pay for future claims or its ability to locate an individual vendor who for example, may emigrate. The retention may also be used as a means of securing a vendor's future obligations under the sale agreement or ancillary document such as not competing with the business or continuing to provide stocks and materials to the business. Whether or not a retention is made is a matter of negotiation.

The vendor's concern is to ensure that the monies retained do eventually become available provided the relevant liability has not crystallised. The vendor is unlikely to grant the purchaser much freedom in its use of the retention. Instead, the vendor will prefer to see the retention monies placed into an escrow account out of the purchaser's control. The account can either be a joint deposit account requiring the signature of both the vendor and the purchaser to release money or it can be placed in an account with an independent trustee. The trustee will want the vendor and purchaser to specify the trust rules before consenting to act.

One issue will be what interest is to be payable on the retention monies. As the retention represents deferred payment, it is reasonable for the vendor to be paid interest on the monies eventually received. Normal arrangements are for the purchaser to be entitled to the interest on the monies subsequently released to it from the retention accounts.

The other main issue will be defining the precise circumstances when part or all of the retention is released to the purchaser. The retention will normally be released to satisfy a claim against the vendor. The purchaser will incorporate an express right of set-off in the sale agreement. The difficulty comes in identifying what constitutes a valid claim. Neither party is likely to want to wait until the matter has been decided on by a court. A suitable compromise is for both parties to rely on the opinion of a leading Queen's Counsel as to whether or not and to what extent the purchaser's claim is likely to succeed.

The vendor may be prepared to accept some of the risk of not having the retention placed into a dedicated account or simply facing deferred instalments rather than a retention. In such circumstances, the vendor should consider the need for security and the risk that the purchaser may fail to make or be unable to make the appropriate payment. One possibility is to seek a parent company or preferably a bank guarantee, though this will involve the purchaser in some expense and may require a deposit to be made with the bank. In addition, the vendor may wish to take a charge over the assets being sold. Unlike a share sale, where this would be financial assistance (CA 1985, s 151) there are no company law objections to such security.

EFFECTIVE DATE OF THE TRANSFER

The parties may sometimes want the transfer to be effective from a date before the completion date, particularly if there is likely to be a long delay while consents are sought. The sale agreement itself cannot be back-dated. Rather its provisions will deem the transfer to be treated as if it took place on an earlier specified date.

There are numerous complications that need to be addressed if an earlier transfer date is to deemed to apply and the complications will outweigh the advantages unless there are exceptional circumstances. The main complications relate to:

(a) taxation in the interim period;
(b) VAT;
(c) liability; and
(d) rescission.

Taxation in the interim period

Despite the fact that the sale agreement will treat income arising after the transfer date as belonging to the purchaser, the Inland Revenue are likely to treat it as income of the vendor. The vendor should only account to the purchaser for post-taxation income earned during the interim stage. The purchaser will not necessarily wish to be paid as if the income had been taxed. The vendor's taxation for the interim period will be difficult to calculate and may not be determinable until the end of the financial year at the earliest, particularly if the business sold comprises one division of the vendor's overall business. Furthermore, it may be difficult to allocate expenditure and income for the period.

Value Added Tax

During the interim period the vendor will have charged and paid Value Added Tax as principal. It will not be possible subsequently to replace the VAT accounting procedures to reflect what the state of affairs was intended to be.

Liability

The deeming provisions will mean that during the interim period the vendor will be treated as acting as agent for the purchaser yet the purchaser will have no control over the vendor's actions. The purchaser is unlikely to want to accept liability for the vendor's actions when it has had no control. At the very most a purchaser may be prepared to accept responsibility only for liabilities arising in the ordinary course of the business.

Rescission

If the purchaser requires the right of rescission to be available between exchange and completion, the vendor is unlikely to agree to the transfer being deemed to occur during the interim period.

CAN THE PURCHASE PRICE EVER BE TOO LOW?

Naturally the objective of all purchasers is to pay as little as possible for the business. However, it is suggested there are some instances, albeit rare, where the purchaser should become cautious if, in reality, the purchase price appears too low particularly if the purchaser is concerned about the vendor's state of solvency. For such instances to be relevant, the purchase price for the assets must be significantly less than market value. The situations that are relevant are:

    (a) breaches by the directors of the vendor of their duties of good faith;

    (b) the vendor becoming insolvent within two years after the transaction;

    (c) transfers within a group of companies.

The duty of good faith

The director of a company has a duty to carry on the business of that company in all respects in good faith for the benefit of that company and not for the benefit of other group companies. Generally the directors owe this duty to their shareholders but as insolvency approaches the duty is owed to creditors (see *West Mercia Safetywear v Dodd* [1988] BCLC 250). Furthermore, the director has a duty not to make a secret profit out of transactions with the company. Any asset sale which is not commercially justifiable as being in the interests of the vendor as a whole will, on the face of it, be a breach of the duties of the directors of the vendor. If the purchaser has actual knowledge that the asset sale carried out by the directors is in breach of their fiduciary duty, the transaction is voidable at the instance of the vendor and the purchaser will hold the proceeds of the sale as a constructive trustee. It is suggested that as a result of CA 1985, s 35 the main difficulties will only arise where the purchaser knows or should have known that the directors of the vendor were abusing their powers, for example, by committing a fraud on the vendor's creditors. Furthermore, any act which falls within the express or implied powers of the vendor contained in its memorandum of association, whether or not a breach of duty on the part of the vendor's directors, will be binding on the vendor if it is approved or subsequently ratified by the shareholders.

Transactions at an under value

Where the purchase price is particularly low, the purchaser may be at risk if the acquisition from the vendor is considered to be a transaction at an under value within the meaning of the Insolvency Act (IA) 1986, s 238. In such circumstances the court has the power to make such order as it thinks fit (IA 1986, s 238(3)) including the right to set aside the transaction. A transaction is at an under value if the transaction constitutes a gift or if the value of the consideration (in money or money's worth) received by the vendor is significantly less than that of the consideration the vendor provides. Section 238 only applies to transactions entered into at an under value within two years prior to the onset of the vendor's insolvency and does not apply to sales by a liquidator as, amongst other things, this is a sale after the onset of insolvency. The onset of insolvency is the date of presentation of an administration petition or the date of commencement of winding up by the presentation of a winding up petition or a resolution by the company to go into liquidation.

It should be noted that for s 238 to apply, the value of consideration received must be *significantly less* than the consideration provided by the vendor. If a purchaser is concerned, it is suggested that it may be appropriate to seek one or more independent valuations of the business though this will of course increase the acquisition costs. Furthermore, a valuation merely provides assurance that the transaction was not at an under value but is not a defence.

A further risk that may be relevant where a purchaser acquires assets and assumes responsibility for some but not all of the creditors, is that the sale may be seen as a preferential treatment of creditors under IA 1986, s 239. This enables a liquidator or administrator to apply to the court where, within two years before insolvency, the vendor has given preferential treatment to creditors. The court can make such order as it thinks fit to restore the position to what it would have been if the company had not given that preference. A preference consists of anything done or suffered to be done by the vendor which has the effect of putting one of its creditors, or any surety or guarantor, into a position which, in the event of the vendor going into insolvent liquidiation, would be better than the position which such person would have been in if that thing had not been done. It has to be shown that, in assuming responsibility for some but not all creditors, the vendor was influenced by a desire to prefer some creditors against others. Where the purchaser is connected with a vendor (connected is defined in IA 1986, s 249) the standard of proof on the vendor is higher in two ways. Firstly, in the case of preferential treatment, s 239 relates to transactions within two years before the onset of solvency rather than six months and the vendor is presumed to have been influenced by a desire to prefer creditors unless the contrary is shown. Secondly, in the case of transaction at an undervalue, it is presumed that the vendor was not solvent at the time the acquisition agreement was exchanged.

One problem sometimes overlooked arises under IA 1986, s 216 and relates to the use of the name of a company which is subsequently insolvent. With effect from the start of an insolvent liquidation of the vendor, unless the court grants leave, the vendor's company name may not be used by the purchaser if the purchaser or directors of the purchaser have been directors or shadow directors of the vendor during the twelve months preceding the liquidation. The restriction on the use of the name extends for five years from the insolvency and breach of s 216 is a criminal offence.

Inter-group transfers

Problems will arise on an asset sale where the vendor and purchaser are members of the same group of companies and the assets are transferred at an under value. Under TA 1988, s 209(4), a transfer of assets between a company and its member at an under value is treated as a distribution. The transfer will be at an under value if the market value of the benefit received by the purchaser exceeds the amount of value of any consideration given by the member. The surplus of market value over consideration given is treated as a distribution and advanced corporation tax will be payable.

The position has been further complicated by the recent case of *Aveling Barford v Perion Limited and others* [1989] BCLC 626. The effect of the decision in *Aveling Barford* is that where a company has no retained earnings, a transfer by it to a sister company which is known to be at an under value may be treated as an unauthorised return of capital. Therefore, where the vendor and purchaser are both wholly owned subsidiaries of a third company and the vendor sells assets to the purchaser at an under value, it is suggested that to the extent the value conferred on the purchaser comes out of the vendor's capital as opposed to distributable profits, then this is treated as an unlawful return of capital by the vendor to the third party holding company. It is suggested that this is an addition to a breach of CA 1985, s 263 which provides that the vendor can only make a distribution out of profits available for the purpose.

In his judgment, Hoffman J considered that 'the court looks at the substance rather than the outward appearance'. The court looks at the whole circumstance of the transaction and considers whether the true nature of the transaction when viewed as a whole is that it is a disguised dividend. It is suggested this is comparable to the manner in which the Inland Revenue will use the decision in *Furniss v Dawson* [1984] 1 ALL ER to view a transaction as a whole rather than each separate step individually.

The consequences for a purchaser of receiving an unlawful distribution are provided by CA 1985, s 277 and will essentially require a purchaser, who at the time of distribution, knew or had reasonable grounds for believing that it was an unlawful distribution sale, to be made liable to repay the distribution to the vendor. The consequences for the vendor are that it will need to account for unpaid advanced corporation tax on the entire amount of the distribution unless there is a group income election in place.

Chapter 3

Purchaser Protection

INTRODUCTION

There are three levels of protection that a purchaser will require.

Firstly, during the negotiations the purchaser will naturally be concerned to be reassured as to what it saw at the outset as being the merits of the proposed acquisition. This will involve identifying the liabilities and risks to be assumed and the state of the assets being acquired.

Secondly, the purchaser will wish to protect itself in the sale agreement against any risks which it was unable to identify during the negotiations but which are discovered after completion and to ensure it is compensated against these by the vendor.

Thirdly, the purchaser will be concerned to ensure that once completion has taken place, the vendor does not establish or participate in a competing business.

Normally, purchasers will achieve these three levels of protection by using the methods described below:

(1) Due diligence.
(2) Warranties and indemnities.
(3) Restrictive covenants.

The relative importance of due diligence and of warranties and indemnities will, to a large extent, depend on the purchaser's assessment of the vendor's current and future financial stature. The warranties and indemnities give the purchaser the right to claim against the vendor after completion. If the purchaser has little confidence in the vendor's ability to pay compensation for breach of warranty, the purchaser will rely heavily on the due diligence exercise. This should enable the purchaser to identify and deal with risks before contract rather than seeking redress from the vendor after completion.

DUE DILIGENCE

Due diligence is the investigation of the vendor's business by the purchaser and its advisers before contracts are executed. The purchaser will have conducted its own investigation of the vendor's business in the negotiations which lead up to either an agreement in principle or a more formal acknowledgement of agreement by the use of heads of terms (see Chapter 1, page 9). During negotiation of the contract, the purchaser will continue to investigate the business but more thoroughly than before and will often instruct both lawyers and accountants to investigate and prepare reports on the business.

If concurrent investigations are to take place, the purchaser should meet its advisers as early as possible to ensure there is no duplication in the areas to be investigated and, more importantly, that all significant areas are covered in the investigation process. The time of the advisers costs money and due diligence will be expensive if its scope and content is not carefully controlled. Due diligence for asset sales is generally cheaper and quicker than for share sales as the investigation covers the specific assets that have been selected rather than investigating hidden liabilities. At this initial stage, the purchaser should discuss carefully with its advisers the scope, aims and objectives of the investigation. The instructions should either be given or confirmed in writing. One way of reducing the cost is to investigate a cross-section of the main assets rather than each separate asset. For example, if the business is heavily dependent on numerous long-term contracts, a purchaser may decide to investigate the contracts equating to a specified percentage of the turnover of the business plus one or two minor contracts. This will give the purchaser assurance as to the main assets and an overview on the minor assets.

The purchaser's lawyers will usually proceed by gathering all information already given to the purchaser and then issuing an information questionnaire to the vendor similar to that set out in Appendix II. It is good practice for the vendor to keep an index and central store of all documents sent in response to the information questionnaire. The vendor will subsequently wish to disclose all such documents against the warranties. Depending on the volume of material and negotiating strength, the purchaser may argue that the vendor can only disclose specific documents against specific warranties. In any event, the vendor will be asked to warrant that all documents and responses supplied are true and accurate. Warranty A1 in the standard sale agreement (see Appendix III) is the sort of warranty a purchaser will normally ask for.

Where the purchaser has commissioned an accountants' report, it is normal practice to request that the vendor warrants the accuracy of the report. Such a warranty, depending on its content, may shorten the warranties that the purchaser requires on specific matters. The purchaser will normally require the vendor to warrant that the report is accurate in all material respects and that there are no facts omitted which make the report misleading. The vendor is likely to resist any warranty as to the accuracy of any expressions of opinion or forecasts contained in the report. At best, the vendor may be willing to warrant that such forecasts and opinions are reasonable. Alternatively, rather than warranting the accuracy of opinions, the vendor may be prepared to warrant that they do not disagree with the opinion.

If the matter was not dealt with at an earlier stage, the vendor is likely to ask the purchaser and perhaps its advisers to enter a confidentiality agreement before the investigations start. A standard confidentiality agreement is set out in Appendix I and discussed in more detail in Chapter 1.

WARRANTIES

Is there any need for warranties?

The purchaser should reject outright any suggestion by any vendor other than a liquidator, administrator or receiver that, unlike a share sale, there is no need to give warranties in an asset sale. There are two reasons that the vendor may give and which the purchaser should not accept.

Firstly, a vendor may argue that, unlike a share sale, the purchaser does not inherit the liabilities of the business. This is true to a large extent in that the liabilities prior to completion remain with the vendor unless the purchaser agrees to accept them. However there are notable exceptions. For example, the purchaser will inherit the employment liabilities if the Transfer of Undertakings (Protection of Employment) Regulations 1981 (SI 1981/1794) apply (see Chapter 5). Also the purchaser is likely to assume responsibility for past liabilities through the assignment or novation of contracts (see Chapter 4), subject to an appropriate indemnity from the vendor. Furthermore, the vendor is being asked not merely to warrant the absence of liabilities but also to warrant the state and adequacy of the assets being sold. Inadequate assets will carry inherent liabilities and the state of the assets therefore requires warranting. The purchaser will also insist that the vendor warrants title to its assets. In addition, the warranties encourage the vendor to make disclosures which relate to the quality of the assets. Basic warranties are contained in the standard sale agreement and discussed throughout this book.

Secondly, the vendor may attempt to argue that sufficient warranties are implied by statutes, such as the Sale of Goods Act 1979, to obviate the need for warranties. The purchaser should not accept any argument that implied warranties are adequate. Although warranties may be implied by statute, not only may they be inadequate, but the vendor will want the purchaser to acknowledge it has not relied on any warranty, representation or undertaking unless expressly set out in the sale agreement. Furthermore, in the absence of express warranties, the common law rule of *caveat emptor* (buyer beware) will apply. Even if implied warranties did apply, they would not address all the purchaser's concerns as can be seen by the fact that the main warranties implied by the Sale of Goods Act 1979 are dealt with within warranties A3 and A4 in the standard sale agreement (see Appendix III). The remainder of the warranties in the standard sale agreement (of which there are many) address the purchaser's other concerns in relation to the business.

Dual purpose of warranties

Warranties serve two purposes. The first is to encourage the vendor to disclose exceptions to the general nature of the warranties. This enables the parties to address the problem areas identified by the disclosures. It is better that the purchaser is aware of the difficulties before contracts are executed as this reduces the possibility of disputes for breach of warranty arising once the transaction is completed.

The second and more important reason is to impose liability on the vendor in the event that the assets are inadequate or defective or the vendor does not have adequate title. The warranties serve as a means of allocating business risk between the vendor and the purchaser. The vendor will seek to reduce the risk by making disclosures and limiting its liability for breach of warranty.

The value of warranties

A breach of warranty will give the purchaser the right to claim damages from the vendor. During negotiations the purchaser should assess the likelihood of a claim arising and the vendor's ability to compensate the purchaser if a claim is successful. The likelihood of a claim arising is a judgment decision which will be influenced by the results of the due diligence exercise. Purchasers are less fearful of the potential for claims if the vendor appears well-managed and well-organised. The assessment of the vendor's ability to pay will depend on the current financial status of the vendor and its plans for the coming years including its use of the sale proceeds. The purchaser should also consider the need for a parent company guarantee.

Depending on these factors a purchaser should consider whether to:

(a) rely solely on its right to claim damages for breach of warranty; or

(b) make a retention of part of the purchase price to deal with identified liabilities; or

(c) reduce the price.

The resulting solution will depend on the relative negotiating strengths of the parties. The purchaser is usually only justified in reducing the price if the due diligence exercise has revealed material inaccuracies in the assumptions used in calculating the initial offer price. For example, the actual profits of the business during the due diligence period may be significantly lower than those forecast.

A retention is often used as a means of resolving a specific difficulty identified by the due diligence exercise (see also Chapter 2, page 51). For example, the purchaser may consider that only 60 per cent of customer contracts expiring in the first year will be renewed, whereas the vendor believes 90 per cent to be a more likely renewal rate. The purchaser will only be willing to pay the price originally agreed if the forecast renewal rate is achieved. Therefore a negotiated sum is retained out of the purchase price and some or all will be released to the purchaser once the actual renewal rate is known. The parties will need to negotiate the period of the retention and define precisely the circumstances in which the retention is released. During the retention period the money should be held in a deposit account. The interest earned is normally paid at the end of the period to the respective parties in proportion to the amount of the retention received by them. An appropriate compromise is for payments from the designated deposit account to require the signature of both the vendor's and the purchaser's lawyers. Alternatively, an independent trustee may be appointed to apply the trust rules negotiated by the parties.

Basis of claims under the warranties

Rescission

Rescission is one remedy available for misrepresentation under the Misrepresentation Act 1967, s 1. It is not within the scope of this book to discuss in detail the circumstances when the purchaser will be entitled to rescind the sale agreement. In principle, rescission may be available if the vendor made a false statement of fact and that statement became a term of the sale agreement. The statement need only be oral and would not need to be expressly repeated in the sale agreement. For this reason it is normal for the vendor to define precisely which documents comprise the sale agreement and to ensure the purchaser acknowledges that it is not relying on any statements of fact unless contained in these documents. The parties should then state that these documents constitute the entire agreement between them.

Even though the vendor may have taken this basic protection, the vendor should be aware of the decision of the Chancery Division in *Goff v Gauthier* 62 P & CR [1991] 388. Mr JAD Gilliland QC (sitting as a deputy judge) permitted the defendants to rescind a contract for the sale of land as a result of a misrepresentation made before contract, despite the fact that clause 10 of the sale agreement provided that the agreement contained all the terms of the contract between the vendor and the purchaser and that the purchaser did not enter into the agreement in reliance on any warranty or representation made or purported to have been made by or on behalf of the vendor other than the vendor's solicitor's written replies to enquiries raised by the purchaser's solicitor. It was held that it was not fair for the plaintiff to rely upon clause 10 to enable him to escape from the consequences of a clear misrepresentation on an important matter which had induced the defendants to exchange contracts even though the representation was not repeated in the contract. It should be stressed that in the *Goff v Gauthier* case, the misrepresentation was of fundamental importance in inducing the defendant to enter the contract and was not a minor misrepresentation which it was suggested that clause 10 would have excluded.

From a commercial point of view rescission as a remedy is more theoretical than practical. It will only be ordered if the purchaser and vendor are capable of being returned to the position they were in before the sale agreement was executed. For this reason rescission is unlikely to be ordered after completion as the purchaser is likely to have affirmed the contract by conduct and third parties may be prejudiced if rescission takes place. Too much may have happened within a matter of days after completion for it to be practical to reverse the sale. However, rescission is an important remedy for the period between exchange and completion. To avoid scope for argument, the purchaser should ensure it is expressly stated in the sale agreement that rescission is available as a remedy for the period between exchange and completion (see clause 13.8 of the standard sale agreement—Appendix III). The purchaser should also include a statement that failure to exercise its right to rescind shall not be a waiver of its right to claim damages.

Damages

The alternative remedy for the purchaser is to claim damages. The purchaser may elect to claim damages for misrepresentation (whether innocent, negligent or fraudulent) and complete rather than rescind the sale. If this is proposed, it is strongly recommended that the purchaser either negotiates and settles the claim before completion or makes a retention.

Under the common law, the measure of damages for a breach of warranty will be to put the purchaser in the position it would have been in if all the warranties had been true. There are many books dedicated to explaining in detail the basis on which damages would be calculated under the common law.

Rather than rely on common law, it is normal practice for purchasers to specify in the sale agreement the basis on which damages will be calculated. This is less important than in a share sale where the difficulty of the purchaser, without an express damage statement, is to show that the shares are worth less than the purchaser paid for them, as a reduction in the assets or increase in the liabilities does not necessarily reduce the price of the shares. A purchaser of assets is more likely to recover the reduction in value of the assets and the consequential reduction in the value of goodwill.

In determining whether to negotiate a specific damages clause such as that in clause 13.3 of the standard sale agreement (see Appendix III), the purchaser should consider the basis on which the price was calculated. If the price is based on net assets, a reduction in assets should be directly reflected in a reduction in price. However, if there is a significant element of goodwill or the price is based on a multiple of earnings, this should be reflected in a formula similar to that used by the purchaser for calculating the price. Purchasers may negotiate alternative formulae and should reserve the right to select the most advantageous formula at the time the claim is brought. The vendor will resist allowing the purchaser such an option.

In rare circumstances a purchaser may seek to argue that the vendor has breached a warranty to such an extent that it considers the vendor to have repudiated the contract. The purchaser may wish to accept repudiation and sue for damages.

Reducing the vendor's liability

The two ways in which the vendor seeks to reduce its potential liability under the warranties are firstly by producing a disclosure letter and secondly by incorporating a limitation of liability clause in the sale agreement.

Disclosure letter

The draft warranties sought by the purchaser will be in general terms. This is dictated by the fact that the purchaser knows little real detail about the business at the time the draft agreement is prepared. For example, the warranty may state that there are and have been no disputes with employees in the last three years. The disclosure letter is then used by the vendor to describe any specific exceptions to the general statement, for example, two claims for unfair dismissal having been brought in the last six months. Traditionally, and to simplify the drafting of the warranties, these exceptions are contained in the disclosure letter generated by the vendor, or its lawyer on its behalf, rather than as amendments to the warranties.

The purchaser should be careful to ensure that the disclosures do not wholly undermine the warranties. The purchaser will want the vendor to warrant that its disclosures are true and accurate and are not misleading and should reject any general disclosures. For example, a statement by the vendor that there have been various disputes by the employees completely undermines the warranty. The purchaser would thereby be deemed to have full knowledge of all disputes. Instead, the vendor should be encouraged to identify, describe and quantify the actual and contingent liabilities arising from these disputes.

It is normal practice for the vendor to disclose various documents to the purchaser as part of the disclosure exercise. As a matter of good practice copies of the documents should either be attached to the disclosure letter or placed in a file of documents delivered with the letter. If claims do arise, it is in everyone's interest to be able to identify easily all the matters that were disclosed. The vendor should be required to refer in the disclosure letter to the reason why the documents have been disclosed. The purchaser should reject at all costs any attempt by the vendor to disclose any other documents which are referred to in the documents presented with the disclosure letter.

The vendor will frequently be tempted to make its disclosure as wide as possible and include all sources of information which the purchaser inspected or could have inspected during negotiations. The clear aim of the vendor is to disclose as much as possible thereby reducing the potential for claims under the warranties. However, it is suggested that the vendor should not adopt this 'scatter gun' approach but instead disclose specific information and salient points expressly or by reference. In *Levison v Farin* [1978] 2 All ER 1149 it was held that it would not normally be enough 'to make known the means of knowledge which may or do enable the other party to work out certain facts and conclusions'.

Clearly the disclosure letter is important as it potentially under-mines the warranties. A preliminary draft of the disclosure letter and all relevant documents should be requested as early as possible in the negotiations for, in many respects, it is as important as the sale agreement. Any attempt to produce the letter for the first time at completion should be resisted and completion delayed until the purchaser has had adequate time to consider the disclosures.

Limitation of liability

It is particularly important and common for the vendor to incorporate provisions into the sale agreement limiting its liability under the agreement, and in particular its liability for breach of warranty. Vendors should not rely on the possibility that protection may be available under the Unfair Contract Terms Act 1977. Vendors would do well to remember the principle illustrated in *Finney Lock Seeds Ltd v Mitchell (George) (Chesterhall) Ltd* [1983] 1 All ER 108 in that the damages incurred and awarded (in that case nearly £100,000) can be far in excess of the purchase price paid for the assets (in that case approximately £100) if the loss is a consequence of a defective asset.

Basic limitation has been included in clause 14 of the standard sale agreement (see Appendix III). Many purchasers will acknowledge that the vendor will wish to limit its liability and incorporate these basic provisions in the initial draft. Common ways of seeking to limit liability are:

(a) agreeing an upper limit on the amount the vendor will pay if the claim is successful (see clause 14.3 of the standard sale agreement—Appendix III). This is normally set at the pur-chase price or the upper limit of the price if this cannot be determined at completion. Whether or not the purchase price is an appropriate or indeed adequate upper limit is arguable but it is only in rare circumstances that a vendor will agree to a higher limit. One such situation is a sale under which the purchaser pays nominal consideration but assumes significant liabilities;

(b) imposing a time limit beyond which, except in cases of fraud and dishonesty, the purchaser is time-barred from bringing a claim (see clause 14.1 of the standard sale agreement—Appendix III). Time limits normally negotiated vary between six months and four years. As a matter of practice most claims come to light within the first two audits of the business by the purchaser;

(c) to set a minimum value which the purchaser's claim must exceed in order for the claim to be brought (see clause 14.2 of the standard sale agreement)—Appendix III. This is described as the *de minimis* and serves as confirmation that the vendor will not be troubled by small claims. In large transactions vendors may also negotiate a lower limit for individual items. For example, the purchaser may agree to ignore all claims of less than £5,000 and not to bring a claim until the aggregate value of all claims over £5,000 exceeds £30,000. The purchaser should reject any suggestion by the vendor that it may then only recover the amount of the claim exceeding the *de minimis*. This implies that the vendor is representing itself as an insurer whereas the real claim is the full value of the damages suffered by the breach of contract;

(d) ensuring the purchaser acknowledges it has not relied on any representation other than those incorporated in the sale agreement and that it shall not have any right to rescind the sale agreement. The case of *Goff v Gauthier* (1991) 62 P & CR 388 has shown that it must be fair and reasonable for the vendor to rely on this exclusion (see page 62);

(e) to state that the vendor will not be liable to the extent that any claim arises out of or is increased by the acts or omissions of the purchaser after completion;

(f) to provide that the purchaser must give credit for the amount by which assets are found to have been understated, or liabilities have been over-provided for in the accounts;

(g) to ensure that the purchaser pays to the vendor all amounts subsequently recovered from third parties relating to claims that have been paid by the vendor. Alternatively, the vendor may require the purchaser to assign to it all rights against third parties but the purchaser will wish to restrict the vendor's ability to commence proceeding against customers as this may affect the goodwill of the business;

(h) to limit some of the warranties to the best of the vendor's knowledge, information and belief. To the extent that the purchaser is willing to accept this reduction of the absolute nature of warranties, it should be on the basis the vendor acknowledges that in all circumstances it has made full and proper enquiries and investigations (see clause 13.6 of the standard sale agreement—Appendix III);

(i) to provide that the vendor shall not be liable if the purchaser completed the sale at the full purchase price despite the fact that it had knowledge of a particular breach of warranty. In the absence of an express statement, it is uncertain whether the purchaser's prior knowledge is a defence available to the vendor. The recent decision of the Court of Appeal in *Eurocopy v Teesdale and others* (1992) BCLC 1067 supports the argument that it is a defence whereas *Goff v Gauthier* P & Ch [1991] 388 supports the contrary view. It is in everyone's interest that the sale agreement contains an express statement as to whether prior knowledge is a defence or whether prior knowledge will not prejudice the purchaser's ability to claim for breach of warranty if the material fact is not disclosed in the disclosure letter (see clause 13.4 of the standard sale agreement— Appendix III). If it is accepted as a defence, the purchaser should limit it to the actual knowledge of specific key individuals involved in negotiating the purchase rather than the knowledge of all its employees and advisers. Ultimately it is for the vendor to prove that the purchaser had such knowledge.

It is suggested that the decision of the Court of Appeal in the *Eurocopy* case is the more equitable solution, particularly in circumstances where a disclosure is expressly brought to the attention of the vendor before completion but is not actually incorporated in the final disclosure letter. In the *Eurocopy* case, the plaintiff and the defendants were the purchaser and the warrantors respectively in a share sale and purchase agreement. The defendants sought to argue that the plaintiff was prevented from claiming breach of warranty since the material fact constituting the breach had been disclosed to the plaintiff at a meeting prior to signing the disclosure letter but had not been eventually contained in that letter. The plaintiff argued that the prior disclosure was irrelevant as the share sale agreement contained clauses stating that the warranties were given subject to the matters set out in the disclosure letter but that no other information whether actual, constructive or imputed would affect any claim made by the plaintiff or reduce any amount recoverable. A further clause provided that the plaintiff would not be entitled to claim for breach of warranty if the material matter had been fairly disclosed to the plaintiff in the disclosure letter but that no other information of which the plaintiff had knowledge would prejudice any claim by the plaintiff under the warranties. In his judgment, Nourse LJ relied on the defendant's argument that the plaintiff had actual knowledge of the position and that the plaintiff had led the defendant to believe that it considered the fact not to be material. The disclosure letter had been drawn up by the defendant on this belief and by its actions the plaintiff was estopped from complaining that the fact should have been included in the disclosure letter. Nourse LJ considered it would be arguable that the defendants were 'entitled to escape literal application of the agreement'. Nourse LJ also considered it was arguable that the plaintiff could not seek to rely on the literal clauses of the agreement when it had known that the disclosure letter was incomplete as to do so would be dishonest. Although Nourse LJ does not categorically state what the law is in this situation, his decision indicates and points towards the view that the defendants may be able to escape the restrictions of the sale agreement where it would be inequitable to allow the plaintiff to rely on the strict wording.

Joint and several liability

Where there are multiple vendors, such as members of a partnership selling their business, purchasers will invariably insist that the vendors give warranties on a joint and several basis. The effect is to enable the purchaser to recover its loss under a breach against any one or more of the vendors and leave the vendor paying the claim to seek compensation from his fellow vendors. There is in fact no need to state in the sale agreement that liability is joint and several (although it is invariably the practice to do so) as this is implied by the Civil Liability (Contribution) Act 1978, s 1(1) and the ability to recover from fellow vendors and their estates is extended by s 6(1) of that Act.

It is helpful for the purchaser and the vendors to understand the implications of both joint liability and several liability. Joint liability is the liability undertaken together by two or more vendors. Although the position has been modified by statute, traditionally a joint liability can only be enforced by bringing the claim at the same time against all the vendors undertaking the liability. A purchaser would have to locate and commence proceedings against all vendors. This is fraught with logistical difficulties for the purchaser.

A several liability is a liability undertaken by the vendors independently of each other and enforceable by the purchaser against each of the vendors independent of the others. Several liability gives the purchaser the choice of which vendor to sue. Once the vendor has been sued successfully it is then up to that vendor to try to recover a proportion of the cost incurred from the other vendors under the Civil Liability (Contribution) Act 1978. Clearly several liability favours the purchaser whereas joint liability favours the vendors. Joint and several liability is a suitable compromise.

If joint and several liability is accepted, there is nothing to prevent the vendors from settling between themselves in a private agreement the basis on which they would each be required to contribute if a successful claim is brought against any one vendor. This will mean the vendors bear the financial risk of not being able to locate fellow vendors or finding that they have inadequate funds. In the absence of an express agreement, under the Civil Liability (Contribution) Act 1978 the court will apportion the contributions between the vendors in such a manner as it considers to be just and equitable. Alternatively, the purchaser may accept that the vendors have limited joint and several liability in that it can only recover limited accounts from each vendor. The purchaser then bears the risk of non-recovery against one or more vendors.

Warranty insurance

A notable development in the last ten years is the availability of insurance cover to protect vendors against possible liability for claims for breach of warranty. The purpose of such insurance is to provide cover against those types of warranty claims which arise out of simple errors made by vendors acting in good faith. The insurance is only intended to cover vendors who at the time of contract had no knowledge of circumstances which eventually give rise to a claim or of the likelihood of claims being made under the warranties.

If insurance is to be sought, the vendor should identify and contact the insurers as early as possible in the negotiations as they will need sufficient time to review the draft documentation and consider the vendor's requirements. The purpose of warranty insurance is not to provide general cover for all possible liabilities under the warranties but to provide cover for specific risks under the warranties. To this end the insurer will require copies of the negotiated transaction documents including, in particular, the sale agreement, the disclosure letter, any side agreements, a copy of the investigating accountant's report (if any) and the last audited accounts for the target business. The vendor will also be required to answer a detailed questionnaire covering not only the vendor's knowledge of claims under the warranties but also explaining the nature of the transaction, the sale price and the basis on which the sale price has been calculated.

The insurers will then review the scope of the warranties and the depth and content of the disclosures being made against the warranties. The insurer will be concerned to see that the vendor has negotiated realistic limitations on its liability including a limit on the aggregate liability.

As with any other policy the insurers will commonly require exclusions against the following:

(1) *The adequacy of insurance arrangements* The view of the insurers is that it should be for the purchaser to determine whether existing insurance cover for the business is adequate and if it is not to increase the level of cover with effect from completion.

(2) *The adequacy of pension funding* Whether or not an insurer

will wish to exclude warranties relating to funding adequacy will depend on whether a recent valuation is available from the managers of the fund and whether the vendor can claim against the valuation if the funding is shown subsequently to be inadequate. If cover for funding adequacy is to be offered the insurer will normally require an additional premium.

(3) *Bad debts*   Insurers normally exclude liability for claims under a bad debt warranty on the basis that cover is available in the conventional insurance market and therefore this risk can be dealt with by other means.

(4) *Defects in goods or services sold or supplied*   As with bad debt liability cover is available in the conventional insurance market in policies for areas such as public liability, product liability and professional indemnity.

(5) *The fraud or dishonesty of the vendor*   In addition to fraud and dishonesty insurers will specifically exclude liability for the wilful failure by the vendor to disclose matters of which it had actual knowledge. Such exclusions may also cover matters of which the vendor ought to have had knowledge and should have disclosed.

(6) *Forecasts*   The insurance policies are only really intended to cover liability for accident or misstatement of fact by the vendor. Consequently, policies will not cover and will exclude forecasts and statements of intention or opinion as opposed to statements of fact.

(7) *Acts or omissions of the vendor after completion*   The exclusions will normally cover liabilities for claims arising due to the failure of the vendor to meet an obligation for which it is primarily liable or which have arisen due to any act or omission of the vendor occuring after completion.

As with any other policy the insurers will always require an excess. The minimum excess is normally £10,000. This may be in addition to any *de minimis* provisions negotiated by the vendor in the sale agreement.

Finally, the insurer will be concerned to see that the vendor has not waived or limited its rights of subrogation. If a warranty claim does materialise and the policy is called upon, the insurers will wish to have all rights to pursue claims against third parties. These would include claims against the vendor's professional advisers if they had been negligent in advising on the negotiation of the transaction.

RESTRICTIVE COVENANTS

One of the purchaser's main concerns is to ensure that, after the sale, the vendor does not immediately re-enter the market in competition with the business that has been sold. This would detract from the goodwill for which the purchaser has usually paid a premium. In order to protect the goodwill, the purchaser should take restrictive covenants from the vendor whereby the vendor undertakes not to compete with the business for a limited period. A purchaser seeking restrictive covenants must consider whether, as a result of the covenants, any prior clearance or approval needs to be sought from the OFT or the European Commission. This is discussed in Chapter 1 at page 31.

As a general rule a restrictive covenant restricts competition and is presumed to be void and unenforceable because such restrictions are contrary to public policy. Despite the general rule, restrictive covenants will be held valid if they are reasonable. They must be considered reasonable by the parties to them at the time of entering into the contract and they must also be seen as reasonable from an objective point of view. In *Allied Dunbar (Frank Weisinger) Limited v Weisinger* [1988] IRLR 60 it was held that ultimately the parties that negotiated the covenants are the best judges of the reasonableness of the terms they have negotiated. The price attributed to the goodwill being protected was considered as being a relevant factor (see also *Alec Lobb Limited v Total Oil GB Limited* [1985] 1 WLR 173, CA). If a covenant is contested it is for the party seeking to rely on the covenant to prove its reasonableness (see *Rex Stewart Jeffries Parker Ginsberg v Parker* [1988] IRLR 483). Therefore if a purchaser is in a strong negotiating position, it should remember not to demand excessive restrictions at the time of contract despite its relative negotiating strength. On the other hand, the covenants need to be sufficiently strong to prevent the vendor from re-entering the market place shortly after completion.

It cannot be overstressed that in every sale the reasonableness of the restrictive covenants must be considered in the particular circumstances. Past cases are only helpful in so far as they act as a guide and some of the main points arising from them are discussed below. Clause 15 of the standard sale agreement (Appendix III) provides a common example of covenants sought by a vendor. Again, it is a starting point for negotiations and should not be seen as a definitive version. Clause 15.1 adopts the common practice of distinguishing in the covenant the separate means by which the purchaser will protect the goodwill. Not only will the vendor covenant not to compete with the business, but it will also covenant separately not to solicit customers or solicit employees. The purchaser hopes that if ever a court considers any one level of protection to be unreasonable, it may sever this from the agreement and leave the other covenants untouched or impose a more reasonable amended form. The parties declare that this is their intention (see clause 15.2) and in clause 15.3

acknowledge that they consider the restrictions to be reasonable.

The main areas to be considered in determining reasonableness tend to be the restrictions on business activities, the territorial extent of the restrictions and the duration of the restrictions. As to business activities, a covenant is likely to be unreasonable if it covers activities which are not relevant to the business sold. For this reason the purchaser should take considerable care in defining the restricted business. It should be no more and no less than the business carried on at the time of completion.

As to the territorial extent, again the restrictive covenant should not cover an area greater than that reasonably necessary to protect the business. It is common practice not to extend the covenant beyond the territory in which the business being sold operates at the time of completion. This was the view taken in *Nutricia v Zuid–Hollandse Conservenfabriek* (OJL 376/22) and was confirmed by the European Court of Justice in *Remia & Nutricia v Commission* (Case 42/84 [1987] 1 CMLR 1).

As to the duration of the restrictions, what constitutes a reasonable period depends largely on the nature of the business sold. It is common to take account of the duration of customer contracts and to allow the purchaser a period that extends beyond the contract renewal point. In the *Nutricia* case the court laid down various guidelines. These involved considering:

(a) how long it will take the purchaser to build up further clientele;
(b) how frequently customers in the market change between the various competitors;
(c) how quickly new products come on to the market and are taken up by customers;
(d) how long it will take the vendor to re-establish itself in the market if there is no restrictive covenant.

As a general warning vendors should not place too much reliance on employment cases. The restrictive covenant in a sale agreement protects goodwill whereas restrictive covenants given by employees protect the employer and employee relationship. A court will also give greater importance to ensuring employees are not prevented from earning a living. In the *Allied Dunbar (Frank Weisinger)* case it was confirmed that sale purchase covenants will be construed less stringently than employee's covenants.

Chapter 4

Contracts, Creditors and Debtors

CONTRACTS

One of the common problems encountered in assets sales is determining how the customer and supplier contracts entered into by the vendor are to be transferred to the purchaser. The transfer of such contracts raises problems which, by and large, are not present in share sales because in share sales the party to the contract with the customer or supplier is not changing. In share sales it is the ownership of the contracting party that is changing rather than the identity of the contracting party. Nevertheless, in share sales problems may still exist if there are change of control clauses in contracts to which the target is a party. Change of control clauses (commonly found in software licences) entitle one party to a contract to terminate the contract if there is a change in ownership of the other contracting party or sometimes a change in ownership of the holding company of that contracting party.

In determining how to transfer contracts pursuant to an asset sale, it is important firstly to understand the legal issues involved in transferring contracts before considering the practical consequences for the vendor and purchaser. The legal issues are best understood by distinguishing between the benefit of a contract and the burden of a contract, or between the rights and entitlements of a contract and the obligations to be performed under a contract. For this reason this section addresses the following three areas:

(1) Transferring the burden of the contract.
(2) Transferring the benefit of the contract.
(3) Practical consequences.

Transferring the burden of the contract

The difficulty in transferring contracts arises because the basic rule is that the vendor cannot be excused from the burden of its contractual obligations by assigning or otherwise purporting to transfer to the purchaser the obligation to perform the duties it has undertaken under a particular contract. However, there are two common alternative legal structures by which the purchaser can assume the vendor's obligation to perform a contract namely:

(a) novation; or

(b) sub-contracting or agency arrangements.

Novation

Novation is the means by which, with the consent of the customer under a specific contract, that contract is replaced by a new contract made between that customer and the purchaser. The old contract between the customer and the vendor is extinguished. The new contract between the customer or supplier and the purchaser must comply with the normal requirements for formation of a contract including intention and consideration. In a novation, the purchaser will assume and be liable for all the obligations of the vendor under the original contract and the vendor will be relieved of its obligations to the customer under the original contract.

The most important fact to note is that novation requires the consent or acceptance of all parties to the relevant contract. Such consent need not be expressed but can be implied by conduct depending upon the circumstances (see *Bilbrough v Holmes* [1876] 5 Ch D 255).

Sub-contracting or agency arrangements

Rather than create a new contract by novation, it may be possible for the purchaser to perform the obligations vicariously on behalf of the vendor under the existing contract. This is normally done by the vendor appointing the purchaser as sub-contractor or as agent. The important point to note is that under such vicarious arrangements the vendor remains responsible directly to the customer and will still be sued by the customer for non-performance or for breach of the contract if the work has not been undertaken in accordance with the terms of the contract. The vendor would then need to recover against the purchaser pursuant to provisions, including indemnities, incorporated in the standard sale agreement.

Such sub-contracting or agency arrangements will not work where the performance by the vendor of its obligations to the customer are of a 'personal' nature. Vicarious performance of a personal contract will not discharge the vendor nor bind the customer. The essence of a personal contract is the significance of the identities of the parties. Is it clear that the parties intended that no one but the actual party in the contract should have the benefit of the contract or the right to call for its performance? Whether or not a contract is of a personal nature is determined on objective grounds and depends on all the circumstances having regard to the nature of the contract and the subject matter of the rights to be assigned and there is no general rule. In the words of Lord Greene in *Davies v Collins* [1945] 1 All ER 247:

Whether or not in any given contract performance can properly be carried out by the employment of a sub-contractor, must depend on the proper inference to be drawn from the contract itself, the subject matter of it and other material surrounding circumstances.

Contracts for services are commonly personal as in such circumstances the customer is likely to have relied upon the individual skill and identity of the vendor.

Transferring the benefit of the contract

The transfer of the benefit of the contract is most commonly dealt with by way of an assignment unless the contract is being novated, in which case the benefit will be dealt with alongside the burden in the novation agreement. In understanding assignment it is important to distinguish assignment from novation. In a novation the old contract is extinguished and the old obligations are assumed in a new contract. Unlike novation, assignment involves the transfer of property namely the rights in relation to a contract which continues to exist and is not extinguished. There are two methods of assignment: assignment under statute and assignment under common law. For the purchaser, it is important to consider whether as a result of the assignment the purchaser will be able to enforce the benefit of the contract directly against the supplier or whether such benefit can only be enforced with the co-operation of the vendor. Generally only a statutory assignment gives the purchaser a direct right. The main question is whether the assignment binds the supplier as well as the vendor.

Assignment by statute is governed by the Law of Property Act 1925, s 136 which provides that:

Any absolute assignment by writing under the hand of the assignor (not purporting to be by way of charge only) of any debt or other legal thing in action, of which express notice in writing has been given to the debtor, trustee or other person from the assignor would have been entitled to claim such debt or thing in action, is effectual in law (subject to equities having priority over the right of the assignee) to pass and transfer from the date of such notice:

    (a) the legal right to such debt or thing in action;

    (b) all legal and other remedies for the same; and

    (c) the power to give a good discharge for the same without the concurrence of the assignor.

What is important to note is that there are three main conditions which must be fulfilled to accomplish an assignment under statute:

(a) the assignment must be absolute;
(b) the assignment must be in writing; and
(c) written notice must be given to the debtor or the supplier as appropriate.

The most important condition for the purchaser to consider is the need for written notice of the assignment to be given to the debtor or supplier.

If any of the three conditions are not fulfilled, the purported assignment under statute will not necessarily be ineffective, as it may constitute an equitable assignment. The disadvantage of an equitable assignment is that if the purchaser is to enforce the contract against the supplier or debtor, the vendor must be joined as a party (see *Performing Rights Society Limited v London Theatre of Varieties Limited* [1924] AC 1). At common law the assignment gives the purchaser a right against the vendor but not an independent right of action against the debtor or supplier.

One distinction between an assignment at equity and under statute is that, for an equitable assignment to be valid, written notice does not need to be given to the supplier whereas it is an essential part of the statutory transfer (see above). Despite the fact that formal notice is not needed, there are two important reasons why the purchaser may wish to give notice of an equitable assignment. Firstly, the purchaser is bound by any payments which a debtor makes to the vendor if it has no knowledge of the assignment (see *Warner Brothers Records Inc v Rollgreen Limited* [1976] QB 430). In such circumstances the purchaser will then need to rely upon the terms of the sale agreement to recover from the vendor. Secondly, the giving of notice will establish the priority of the purchaser against the debtor ahead of any other assignee of the vendor who has failed to give notice of assignment to the debtor (see *Dearl v Hall* [1828] 3 RUS 1). Provided that the purchaser did not have actual or constructive notice of the prior assignment at the time the asset sale agreement was completed, the purchaser is not prejudiced, if between completion and giving notice to the debtor, the purchaser discovers the existence of a prior assignment by the vendor (see *Mutual Life Assurance Society v Langley* [1886] 32 Ch D 460).

The main exception to the procedures for statutory and common law assignments is where the benefit to be assigned relates to a personal contract (see above). If the contract is personal, the benefit of that contract must be novated, it cannot be transferred by way of assignment. An express prohibition on assignment does not in itself render the contract personal. It is a matter of construction of the contract and the surrounding circumstances as to whether the prohibition is intended merely to place the vendor in breach of contract and exposed to a claim for damages or whether the prohibition is intended to render the assignment ineffective and make it clear that the contract is personal. If the contract is not personal but contains an express prohibition on assignment, such prohibition will only prevent an assignment of the benefit if on its wording it is clear and precise.

If there is an express prohibition on assigning the benefit it is important to distinguish between the benefit *of* the contract, namely the right of each party to have a contract performed in accordance with its terms, and the benefits which arise *under* the contract, namely those rights which arise incidentally from the performance of the contract and are sometimes known as the fruits of performance such as the right to claim for damages under the contract. The fruits of performance are proprietary rights and choses in action assignable under statute even if the contract is personal (*Linden Gardens Trust Limited v Lenesta Sludge Disposals Ltd* and *St Martins Property Corporation Ltd and Another v Sir Robert McAlpine and Sons Ltd* 57 BLR 57, both cases have been joined and are being heard in an appeal to the House of Lords at the time of writing). The benefit of the contract is only assignable if it makes no difference to the person on whom the obligation lies as to whether the obligation is discharged to the vendor or to the purchaser.

Practical consequences

The level of complexity with which the sale agreement addresses transferring the vendor's contracts to the purchaser will vary enormously depending upon the nature of the vendor's business and the parties' relative negotiating strengths. Understandably, despite such possible complexity, the purchaser will not be interested in the legal semantics of how the contracts are to be transferred but will be interested in two main practical concerns: firstly, in receiving the benefit of the contracts in return for performing the burden and secondly, in not paying for a contract if the purchaser cannot benefit from it.

The simplest situation to deal with is where the benefit of the vendor's contracts is freely assignable. The main concern of the purchaser will be whether to rely on the sale and purchase contract as constituting the assignment between the purchaser and the vendor or whether to issue notices of assignment to each party to the contracts after completion and so achieve a statutory assignment rather than an equitable assignment. The statutory assignment has the advantage of enabling the purchaser to enforce the contracts directly against the supplier rather than through the vendor. The purchaser should ensure that it is not restricted from issuing notices of assignment by any of the announcement or confidentiality restrictions in the sale and purchase agreement.

The difficulty occurs where consent to the transfer of contracts is needed, whether it be consent to transfer of the benefit or of the burden. Consent will be needed where there is a clear express prohibition in a relevant contract or where that contract is 'personal'. If consent is needed any purported transfer by the vendor may be a repudiatory breach of that contract by the vendor exposing the vendor to a claim for damages from its customer and possibly a claim by the purchaser against the vendor if the customer treats the contract as terminated particularly if the vendor warranted that no consents were needed. To avoid such problems, where a consent is needed, the normal practice is for the sale agreement to provide that the vendor will hold the benefit of such contract on trust for the purchaser and pay any sums which the vendor receives after completion to the purchaser immediately upon receipt (see clause 8.2(a) of the standard sale agreement—Appendix III). In return the purchaser will undertake to perform the vendor's obligations under such contract. However, the purchaser should ensure that this only applies to obligations to the extent that they have been disclosed and ensure that it will not be required to perform the obligations if such vicarious performance would be a breach of the relevant contract (see clause 8.2(b) of the standard sale agreement—Appendix III). The purchaser should also ensure that the vendor is under an obligation to provide all necessary assistance and co-operation in obtaining the consents after completion either by relying on the general further assurance clause or by incorporating a dedicated further assurance clause such as that in clause 8.4 of the standard sale agreement (see Appendix III). Problems arise where consent to an assignment or agreement to novation is sought but is refused. In such circumstances the purchaser will wish to absolve itself of any responsibilty to perform obligations under the relevant contract and will seek an indemnity from the vendor for any liability in respect of such contract (see clause 8.3 of the standard sale agreement—Appendix III). Whether this is acceptable to the vendor is a matter of commercial negotiation and depends on who agrees to bear the risk that a consent is refused or not forthcoming within a specified period. The difficulty for the vendor is that, as a result of the sale, the vendor may be left with no facilities to perform obligations under such contract and may face a claim from the party to that contract for breach.

The contracts for which consents are required are likely to have been revealed by the purchaser's due diligence exercise and by the vendor's disclosures. The vendor will be required to disclose such contracts against the warranty that no consents to transfer are required (see warranty F1 in the standard sale agreement—Appendix III). In an ideal world, the purchaser will wish to receive formal consent from every customer and supplier before completing the acquisition. This will normally be impractical and it is suggested that the purchaser may wish to distinguish between the following three levels of consent:

  (a) critical consents;
  (b) material consents;
  (c) ancillary consents.

Critical consents

Critical consents are those which it is essential for the purchaser to obtain if it is to conduct the business after completion. An example of such consent is the transfer of the vendor's contracts with its main suppliers particularly if the business cannot operate without an assurance of a constant supply of products. In such circumstances the purchaser is likely to insist that the obtaining of these critical consents is a condition precedent to completion of the acquisition and it is difficult for the vendor to oppose this if the consents are truly critical. The main concern of the vendor will be the commercial effect upon its business in approaching individuals for critical consents if completion does not take place because one or more have withheld their consent. The further risk both the vendor and purchaser will wish to minimise is alerting the particular customer or supplier as to how significant they are in relation to the business. In extreme circumstances the customer or supplier may seek to use its strong position and extract personal benefits in return for giving its consent. Alternatively, the customer or supplier may look on the purported transfer as an opportunity to terminate or renegotiate the contract.

Material consents

A less important category is those contracts which are material to the continuing conduct of the vendor's business but without which the business can still be operated after completion, albeit on a smaller scale. Material consents relate to those contracts, normally the vendor's customer contracts, which the purchaser would like to receive formal consent for and if such contracts are not transferred failure to take over such contracts may materially reduce the value of the business acquired. One possibility is for the purchaser to provide that part of the purchase price will be reduced and repaid to the purchaser if certain material consents are not received or if only a proportion of material consents are received. Ideally, the purchaser would prefer to make a retention of part of the purchase price and only pay this to the vendor once certain levels of material consents have been received. The vendor may not be willing to agree to a retention particularly if the purchaser is unable to offer adequate security for the future payment or is unable to pay retention monies into a joint account pending receipt of the consents. The vendor may simply refuse to consider a retention or deferred payment since after completion it will simply not have the facilities to perform any remaining contractual obligations and vicarious performance by the purchaser is not possible or is inappropriate. Ultimately, it is a question of who, commercially, is to take the risk that a consent may be refused.

Ancillary consents

Ancillary consents are those which technically require formal consent but which the purchaser does not consider as being significant to the business. In such circumstances the purchaser may be willing either to take the risk that consent is refused or withheld or alternatively to proceed without obtaining formal consent and if necessary argue that the relevant party to the contract has consented by its conduct after completion. Such conduct may include regular payments which are clearly made by the purchaser after completion for invoices submitted by the other party to the contract to the vendor. It may also be possible to argue that where the party has failed to respond to a notice of assignment from the purchaser, such lack of action over a long period is an implied consent where that party has dealt with the purchaser after completion.

DEBTORS AND CREDITORS

One of the issues to be resolved between the vendor and purchaser is the question of whether the purchaser is willing to take over either of the debtors or creditors of the business or whether one or both of these will remain with the vendor after completion of the sale. The issue is not dissimilar to the general question of identifying what assets are included in the sale and what are excluded. However, the issue is discussed here as it does to a certain extent relate to customer and supplier contracts that are being assigned. For example, the purchaser may consider that certain supplier contracts are essential to the business but at the same time is not willing to accept responsibility for the vendor's debts to the supplier.

It is worth examining separately:
(1) The reasons for excluding debtors and creditors.
(2) The reasons for including debtors and creditors.
(3) Common solutions for the issue.

The reasons for excluding debtors and creditors

The following are the main reasons that the vendor will wish to exclude both debtors and creditors and will normally outweigh the reasons for including debtors and creditors in the sale.

Stamp duty

The purchaser will have to pay *ad valorem* duty at the rate of one per cent on the gross value of the debtors (Stamp Act 1891, s 57) and at one per cent on the total value of the liabilities to creditors assumed. The important point is that stamp duty is payable not on the net position (ie debtors less creditors) but on the value of debtors plus the value of liabilities. Furthermore, duty is payable on the gross value of the debtors and ignores the possibility of any bad debts and the purchaser will be paying stamp duty on an asset for which he has received no benefit.

Bad debts

If debtors are to be transferred, the purchaser should seek a warranty in the sale agreement that all the debts will be realised in full within a fixed period after completion and that none of the debts is subject to any counter-claim or is disputed. An appropriate warranty is included as warranty A.7 in the standard sale agreement, see Appendix III. In addition, the purchaser should seek from the vendor a specific indemnity against bad debts but on the basis the purchaser acknowledges that it will not be able to recover twice for both breach of warranty and under the bad debt indemnity. The disadvantage of a bad debt warranty and indemnity is that all it does is provide a remedy for the purchaser. Ideally, the purchaser would prefer to leave the risk of bad debts with the vendor, after all, the vendor is the person best able to assess the position.

Creditors

The risk for the purchaser is that the vendor may have understated the scope and extent of the creditors. As with bad debts, the purchaser will insist on warranties covering the scope and extent of creditors and the fact that all creditors have been paid in accordance with usual practice in the ordinary course of business and that the vendor has not delayed payment of the creditors as completion approaches. The purchaser should also impose a financial limit on the value of the creditors that it assumes. Although a limit can be imposed, it is difficult to know how as a matter of practice what limit can be operated. Furthermore, the protection of warranties and imposing a limit is only the second best option. Ideally the purchaser would prefer to leave the risk of creditors with the vendor.

Price and cash flow

The purchaser and vendor will need to negotiate how the assumption of debtors and creditors is to be reflected in the price paid for the business. The purchaser is unlikely to be willing to pay for the gross value of debtors less gross creditors in full on completion. There are three main reasons. Firstly, there is no reason why the purchaser should pay for items which eventually materialise into bad debts. Secondly, there is no reason why the vendor should receive payment from the purchaser for the debtors earlier than the vendor would have received such payment from the debtors themselves. This would put the vendor in a better position than it would have otherwise been in had the sale not taken place. Thirdly, there will be considerable cash flow implications for the purchaser, particularly if the creditors fall due to be paid before the debts are collected from the debtors. There is no reason why the purchaser should bank roll the vendor's cash flow position.

Reasons for including debtors and creditors

The following are the main reasons for including the debtors and creditors in the asset sale:

The availability of staff, books and records

It is probable that the purchaser will have taken over all the books and records of the vendor relating to the business and the purchaser may have also taken over all of the vendor's accounting staff. In such a situation the vendor is left without the means to discharge the creditors and pursue the debtors.

Continuity

It is easier for the purchaser to deal with the creditors and debtors as they are likely to continue to be customers and suppliers of the business after completion. Excluding the creditors and debtors may cause confusion amongst them as they will be uncertain as to whether they are meant to be dealing with the vendor or the purchaser for particular debts and liabilities. It is far easier from their point of view if they only need to deal with one entity and they will probably prefer that to be the purchaser as it is the purchaser that has taken over the business.

Goodwill

If debtors and creditors are excluded the natural inclination of the vendor will be to pursue the debtors and delay paying the creditors for as long as possible. Irrespective of the fact that the business has changed hands, creditors may associate the delay in payment with the business itself rather than the identity of the vendor. Furthermore, if the vendor commences debt recovery proceedings against debtors who continue to be customers of the business this may jeopardise goodwill.

Common solution  —good

The common solution is for both creditors and debtors to be excluded from the sale and to remain with the vendor as this is to the clear advantage of the purchaser. As a compromise, the purchaser is normally willing to act as agent for the vendor both in collecting the debts and paying creditors. By adopting this solution the purchaser avoids the risk of bad debts and understated creditor liability and will not incur stamp duty costs. By acting as agent the purchaser will overcome the problem that the vendor no longer has the books and records of the business and may no longer have any accounting staff.

The risk to the purchaser in this solution is that the vendor may still wish to pursue debtors. For the purchaser, it is important to establish in the asset sale agreement an undertaking by the vendor not to pursue debtors without the consent of the purchaser. The vendor is only likely to be willing to accept this restraint in respect of debtors that continue to be significant customers of the business after completion. The vendor will also be concerned to know how quickly the cash will be returned to it by the purchaser. At the same time, the purchaser will not wish to return cash to the vendor that he has not yet collected from debtors, nor will the purchaser be willing to use its own funds to satisfy creditors on behalf of the vendor. A practical solution is for the purchaser to pay all debts collected on behalf of the vendor into a designated deposit account and to satisfy the excluded creditors out of the proceeds of that account. The vendor should be entitled to any interest that is earned on the balance and should receive either weekly or monthly statements from the purchaser or from the bank. Alternatively, where it is likely that the creditors will need to be paid before the debts can be collected, the purchaser may wish to make a retention out of part of the purchase price which it then uses for satisfying the creditors. The purchaser should reserve the express right to pay the creditors directly out of the retention on behalf of the vendor. A formula can be developed which may be complicated but under which the purchase price is paid in instalments and the precise amount of the instalments will decrease depending on the extent to which the purchaser has had to satisfy the debts to creditors on behalf of the vendor.

Where the excluded creditors continue to be customers of the business, the purchaser would understandably prefer to use monies received from that creditor to satisfy invoices that the purchaser has issued rather than those which were issued previously by the vendor.

Ignoring the bargaining strengths of both parties, there is no clear reason why a vendor should be willing to agree to this and as a matter of practice should establish the order of priority of satisfaction of liabilities within the terms and conditions of the sale agreement. The vendor should insist that monies received are used to satisfy the oldest liabilities first.

Chapter 5

Employment

THE GENERAL RULE AND ITS CONSEQUENCES

As a general rule the liabilities associated with persons employed in a business being sold are normally governed by the Transfer of Undertakings (Protection of Employment) Regulations 1981 (SI 1981/1794—the Transfer Regulations). The Transfer Regulations, which were enacted to give effect to the EC Acquired Rights Directive 77/187, will usually apply to a business sale if the vendor's business is transferred to the purchaser 'as a going concern'. This is the position adopted in the standard sale agreement (see Appendix III). Broadly speaking, although it is discussed in more detail below, a business is transferred as a going concern if the purchaser carries on that business in succession to the vendor as distinct from the purchaser selectively choosing specific assets of the vendor for use in the purchaser's own business. In other words, as a result of the sale, the vendor's business has been taken over by and is being conducted by the purchaser to the exclusion of the vendor. If the business is not transferred as a going concern the common law position will apply, and the employees will remain with the vendor if the purchaser does not wish to employ them.

The effect of the Transfer Regulations is that the contracts of employment of the persons working in the business immediately before it is transferred are novated automatically to the purchaser on completion of the transfer. The Transfer Regulations reverse the common law position which is that persons employed in that business will be redundant unless the vendor has other business in which they can be redeployed. If the common law position applies, the purchaser is free to offer employment, but upon whatever terms he chooses and to whomever he chooses. Instead, by virtue of the automatic novation when the Transfer Regulations apply, the contracts of employment continue to have effect after the transfer as if they were originally made between the purchaser and the employee.

This is a particularly important consequence for all purchasers. The general advantage of asset sales over share sales is that the purchaser can be selective as to which assets and liabilities he buys or assumes. The Transfer Regulations reverse the position with respect to employees. Due to the Transfer Regulations, the purchaser is in much the same and in no better a position than if he had bought the shares of the vendor company. As a result of the Transfer Regulations the purchaser becomes responsible for all the rights, obligations and liabilities of the vendor under the employment contracts for all persons employed in the business transferred. Moreover, if the purchaser wishes to rationalise the workforce he runs the risk of becoming liable for automatically unfair dismissals where employees are dismissed as a result of the transfer of the business. The purchaser takes over each employee subject to that employee's accumulated statutory rights. Due to the statutory novation it is normal practice for the vendor to indemnify the purchaser against all liabilities concerning the employees up to the time of completion. This approach, which is reflected in clause 9 of the standard sale agreement (see Appendix III) attempts to reinstate the advantage of an asset sale. The indemnity is, of course, only as good as the vendor and, if appropriate, its guarantor.

THE NEED FOR INFORMATION AT AN EARLY STAGE

Since the purchaser is to assume the liabilities for all persons employed in the business (including any claim by the employees against the vendor) it is important for him to collect, as early as possible, full details of all employees. This is particularly important if the purchaser is buying a service business and one of the main assets (or possibly liabilities) is the vendor's employees. Points which the purchaser may wish to raise with the vendor are set out in the information questionnaire (see Appendix II).

The terms of employment may have an impact on the purchaser's assessment of the merits of the transaction. For example, the employees that he takes over may have more generous terms of employment than his existing staff, or the vendor may have a collective agreement with or have recognised a trade union. To reduce the benefits of the new staff may be constructive dismissal yet to have staff doing similar work but on different terms will cause friction within the purchaser's workforce.

Alternatively, the purchaser may decide that he can operate the business more efficiently than the vendor either by a general reorganisation of job responsibilities or by his existing staff taking on a greater workload. Either way the purchaser will need full details of the vendor's employees in order to assess the costs of redundancies, wrongful and unfair dismissal claims and identify which of the vendor's employees he may prefer to retain. Depending on the likely cost of redundancies and the scale or likelihood of claims by the vendor's employees relating to their past relations with the vendor, the purchaser may wish to negotiate a contribution from the vendor or a reduction in the price.

The purchaser may also wish to ensure that the vendor's important employees will be transferred with the business. Further, the purchaser will wish to consider carefully the position of any person described by the vendor as an independent contractor (see below).

PENSION ENTITLEMENT

Until very recently it was commonly thought to be a peculiar anomaly of the Transfer Regulations that reg 7 specifically excludes from the statutory novation the rights of employees in respect of occupational pension schemes. It was thought that the purchaser automatically took on board liability for all of the employees' rights except those in respect of pension schemes, save in the case of contractual rights to receive payments into personal schemes which would be unaffected. Pension entitlements are dealt with separately in Chapter 6.

However, the effect of the recent tribunal decisions in *Warrener v Walden Engineering Co Ltd* (Case No 22672/91, Hull 21 October 1991) and in *Perry v Intec Colleges Ltd* [1993] IRLR 56 is that there is a major risk for a purchaser that he is now obliged to provide occupational pension benefits to the employees equivalent to those enjoyed by them while employed by the vendor. *Warrener* and *Perry* are discussed in more detail in Chapter 6. What remains to be answered, even if pension rights are capable of transfer, is what are the precise obligations of the purchaser in this regard, and how should compensation be calculated in the event of a breach by the purchaser of these obligations? It is suggested that if there is a breach, an employee is under a duty to mitigate the loss and this would probably involve joining the purchaser's existing pension scheme even if the benefits are not as generous as under the vendor's scheme. It would be a matter of negotiation as to whether the employee consented to the resulting change in employment benefits at the same time as agreeing to participate in the purchaser's scheme.

THE TRANSFER REGULATIONS

When do the Transfer Regulations apply?

Subject to the important exceptions below, the Transfer Regulations apply to the 'transfer from one person to another of an undertaking situated immediately before the transfer in the United Kingdom or a part of one which is so situated'. An undertaking is defined in reg 3 of the Transfer Regulations as including any trade or business, and as a result of a series of cases (*Kenmir Ltd v Frizzell* [1968] 1 All ER 414; *Batchelor v Premier Motors (Romford) Ltd* COIT 1359/181 19.11.82; *Premier Motors (Medway) Ltd v Total Oil (GB) Ltd* [1984] ICR 58; *Spijkers v Gebr Benedik Abattoir CV* [1986] 2 CMLR 296) it is well established that there will be a transfer of an undertaking for the purpose of the Transfer Regulations only if 'the business concerned is transferred as a going concern'.

What is the transfer of a business as a going concern?

There is no hard and fast rule as to what constitutes the transfer of a business as a going concern. However, it must be stressed that it is a question of fact in each individual transaction, and the question one has to ask objectively in every single situation is whether the purchaser is merely selecting specific assets for the use in his own business or whether he is buying assets in order that he can carry on the business in succession to and in place of the vendor. The former is an asset sale whereas the latter is the transfer of a business as a going concern.

There are many cases (noted below) on whether a business is transferred as a going concern. All the cases should be used with care and should always be related to their unique facts. However, as a result of past cases, several factors have now evolved as being helpful guidelines in answering the question. The factors which, if present, indicate the transfer as a going concern largely relate to intangible assets.

Goodwill

The transfer of goodwill is generally considered to be the single most important factor (see *Luckey v Hockley* [1966] 2 KIR 17; *Douglas v Merchants Facilities (Glasgow) Ltd* [1966] 1 ITR 374; *Seymour v Barber and Heron* [1970] 5 ITR 65; *Bonser v Patara* [1967] 2 ITR 76), but not an overriding one, in support of the transfer as a going concern. Where many of the other factors below are missing from a sale, the exclusion of goodwill from the sale will almost certainly make the transfer not a going concern.

Customer list

Again, a customer list is not a conclusive factor but is a helpful factor (see *Rencoule v Hunt* [1967] 2 ITR 475 and *MacDonald v Bull and Patterson* [1966] 1 KIR 734) particularly if the vendor assists in the transfer of its customers to the purchaser.

Work in progress

Work in progress must be the genuine transfer of the vendor's work in progress to the purchaser. It is unlikely to be the transfer of a business as a going concern if the purchaser merely completes work for the vendor after completion under a specific contract with the vendor (*Melon v Hector Powe Ltd* [1981] 1 All ER 313).

Restrictive covenants

Covenants by the vendor not to compete with the purchaser, particularly in respect of the business, support the fact that the purchaser bought the business as a going concern (*Robert Seligman v Baker* [1983] ICR 770). This factor tends to be linked with goodwill as it would be unusual for a purchaser not to take restrictive covenants to protect any goodwill he has purchased.

Trading names and trade marks

The transfer to the purchaser of the trade names and trade marks used in the business sold by the vendor is synonymous with the succession by the purchaser to the vendor's business.

Irrelevant factors

It is also helpful to bear in mind that the following factors tend to be of little or no relevance in determining whether a business is transferred as a going concern.

Statement by the purchaser and the vendor

As it is a question of fact, a statement in the sale agreement by the purchaser and the vendor that they consider the transaction to be the transfer of a business as a going concern is of little relevance. Such a statement merely indicates that the vendor and purchaser agree as between themselves that the Transfer Regulations should apply. To the extent that an industrial tribunal disagrees as a matter of fact and considers that the common law position applies instead, to the warranties and indemnities, will adjust the position between the vendor and the purchaser accordingly.

Tangible assets

The fact that a transaction includes the transfer of machinery, factory or office premises, stock, plant and equipment, tools and other tangible assets is not relevant if no intangible assets are transferred (*Woodhouse v Peter Brotherhood Ltd* [1972] 2 QB 520).

The opinion of the employees

It is irrelevant that, so far as the employees are concerned, they are working in the same premises with the same equipment and on the same job as before the sale and perhaps have not even been informed that a sale has taken place (*Woodhouse v Peter Brotherhood Ltd* [1972] 2 QB 520; *Woodcock v Committee for the Time Being of the Friends School Wigton and Genwise Ltd* [1987] IRLR 98, CA).

Similarity of work

It is not conclusive that the purchaser carries on work similar to or the same as that previously carried on by the vendor, especially if this work is undertaken pursuant to a contract between them.

Specific situations when the Transfer Regulations do not apply

Even if a sale clearly appears to involve the transfer of a business as a going concern, it is still important to consider whether the Transfer Regulations are relevant. The following are common situations in which the Transfer Regulations will not apply. In these situations the position will be governed either by the common law or the Employment Protection (Consolidation) Act 1978.

Business operated under franchise or licence

A detailed analysis of the sale of businesses operated under licence or franchise is outside the scope of this book. Common examples of such businesses include petrol stations, public houses, fast-food restaurants and shops within shops often found in department stores. The basic difficulty is that although the vendor is usually the employer and owns the assets used in the business being sold, the right to conduct the business is not his to transfer. The Transfer Regulations only apply to those persons employed by the vendor in the undertaking transferred by the vendor. In the case of franchises and licences the business is not transferred by the vendor and the vendor will normally have to arrange for a new licence or franchise to be granted to the purchaser by the licensor or franchisor on the surrender of the vendor's licence or franchise.

However, it is important to note that following the recent decision of the European Court of Justice in *Rask and Christensen v ISS Kantineservice A/S* (1992) 12 November, ECJ No: C-209/91 there is an increasing risk that the Transfer Regulations will apply to businesses operated under a franchise or licence. The *Kantineservice* case did not cover franchise or licence businesses but covered the contracting out of services by a customer to an independent contractor. The European Court of Justice said that the Acquired Rights Directive applies whenever there is a change in the person or legal entity responsible for running the undertaking and who, as a result of the change, enters into the obligations of employer in relation to the employees of the undertaking. The European Court of Justice held that it was not relevant whether the ownership of the undertaking was transferred. The risk of the *Kantineservice* decision is that, although there is no true transfer of an undertaking when the franchisor is changed, the person acquiring the franchise may be seen as taking over responsibility for running the undertaking and will normally retain the original employees. In such circumstances a tribunal may chose to construe the Transfer Regulations purposively and decide that they apply. However, the situation is not clear at present.

Independent contractors

The Transfer Regulations only protect employees and not independent contractors. Clearly there is always the danger that a vendor may describe people as independent contractors solely in order to avoid national insurance contributions, settling PAYE and difficulties in eventually dismissing such people. A purchaser should always make careful enquiries to satisfy himself that persons described by the vendor as independent contractors are not in fact employees. If the purchaser does not take on such persons and they are subsequently shown to be employees, they will be protected by the Transfer Regulations and the purchaser will be liable for any costs of redundancy or dismissal.

NATIONAL INSURANCE—CONSEQUENCE OF INCORRECT CATEGORISATION

If the persons are found to be employees, the vendor will be liable to the Inland Revenue and Department of Social Security (DSS) for PAYE and national insurance contributions due in respect of emoluments paid to the employees before the date of the transfer. On the sale, the purchaser should not assume any such liabilities as they are not liabilities to the employees.

All payments made will be treated as earnings and will be assessed to primary and secondary class 1 contributions. The vendor is liable for the full amount of the assessment subject to credit being given, at the DSS's discretion for any class 2 contributions paid by those persons. The employer cannot recover the secondary class 1 nor indeed the primary class 1 contributions from the employee.

Employees based overseas

The Transfer Regulations only apply where there is a transfer of an undertaking situated inside the United Kingdom. If an employee of an undertaking situated inside the United Kingdom is located overseas (for example a salesman based in Sweden for an English business) notwithstanding the application of the Transfer Regulations to the sale, the employee may be unable to bring a claim due to being employed abroad.

Non-commercial ventures

It is now thought that the Transfer Regulations will apply to undertakings or parts of undertakings that are not in the nature of commercial ventures. This is a peculiar anomaly in that the Transfer Regulations currently exclude undertakings in the nature of commercial ventures. However the Trade Union Reform and Employee Rights Bill currently before Parliament will reverse this position. Indeed the European Court of Justice has recently held in *Dr Sophie Redmond Stichting v Bartol* [1992] IRLR 366 that the 'fact that ... the transaction arises out of the grant of subsidies to foundations or associations whose services are not remunerated does not exclude the transaction from the scope of the EC Acquired Rights Directive'. Therefore the exclusion of non-commercial ventures currently contained in the Transfer Regulations is in conflict with the EC Acquired Rights Directive and the exception is likely to be meaningless.

Group service companies and group reorganisations

Care should be taken where the vendor is a member of a group of companies. The Transfer Regulations only apply to persons employed by the vendor in the undertaking transferred by the vendor. It is sometimes the case that all persons within a group are employed by one service company set up specifically for providing services such as staff and property to all other group companies. If the parties want the Transfer Regulations to apply to these persons, the vendor will need to become their employer prior to the sale, or the service company will have to become a party to the transaction. The substitution of the vendor before the sale would need the consent of each affected employee.

Who transfers?

The persons transferred automatically to the purchaser are all persons employed within the business being sold at or immediately before the time of sale whose contracts would otherwise (at common law) have been terminated by the sale. The Transfer Regulations apply to all employees irrespective of their length of service in the business or whether they are full-time or part-time. However, purchasers should not be concerned about part-time employees (less than eight hours per week) as they cannot claim unfair dismissal rights.

now changed by recent cases/HL decision

Dismissals under the Transfer Regulations

If there are to be dismissals in connection with a sale, and there often are, the key questions that the parties will want answered are:

(1) What are the liabilities in respect of any dismissals?
(2) Who bears the cost, the vendor or the purchaser?
(3) How can the liability be avoided?

What are the liabilities for dismissal?

The three main liabilities are for unfair dismissal, redundancy and wrongful dismissal.

UNFAIR DISMISSAL

Any dismissal (either express or constructive) which is in connection with a sale governed by the Transfer Regulations is, as a result of reg 8(1) of the Transfer Regulations, automatically presumed to be an unfair dismissal. Only employees with two or more years' continuous service qualify for unfair dismissal rights. The automatic presumption is rebutted if the dismissal is for an 'economic, technical or organisational reason entailing changes in the work force' (see reg 8(2) of the Transfer Regulations). Notwithstanding the rebuttal of the presumption, the employer must still show that he acted reasonably in dismissing the employee and that the dismissals were fair under the Employment Protection (Consolidation) Act 1978, s 57(3). It is particularly important to note that redundancies may, therefore, be deemed to be unfair dismissals, thereby increasing considerably the question of compensation payable.

The words 'economic, technical or organisational' are given a wide interpretation and can, to a degree, be interrelated. 'Economic' suggests the saving of money in the management of the business and does not mean the economic value of the sale to the vendor. It does not cover the dismissal by the vendor prior to the sale for the reason that the purchaser will either not buy the business if it contains certain employees or alternatively will pay a lower price (see *Wheeler v Patel* [1987] ICR 631). There do not appear to be any significant decisions on the word 'technical', but it is not difficult to contemplate circumstances where the purchaser may wish to absorb his purchase into an existing business which operates with different technology. 'Organisational' reasons appear to overlap with 'economic' reasons and tend to be where the purchaser, in merging his work force with the vendors, dismisses a person because the purchaser will have too many people doing the same job. It is these horizontal economies of scale that are sometimes of key benefit to the purchaser. Even if the reason is economic, technical or organisational the employer must still act reasonably in selecting and dismissing each employee.

If employees are to be dismissed during negotiations, the purchaser and probably the vendor will want to quantify the potential cost of the dismissals. It is assumed that a tribunal will not be willing to make an order for reinstatement or re-engagement. For this, the purchaser will need detailed information as to the age, length of employment, salary and benefits for each employee.

There are four statutory awards which an employee may possibly claim under the Employment Protection (Consolidation) Act 1978. The levels of compensation are subject to statutory limits which are usually increased annually. The limits set out below are as at 1 June 1993. There are factors outside the scope of this book which a tribunal may consider and thereby reduce the amount the employee is awarded. Such factors relate to the conduct of the employee and the total compensation received. Ultimately a tribunal will award what they consider to be just and equitable on the facts of each case.

(i) *Basic award* The maximum basic award is £6,150. The basic award for each employee is calculated as one and a half week's pay for each year of continuous employment over the age of 41, one week's pay for each such year between the ages of 22 and 40, and half a week's pay for each year between the ages of 18 and 21. The calculation is limited to the 20 most recent years of continuous employment subject to a maximum week's pay of £205.

(ii) *Compensatory award* The maximum compensatory award is £11,000. A tribunal must make a compensatory award if it has made a basic award. The award compensates the employee for any loss sustained as a result of the dismissal itself and the employer's actions but each employee is under a duty to mitigate the loss and the tribunal will make a deduction if the employee's actions contributed to the dismissal.

(iii) *Additional award* The maximum additional award is either £5,330 for ordinary cases or £10,660 for discriminatory cases. Additional awards are not common as they are only made on top of the basic and compensatory awards in cases where the employer has failed to comply with earlier orders either to reinstate or re-engage an employee. The award is higher where the employer is found to have discriminated against the employee under the Rehabilitation of

Offenders Act 1974, the Sex Discrimination Acts 1975 and 1986 and the Race Relations Act 1976.

(iv) *Special award*   Special awards are made where a dismissal relates to trade union membership. The provisions are complex and specialist advice should be sought. In general, the maximum special award is £26,800. If the employer failed to comply with an order to reinstate, the maximum special award is the greater of £20,100 or 156 weeks' pay without there being any limit on a week's pay.

REDUNDANCY

The concept of redundancy is defined in the Employment Protection (Consolidation) Act 1978, s 81(2). In the context of a business sale an employee will be redundant if his dismissal was wholly or mainly attributable either to the change in location of the business or to the fact that fewer employees are now required for the business. This latter ground is usually inevitable if the purchaser combines the vendor's workforce with his own.

An employee will not be eligible for a redundancy payment unless he has had two years' continuous employment. The maximum payment is the same as the basic award for unfair dismissal, namely £6,150. The payment is calculated as one and a half week's pay for each year of continuous employment over the age of 40 up to 65 for a man and 60 for a woman, one week's pay for each year between the ages of 22 and 40, and half a week's pay for each year between the ages of 18 and 21. The calculation is limited to the 20 most recent years with the employer and subject to a maximum week's pay of £205. The payment will be reduced under statutory provisions if the employee is approaching retirement age.

WRONGFUL DISMISSAL

Whereas redundancy and unfair dismissal are statutory claims, wrongful dismissal is a contractual claim where the employer terminates the contract of employment without giving proper notice. It is of greatest significance for persons employed under fixed-term contracts where the term has not expired at the time of the sale but the purchaser does not wish to take them on, and for employees with long notice periods such as three to six months. They are normally the senior employees and therefore the high earners of the business and it is important for the purchaser to assess the cost at an early stage. However, a degree of sensitivity is required as the purchaser may need their assistance in any due diligence exercise it is undertaking, and to effect a smooth handover of the business.

The damages will be based on the amount the employee would or could have otherwise earned and the benefits he would have otherwise received during the unexpired term of his contract if he had not been dismissed. Allowance will be made for the early payment of a lump sum to the employer which he would have earned over a period of time. Naturally the employee is under a duty to mitigate his loss by finding suitable alternative employment.

Who is liable for the dismissal?

Purchasers should be aware that the recent House of Lords' decision in *Litster v Forth Dry Dock Engineering Company Ltd* [1989] IRLR 161 has radically altered the position of purchasers for liability where persons are dismissed in connection with a business transfer. The new position as a result of *Litster* is that the purchaser can be liable for any dismissal in connection with a sale irrespective of whether the dismissals take place before, on or after completion.

It is important to understand the position before *Litster*. Under the old law, the Court of Appeal in *Secretary of State for Employment v Spence* [1987] QB 179 gave a strict literal interpretation to reg 5 of the Transfer Regulations. Regulation 5 provides that the Transfer Regulations only apply to those persons employed within the undertaking 'at the time of transfer or immediately before it'. The Court of Appeal decided that the Transfer Regulations did not cover employees employed in the undertaking but dismissed shortly prior to completion. Therefore, a purchaser would avoid automatically assuming liabilities by requiring a vendor to dismiss all or some employees prior to completion. The purchaser could then select employees on its own terms and conditions. The position is particularly sensitive in the case of an insolvent vendor, without assets to compensate the employees.

In *Litster* the House of Lords reversed the old law. As a result, the purchaser can now be held responsible for all dismissal claims by employees dismissed in connection with the sale even if the dismissals took place at a time earlier than literally 'immediately before' the transfer. The Transfer Regulations were an enactment of the EC Acquired Rights Directive 77/187. In order to give effect to the original intention of the Directive, the House of Lords held that the Regulations should be construed purposively and read as if after the words 'immediately before the transfer' the following words were added 'or would have been so employed at the time of the transfer if he had not been unfairly dismissed in the circumstances described in reg 8(1)', (ie for a reason in connection with the transfer).

It is important to note that the House of Lords in *Litster* approved *Spence*. The distinction between *Spence* and *Litster* is that in *Spence* the dismissals had nothing to do with any transfer of a business. In *Spence* the deadline stipulated by the purchaser for the sale of the business by a receiver had passed and the receiver ceased trading and dismissed the employees. Later the same day, the receiver successfully completed a sale agreement with the same purchaser. In *Litster*, even though the sale was by a receiver, it was clear that the employees had been dismissed immediately prior to completing the sale of a business solely to avoid the effect of the Transfer Regulations on the sale.

How can the liability be avoided?

A purchaser is only likely to avoid liability for dismissals before completion if either the dismissal was for a reason unconnected with the sale (eg gross misconduct) or the dismissal was sufficiently far in advance of completion that it was not connected with the sale. Quite how far in advance a dismissal must be no one yet knows. It is in the purchaser's interests for dismissals to be as early as possible but the vendor runs the clear risk that the sale may not complete.

SALES WHEN THE TRANSFER REGULATIONS DO NOT APPLY

The common law

If the Transfer Regulations do not apply, but it is the transfer of a business as a going concern, the position is governed by the Employment Protection (Consolidation) Act 1978 (although a discussion of this Act is outside the scope of this book).

However, if the Transfer Regulations do not apply and it is not the transfer of a business as a going concern, the position is governed by the common law. Under common law, an employment contract is by its nature a contract for personal services. Due to the personal nature of the contract several problems will arise:

(1) A vendor cannot transfer an employee unilaterally against his will.
(2) If an employee does consent to being transferred to the purchaser he will lose all accrued statutory rights.
(3) The transfer of an employee is a constructive dismissal of that employee by the vendor (*Nokes v Doncaster Amalgamated Collieries Ltd* [1940] 3 All ER 549; *Lee v Barry High Ltd* [1970] 3 All ER 1040). All claims by the employee, whether they be for unfair dismissal, wrongful dismissal or redundancy are claims against the vendor.

Consultation

Under reg 10 of the Transfer Regulations, the vendor is under a duty to give recognised trade unions certain information about the business sale and the vendor is under a duty to consult with the unions if either the vendor or the purchaser envisages he will take 'measures' in relation to the transfer. The Transfer Regulations do not impose a duty to consult employees in general if there is no recognised trade union. There is no specified consultation period but the employer must give the specified information to the union 'long enough' before the sale to enable consultations to take place. However, the vendor will wish to delay consultation until as near to completion as possible or he will risk affecting the morale of his workforce if completion does not take place. Once a vendor has consulted he may find himself under moral pressure from his employees to complete as soon as possible and hopefully re-establish certainty for them over their future.

If a union complains to an industrial tribunal of failure by the employer to consult, the employer may be liable for a compensation award of up to two weeks' pay per employee affected with a week's salary being limited to £184.

If it is proposed to make employees redundant, it is suggested that the vendor should commence consultation with the unions no later than the same time as the statutory consultation period imposed upon him by the Trade Union and Labour Relations (Consolidation) Act 1992, s 188. This period will vary depending upon the number of redundancies.

There is an obligation to notify employees within one month of the change of the identity of the employer.

What should the warranties cover?

The following are the main areas the vendor will be asked to warrant and are covered in the main sale agreement (see Appendix III) though not in the same order as they appear below.

Terms of employment

Given the effect of the Transfer Regulations, the purchaser will be particularly concerned to ensure the vendor warrants that it has disclosed accurate details of all the terms of employment of all the employees. The terms include not only basic matters such as salary, bonus entitlement, company car and medical insurance but also the date of commencement of employment, age and a description of the function of each employee in the business.

Breach of contract

The vendor will be required to warrant that it is not in breach of any of the contracts of employment nor, so far as the vendor is aware, are any of the employees.

Industrial action

The vendor will be required to warrant that no industrial action has been taken or threatened in the last few years.

Trade unions

The vendor will be required to warrant that no trade unions have been recognised and that there are no collective agreements.

Independent contractors

The purchaser will be concerned to ensure that the vendor has given full and accurate details of all independent contractors used by the business and to warrant that no such person is an employee.

Chapter 6

Pensions

INTRODUCTION

The transfer values involved in pensions sometimes exceed the purchase price for the business, yet pensions is one of those areas which most general practitioners immediately pass on to a specialist. The purpose of this chapter is not to eliminate the need for the specialist but to provide the general practitioner with an understanding of the main principles and concepts involved. It is important, particularly in the early stage of negotiations, to have an understanding of the issues and, before addressing them, to have an understanding of:

(1) The different types of pension schemes and the different categories within these types.
(2) The concept of funding.

Types of pension schemes

The first thing a purchaser needs to do is to identify the nature of the vendor's scheme. There are two basic types of scheme and various categories within these types. The two basic types are either:

(a) money purchase schemes, sometimes described as defined contribution schemes, or
(b) final salary schemes or salary related schemes, sometimes described as defined benefit schemes.

Money purchase or defined contribution schemes

In terms of business sales, money purchase schemes are of less financial significance and are far simpler to deal with than final salary schemes. A money purchase scheme is like a bank deposit account. The benefit available on retirement is based on the amount of the contributions made during the period of membership plus the investment returns received on these contributions. In theory, the greater the contribution, the greater the benefit. For example, if £1,000 has been contributed each year during 20 years of service the benefit is that which can be bought with £20,000 plus the investment return earned during the 20 years.

Final salary or defined benefit schemes

The benefit an employee expects to receive from a final salary scheme is defined by the individual's salary either on the day of retirement or in a period, typically one or more years before retirement. The benefit received under such a scheme is a fraction of final salary (usually between one sixtieth and one eightieth) multiplied by the total number of years of pensionable service. The aim of the trustees managing the scheme is to receive sufficient contributions during those years of service and to invest those contributions well enough to ensure that adequate funds are available at the point of retirement to pay the appropriate level of benefits.

An employee of a business which is sold may, without some commitment on the part of the vendor to use powers under its scheme (and usually the agreement of its trustees), be treated as having left service at the date of sale. The employee's right will be to a deferred pension payable from normal pension age, and based on his pensionable earnings at the date of the sale. Where the employee continues in employment, albeit with the purchaser, the employee's expectation is that his pension earned with the vendor will continue to be linked with his earnings which are likely to grow between the date of sale and his actual retirement. The scope for and willingness of the vendor to increase the deferred pension is likely to be limited. Effect can however be given to the employee's expectations by arranging the assumption of liability by a scheme set up by the purchaser, in return for the payment of a transfer value, which can be calculated (consistent with Inland Revenue requirements) with an allowance for the effect on the past service liability of future increases in salary.

Occupational schemes and personal pension schemes

Individuals may fund their own personal pension schemes or, alternatively, the contributions may be made by an individual's employer and this is described as an occupational pension scheme. If employers contribute the only contractual commitment is between the employer and the employee. The employer does not undertake commitments to the scheme. The usual occupational pension scheme will be 'exempt approved' by the Inland Revenue so that certain tax relief can be obtained. A personal pension scheme will always be a money purchase scheme whereas an occupational scheme can be either a money purchase or a final salary scheme.

Self-administered schemes and insured schemes

This distinction is based on the method used for investing the contributions made to either a money purchase or to a final salary scheme. An insured scheme is one under which contributions are paid to and managed by an insurance company under a policy. A self-administered scheme is one under which contributions are either managed by in-house investment advisers or by banks and investment houses. The increasing trend in the United Kingdom is for the majority of schemes to be insured.

The concept of funding

Funding is a description of the level of monies paid into a scheme by both employers and employees and reflects the value of the scheme or perhaps the potential liabilities inherent in a scheme. Largely due to Inland Revenue requirements most exempt approved occupational schemes are under trust to which contributions are paid. One of the most significant pension issues on a business acquisition is the financial position of that Trust fund.

Money purchase schemes

As regards money purchase schemes, the question of whether the scheme has been fully funded by the employer is uncontentious. Funding arrangements for money purchase schemes are straightforward as all that is required is for pre-determined monthly contributions to be paid. A purchaser's primary concern is to verify that at the time of the transfer all contributions due to the money purchase scheme have been paid and consider whether the purchaser will be required to make the same commitment to the employees since this directly affects future employment costs and the financial attraction of the transaction. A purchaser should seek a warranty to this effect and verify the matter from financial statements.

Final salary schemes

Funding as a concept is quite simple, yet, in relation to final salary schemes, it is one of the most important and sometimes the most contentious area to be discussed by the purchaser and vendor. This is due to the fact that the benefits cannot be determined at the time of the sale as they are defined by reference to final salary and therefore depend on future circumstances. Also, in the mid 1980s investment returns at the time led to large surpluses. The contentious issue in such a situation is whether any of the surplus is to be transferred to the purchaser's scheme assuming the purchaser intends providing similar benefits. If the purchaser receives no surplus, the purchaser will face immediately increased pension costs on transfer.

The prime concern of a purchaser who takes over a final salary scheme is to ensure that the scheme is sufficiently well funded to meet its future liabilities. To satisfy this concern the purchaser needs to consider:

(a) what is the appropriate level of funding for the scheme; and
(b) given the information available, what can the purchaser assume will be the future growth in both the scheme's assets and its liabilities.

THE LEVEL OF FUNDING

The concept of what is an appropriate, or adequate, level of funding can be considered using the analogy of water in a bath tub. The flow of water into the bath represents the financial contributions into the scheme, namely the employer's and employee's contributions, and the investment return on the fund's assets. The higher the level of water in the bath the greater the value of the scheme's assets. The flow of water out of the bath represents the drain of assets paid as benefits to individuals who have retired. The level of water left in the bath is the reserve of assets needed to meet future liability in respect of current pensioners and the benefits accrued for present and former employees who have yet to retire. The difficulty arises in that, at the time the contributions are put into the scheme, the future outflow in years to come can only be estimated. There is no golden rule as to what is the correct or appropriate level of funding required to ensure that there will be sufficient assets to pay future benefits.

The vendor's objective is to justify as low a level of funding as possible and retain the amount by which the current perceived level exceeds this. The excess is commonly referred to as the surplus. Care must be taken to define surplus as it means different things to different people. The purchaser's objective is to minimise the amount of the excess retained by the vendor's scheme and argue that there is a deficit which the vendor must remedy at the time of sale. As there is no prescribed level of funding, different schemes will usually aim for different target levels. The four main levels are:

(1) The lowest level is that required by the Occupational Pensions Board if the scheme is contracted out of the State Earnings Related Pension Scheme (as most schemes are). This level represents the value of assets that is required if the scheme were to be wound up in order to secure all accrued guaranteed minimum pensions. Guaranteed minimum pensions are the minimum benefits which a scheme must provide in replacement of the State Earnings Related Pension Scheme.

(2) The next level is the value of assets which would be required if the scheme were to be wound up immediately.

(3) The third level is the value of assets required to provide for all

benefits that will eventually become payable as a result of pensionable service already completed after taking into account future salary increases. This is the target level for the majority of schemes.

(4) The highest level is the level beyond which the Inland Revenue regards the funding as excessive. Any investment returns from funding above this level are ineligible for the income and capital gains tax exemptions normally available on pension fund investments.

THE ASSUMPTIONS

The appropriate level of funding depends on forecasts as to the size and rate of flow into and out of the fund in future years and the rate at which the value of assets in the fund will increase before then. These forecasts are commonly referred to as assumptions and are made by actuaries. The two main categories of assumptions are demographic and financial. The assumptions are the most important part of valuing a scheme as only a slight variation in one assumption can result in an enormous change in the perceived solvency of the fund or adequacy of a transfer value reducing it from surplus to deficit.

Demographic assumptions are based on statistical studies of the population. Assumptions are made as to life expectancies, both in service and after retirement, and to the likelihood of either early retirement or people changing jobs before retirement.

There are three key financial assumptions. The first is the rate of future salary increases as the benefits to be paid in respect of service under the vendor's scheme depend on future final salaries. The second assumption is the rate of interest or the rate at which the assets contributed to the fund will grow in value. This is described as the investment yield. The third is the assumption as to future inflation and hence the growth in pensions liabilities. This is particularly important if the benefits payable are increased each year. The rates are invariably expressed as percentages. What is important is the relationship between the three rates and, in particular, the amount by which interest exceeds salary increases. This is 'the assumed real rate of return' and represents the rate at which the assets in the fund will increase faster than the benefits paid out of the fund before any further contributions need to be made. Most funds aim for an assumed real rate of return of between one and three per cent. Actuaries will describe assumptions as more or less 'conservative'. The smaller the assumed rate of return the more conservative the assumption.

PURCHASER'S MAIN CONCERNS

The main concerns

There are four main concerns which the purchaser needs to consider and which are discussed in the remainder of this chapter.

(1) The purchaser needs to consider whether or not it wants to or, is indeed able to, take over the existing pension scheme. This is only likely to be possible where the whole of the business to which the vendor's scheme relates is being acquired. When it is not the purchaser has to decide whether to make arrangements for the assumption by its own scheme of transfers in respect of past service under the vendor's scheme or perhaps establish a new scheme. Ultimately it is a commercial decision.

(2) The purchaser needs to consider whether or not the vendor's scheme is in surplus or deficit and whether or not this will be reflected in the purchase price. The purchaser should also consider the financial implications of funding the scheme after transfer, and in particular what effect this will have on the profitability of the business in its hands.

(3) If the vendor is to retain part or all of the existing scheme, the purchaser needs to consider what is the appropriate amount that needs to be transferred from the vendor's scheme and when this will take place.

(4) The purchaser needs to consider whether the trustees of the existing scheme will consent to whatever arrangements the purchaser agrees with the vendor.

(5) The purchaser needs to consider whether it wishes to join the vendor's scheme for an interim period and, if so, for how long and on what terms. The purchaser should consider whether there are any legal liabilities arising from joining the vendor's scheme.

However, before the purchaser can address any of these concerns, as much information as possible should be obtained concerning the vendor's existing pension arrangements.

The need for information

The information questionnaire (see Appendix II) contains a detailed list of the information the purchaser may require. The vendor should also be required to warrant the completeness and accuracy of all information supplied. The most important points the purchaser will wish to clarify are:

(a) whether or not the employees being transferred are members of any scheme or have any contractual entitlement to have pension contributions made;

(b) is it a money purchase or final salary pension scheme?

(c) if it is a money purchase scheme, what are the employer's monthly contributions and are these paid up to date?

(d) if it is a final salary scheme, the purchaser will want as much information as possible about the scheme. This includes:

   (i) a copy of the scheme's trust deed and rules, including all variations to the original trust deed and details of any patterns of granting discretionary benefits;

   (ii) details of all members of the scheme employed in the business and current beneficiaries including details as to their sex, age, retirement ages under the scheme and current salaries;

   (iii) copies of all members' booklets;

   (iv) the most recent actuarial valuation;

   (v) details of employer's contribution rates in recent years;

   (vi) details of special benefits provided for specific classes of member.

   (vii) disclosure of pension costs in the vendor's accounts in relation to the business.

Actuarial valuation

The vendor is unlikely to be willing to provide copies of the scheme's accounts and even less willing to provide the actuarial valuation unless the purchaser is to take over the entire scheme. The vendor may not want to disclose the valuation as this will restrict his ability to argue about the size of any surplus or deficit in the scheme. The vendor may find it difficult to argue that the actuarial assumptions used for calculating the value of the fund and the resulting transfer payment should be more conservative than those used in recent valuations. Whether or not the vendor will disclose the valuation is a matter of negotiation. However, in certain cases, such as management buy-outs, the purchaser may be a member of the vendor's scheme and therefore entitled as of right under the Occupational Pension Schemes (Disclosure of Information) Regulations 1986, SI 1986/1046 to see the most recent valuation. In such cases the purchaser must be careful not to breach any fiduciary duties it owes the vendor or any duties of confidentiality. Actuarial valuations tend only to be produced once every three and a half years, the common interval being once every three years. There is a risk that, as well as being out of date, for financial purposes the assumptions may be completely inappropriate due to changing circumstances.

Trust deed

The trust deed is one of the most important pieces of information. The deed and rules set out provisions such as the identity of the trustees, who can appoint and remove the trustees, who can decide transfer values and benefit levels, who is entitled to be a member of the scheme, and any restrictions on withdrawing surplus from the scheme.

A point not to be overlooked is that the vendor and purchaser are not parties to the pension scheme. The scheme is controlled by its trustees who are distinct from the vendor. The trustees will not be parties to the sale and purchase agreement and will not automatically accede to whatever the vendor and purchaser have agreed between themselves, as they owe fiduciary duties to the beneficiaries of the scheme, not to the vendor or purchaser. In many schemes, the purchaser may require the vendor to underwrite the risk that the trustees do not consent or only consent to part of the negotiated transfer payment. Alternatively, completion of the business sale agreement can be conditional on the trustees consenting to the negotiated transfer though in practice this is rare since neither the vendor nor the purchaser will want the transaction to collapse for this reason alone unless a particularly significant transfer payment is involved.

Future cost

One of the purchaser's main concerns is to know how much the pension obligations assumed under the transaction will cost in future years. The cost to the purchaser may be far greater than that assumed by the vendor in recent years if the purchaser is not to receive any surplus. Purchasers rely to some extent on the audited accounts of the vendor's business to know how much the obligations the purchaser assumes have cost the vendor on a year by year basis, for example, salaries and the rent for properties. Unfortunately, when assessing pension costs, although some disclosure will be contained in the audited accounts of the business, these are only of limited value. Until recently it was normal practice for a company to illustrate in its profit and loss account the exact amount of the contributions paid by it to the pension scheme during the relevant period. The effect of this was that, if a company was enjoying a pension contributions holiday, the pension cost for that period would be nil and would inflate company profits for that period. To avoid this distortion the accountancy profession issued Statement of Standard Accounting Practice (SSAP) 24. The objective of SSAP 24 is to ensure that there is a charge for pension costs in the profit and loss account irrespective of actual contributions in that period. SSAP 24 requires that the charge for pension costs represents a reasonable estimate of the cost of the pension benefits accruing over the remaining service lives of the workforce as opposed to representing the actual pension contributions paid. To comply with SSAP 24 when preparing its accounts, a company will ask the fund's actuary to give its best estimate of the cost of providing the pension benefits promised in respect of the relevant accounting period. The estimate and the assumptions used to make the estimate are not necessarily the same as the methods and assumptions used for assessing actual contributions to the scheme and target funding levels.

There has been criticism of SSAP 24 because it allows a variety of options in its implementation and is subject to the judgment of the actuaries in their methods and assumptions. Furthermore, any deviation from a normal rate of contribution because of a surplus or deficiency in the vendor's scheme has to be spread over the remaining service lives of perhaps 15 to 20 years. As a result, purchasers should not rely on the pension costs for the business stated in the audited accounts as they will not be directly comparable to how the purchaser's own actuary will advise the same costs be represented in its accounts in future years. Usually there is insufficient disclosure made in the vendor's accounts to enable a suitable comparison to be made. The main advantage of SSAP 24 is that there will be greater consistency in the accounts for the business for preceding years.

One of the difficulties of SSAP 24 is dealing with the regular costs or benefits that arise due to the emerging surpluses and deficiencies in the vendor's scheme. SSAP 24 causes these benefits and liabilities to be allocated over the expected remaining service lives of the current active members. The variation caused by large surpluses may result in negative pension costs in the profit and loss account boosting profits even more than if SSAP 24 had not been applied. The differences between the cost recognised and the contributions actually paid will be reflected by a provision or prepayment in the balance sheet.

The vendor's accounts may also be distorted by the manner in which it first applied SSAP 24. In applying SSAP 24 for the first time, the company has an option in relation to accumulated adjustments either to make a prior year adjustment or to spread forward over the remaining service lives. If the company is enjoying a contributions holiday due to the surplus, a prior year adjustment will result in a large prepayment in the balance sheet and higher pension costs in the profit and loss account. Alternatively, if the benefit of the surplus is spread forward there will be lower pension costs in the profit and loss account with a small provision in the balance sheet. For surpluses refunded from the scheme to the employer it is possible to take the full amount into the profit and loss account immediately rather than spreading forward.

DO THE TRANSFER REGULATIONS AUTOMATICALLY TRANSFER THE PENSION OBLIGATIONS?

As explained in Chapter 5, the effect of the Transfer Regulations is a statutory novation of the contracts of employment putting the purchaser in the same position as if he had always employed the employees of the business. The purchaser is required to provide the employees with contractual benefits equivalent to those they received from the vendor. One would expect the general novation to include the assumption by the purchaser of all pension obligations in relation to the employees. Until very recently the common view was that reg 7 of the Transfer Regulations was effective to exclude the Transfer Regulations from applying to any term in a contract of employment to the extent that it relates to an occupational pension scheme. At the time of writing this remains the position. However, the view as to whether the Transfer Regulations apply to pension obligations was called into question by the recent industrial tribunal cases of *Warrener v Walden Engineering Co Ltd* (Case No 22672/91 Hull, 21 October 1991) and *Perry v Intec Colleges Limited* [1993] IRLR 56. The present position is that reg 7 of the Transfer Regulations was accepted as meaning that the purchaser is not obliged to provide an equivalent occupational pension scheme. If reg 7 is given this strict interpretation, the employees' only recourse for failure by the purchaser to provide an occupational scheme or equivalent benefits would be against the vendor.

Although the decision in *Warrener* was overturned on appeal, it is still worth understanding the initial tribunal decisions. The tribunal in *Warrener* considered that reg 7 was narrower than the scope intended by the EC Acquired Rights Directive 77/187 which the Transfer Regulations were enacted to implement. In *Warrener* the tribunal distinguished between the general right to receive a pension and the specific right to participate in the vendor's occupational scheme. More specifically, reg 7 was enacted to give effect to Article 3(3) of the EC Acquired Rights Directive 77/187 which permits an exclusion in relation to employees' rights 'under *supplementary* company or inter-company pension schemes outside statutory social security schemes in Member States'.

However Article 3(3) also provides:

Member States shall adopt the measures necessary to protect the interests of employees and of persons no longer employed in the transferor's business at the time of the transfer . . . in respect of rights conferring on them immediate or prospective entitlement to old-age benefits including survivor's benefits under [such] supplementary schemes.

In *Warrener* the tribunal decided that a contracted-out scheme (ie, one providing a benefit in place of State benefit) is not a supplementary scheme described in Article 3(3) because, by virtue of the fact that it is contracted-out, it replaces the State scheme. This reasoning, if followed, would have the peculiar effect that the Transfer Regulations would apply to contracted-out schemes but not contracted-in schemes.

It is suggested that the reasoning of the tribunal in *Perry* represents a more practicable approach to the issue. The tribunal considered that reg 7 was only consistent with the first part of Article 3(3) in that a transferring employee could not as a matter of practice have the right to continue in the vendor's scheme after the transfer. However, the tribunal considered that the Transfer Regulations did not give effect to the second part of Article 3(3) in terms of adopting measures necessary to protect the interests of employees. Consequently, the tribunal considered that reg 7 was inconsistent with Article 3(3) and effect should be given to Article 3(3).

Neither tribunals are binding precedents, and the decision in *Warrener* has been overturned on appeal. In summary, the purchaser should assume that it will not be obliged to provide future pension benefits to the employees equivalent to those they would have received under the vendor's scheme and the vendor may seek an indemnity from the purchaser against failure to provide an equivalent pension.

STRUCTURING PENSION ARRANGEMENTS

The precise transitional arrangements to be effected between the vendor and purchaser are a matter of negotiation. Money purchase schemes are far easier to deal with than final salary schemes. With money purchase schemes, the purchaser will be concerned that all payments due from the vendor and any employees have been made and will want the vendor to warrant the precise amount of monthly payments and the fact that there are no other pension obligations. It will usually be possible for the purchaser to join in the vendor's money purchase scheme temporarily and the terms of participation should not be problematic.

Final salary schemes are more complicated. How these are dealt with depends on a variety of factors. The main factors are:

(1) Whether the vendor's scheme is a stand-alone or a group scheme?
(2) What are the purchaser's existing pension arrangements for its own staff and what does it want to provide for the transferring employee?
(3) Is the purchaser to pay for the surplus?

Stand-alone or group scheme

A stand-alone scheme is restricted to employees of the business being sold whereas a group scheme is maintained for the benefit of persons employed in other businesses of the vendor or a scheme operated by a parent company of the vendor for all employees in the group including those being transferred.

Stand-alone schemes

If the vendor's scheme is stand-alone, the purchaser may either provide an alternative scheme for the benefit of the employees or take over the existing scheme. If the vendor retains the scheme a transfer payment will need to be made to the purchaser's scheme. The vendor is only likely to want to retain the existing stand-alone scheme if there is a hope of retaining any surplus after the transfer payment has been made to the new scheme. If instead, the purchaser takes over the scheme, the purchaser needs to make a thorough investigation of the scheme's assets and liabilities and the trust deed will need to be amended to replace the purchaser as the principal employer. In addition, if the scheme is to be taken over, the purchaser should require full warranty cover and full disclosure and some assurance that the trustees will consent to the new arrangements if consent is necessary.

Group schemes

If the vendor's scheme is a group scheme, the vendor will wish to retain the group scheme and the purchaser will have to decide whether to provide replacement benefits for the employees either by establishing a new scheme or by offering membership of the purchaser's existing scheme. Either way the purchaser will normally seek the vendor's agreement to a transitional period. This is a period during which after completion of the acquisition the purchaser participates in the vendor's scheme until the purchaser has been able to make and fulfil offers to the employees to join the purchaser's scheme. The sale and purchase agreement should set out in detail the basis on which the purchaser will be required to contribute during this period (see later). The agreement should also provide the basis on which a transfer payment is to be made from the vendor's scheme. The calculation of transfer payment and the mechanics of achieving the transfer are discussed below.

Purchaser's existing pension arrangements

An important factor for the purchaser in deciding whether to take over the vendor's scheme will be what arrangements are already in place for its existing employees. If the purchaser has a long established scheme he may not wish to complicate matters in terms of administration by adopting a second scheme. This may cause administrative difficulties in future transfers of employees within the purchaser's group and may cause disunity within the workforce if one scheme is perceived as more beneficial than the other. Equally the vendor may be part of a much larger group than the purchaser. In this instance, the purchaser will prefer to integrate a transfer payment into its existing scheme rather than adopt a scheme too complicated for its needs. The more complex the scheme the more expensive it will be to administer. If the employees are to be integrated into the purchaser's existing scheme the purchaser should insist that the payment is made on at least a past service reserve basis (see below).

Payment for the surplus

If the scheme to be taken over by the purchaser is in surplus, the vendor will request a contribution from the purchaser to recognise the receipt of the surplus. However, for two main reasons the purchaser should reject any request by the vendor to increase the purchase price of the business by the amount of the surplus.

Firstly, there is no guarantee that the purchaser will be able to extract the entire cash value of the surplus. The maximum the purchaser could ever extract is 60 per cent of the surplus as there is an immediate charge of tax of 40 per cent on any repayment of surplus irrespective of the purchaser's financial position.

Secondly, the ability to extract the surplus will probably be restricted by the terms of the scheme's trust deed. Further, under the Social Security Act 1990, sufficient funds must be retained to guarantee statutory minimum increases in pension payment. Attempts to withdraw any surplus may also be challenged by the employees and in the light of recent events such as the *Maxwell* case the courts will tend to protect the employees or beneficiaries rather than the employer.

If the purchaser is willing to pay for the surplus, the payment should only be related to the value of the benefit actually received by the purchaser and should only be payable at the time of receipt.

No doubt the vendor would prefer to extract the surplus before the scheme is passed to the purchaser. However, there is unlikely to be sufficient time to extract the surplus before the business is transferred and the purchaser will be concerned in case the vendor's action has reduced the scheme to a deficit.

TRANSFER PAYMENT—AMOUNT AND TIMING

Amount of payment

The calculation of the transfer payment depends on what the vendor and purchaser, or rather their actuaries, have agreed as the appropriate level of funding and the basis of valuing the scheme's assets and liabilities to reach this agreed appropriate level. There are three main categories of payment:
  (1) Cash equivalent.
  (2) Share of fund.
  (3) Past-service reserve.

Cash equivalent

This is the smallest transfer payment and benefits the vendor. The cash equivalent is based on current salaries and is calculated as if the members of the scheme were resigning at the time the business is transferred. This would only entitle the members to a deferred pension and to take the cash equivalent of that deferred pension to a different occupational scheme.

Past-service reserve

The past-service reserve is the amount necessary to transfer the employees at a level of no surplus and no deficit. It is based on the accrued rights of members but with salary projected forward to normal retirement age. It is usually a higher level than the cash equivalent as it takes into account future increases in salaries. A peculiar anomaly is that many pension trust deeds specify that, in shares sales, the transfer will be on a past-service reserve basis but are silent as to what happens in asset sales. However, as a result of negotiation, the majority of business transfer agreements tend to follow the line of share sales and calculate the transfer payment on a past-service basis.

Share of fund

The share of fund method transfers a proportion of the total asset value equal to the proportion that the liabilities of the transferring members bear to the total liabilities in respect of all fund liabilities.

The share of fund method is most favoured by the purchaser whereas the vendor will prefer the past-service reserve.

Timing of transfer

It is often the case that it has not been possible within the time involved in negotiating the sale, to agree and finalise the method of dealing with the pension issues and the amounts to be transferred. If the scheme itself is to be transferred, the purchaser will need to be substituted as the participating employer and this will require the consent of the trustees. If, instead, a transfer payment is to be made, time needs to be allowed to enable the members to decide whether they wish to join the purchaser's scheme as, under the Social Security Act 1986, s 15, an employee cannot be compelled to join the purchaser's scheme. The purchaser may also need time to obtain a contracting-out certificate or amend the certificate for its existing scheme. As a result it is common for there to be a delay after completion of the sale. During this interim period the employees being transferred to the purchaser will remain in and participate in the vendor's scheme.

The purchaser and vendor need to establish in the business transfer agreement the basis on which the employees will participate in the vendor's scheme during the transitional period if one is to apply. This is usually dealt with by a deed of adherence similar to that in schedule 6 to the standard sale agreement (see Appendix III). The usual length of an interim period is between six and twelve months. The purchaser should also consider the provisions of the Social Security Pensions Act 1975, s 58(*b*) (as amended), as in certain circumstances, the provisions may make the purchaser, in its capacity as employer, liable for deficits in the vendor's scheme during the interim period.

The main issue to be resolved is the size of contributions to be paid by the purchaser during the interim period. This may already be provided for by the scheme's trust deed. However, scheme rules normally enable the employer to pay a reduced contribution or to take a pensions holiday if the fund is in surplus. If the vendor is not prepared to allow the purchaser the benefit of the surplus, and this is a matter for negotiation, the purchaser may be required to contribute as if there were no surplus.

During the interim period the vendor will wish to restrict the size of any pay increases awarded by the purchaser to transferring employees if this would increase the size of the transfer payment.

BARBER v GUARDIAN ROYAL

In *Barber v Guardian Royal Exchange Assurance Group* [1990] 2 CMLR 513 the European Court of Justice decided that employers should not discriminate between men and women by imposing different retirement ages in occupational pension schemes. Such discrimination would be in breach of Article 119 of the Treaty of Rome. In *Barber* it was successfully argued that the traditional relevant ages of 60 for women and 65 for men discriminates against men as a man who retires at 60 (ie early) will get a smaller pension than a woman retiring at 60 even if both have the same employment record.

The result of *Barber* is that all schemes should now have equal retirement ages. Unfortunately, although clarifying the issue of sex discrimination, the judgment in *Barber* leaves various important questions unanswered mostly relating to how equality is to be implemented. One of the matters which is not clear is the extent to which the *Barber* judgment, made on 17 May 1990, is retrospective. One major question is whether the *Barber* judgment is completely retrospective, so enabling members to claim discrimination prior to 17 May 1990. The view favoured by employers is that there is a liability to equalise in respect only of benefits attributable to service after 17 May 1990. This is the interpretation that is proposed to be adopted in a protocol to the Maastricht Treaty. At the time of writing it is uncertain whether the Treaty will be ratified by all 12 Member States and hence the matter may instead be resolved by the European Court of Justice in the joined test cases in the ECJ including the case of *Coloroll Pension Trustees Limited v Russell and Others*. The Advocate General delivered his opinion at the end of April 1993 which largely endorses the view stated above. Judgment of the ECJ in the *Coloroll* case is expected to be delivered at the end of 1993.

The purchaser should take care to ensure that all transfer payments are calculated on the basis that benefits are payable by reference to equal retirement ages if the vendor's scheme discriminates, at the very least in respect of periods of employment after 17 May 1990. Claims for sex discrimination from people who have retired before the acquisition will be against the vendor whereas if the purchaser had bought shares they would be against the target company acquired by the purchaser.

DIRECTORS AND SENIOR EMPLOYEES

An approved scheme will lose its beneficial tax status if its employees contribute more than 15 per cent of their gross earnings. Until recently there was no cap on the monetary value of employee contributions provided that they did not exceed 15 per cent of the employee's gross salary. However, for members joining an exempt approved scheme after 31 May 1989, there is a limit on the amount of salary that can be treated as pensionable. The current limit is £75,000 and therefore the maximum contribution is £11,250.

Care must be taken if any of the employees transferring earns more than the limit. If his gross income exceeds £75,000 the limit does not apply if he was a member of the scheme before 31 May 1989. However, the moment the employee leaves the scheme, the limit will apply unless he joins a 'replacement' scheme. The rules as to what constitutes a replacement scheme are particularly complex but include where a member's employer changes hands and he is moved to the new owner's scheme.

WHAT SHOULD THE WARRANTIES COVER?

Despite the fact that the vast majority of work relating to pensions, particularly where a final salary scheme is concerned, will be in the negotiation of the actuarial assumptions, negotiating the right to share in any surplus and evaluating the implications of funding costs to the purchaser, the purchaser should not overlook the need for warranties. The prime reason for seeking warranties relating to pensions is to give the purchaser a remedy if the information on which it negotiated the transfer from the vendor's fund was inaccurate. Warranties will be particularly important if the purchaser takes over the vendor's scheme. The following are the main areas the vendor will be asked to warrant and are covered in the standard sale agreement (see Appendix III), though not necessarily in the same order as they appear below.

No unidentified schemes

The purchaser should insist the vendor warrants that, apart from the scheme disclosed to the purchaser, there is no other legal or moral obligation to provide retirement, death or disability benefits to the transferring employees.

Full details disclosed

The vendor will be required to warrant that it has disclosed to the purchaser full details of all relevant schemes. Some purchasers will then specify in the warranty the details which they consider to be relevant and necessary. These would normally include the information listed on page 106.

Adequacy of the fund's assets

The vendor should resist any outright requests by the purchaser to warrant in absolute terms that the fund has sufficient assets to meet present and future liabilities. The vendor should be prepared to warrant factual information but not future expectancy. A compromise would be for the vendor to warrant that on the basis of the actuarial valuation the vendor, in its opinion, considers that there are sufficient assets.

Exempt approved scheme

The vendor will be required to warrant that the scheme is an exempt approved scheme within the meaning of TA 1988, s 592. A scheme that is approved is exempt from income tax and corporation tax on investment income and capital gains. Contributions by the vendor to the scheme will be treated as deductible expenses under Schedule E.

Claims and disputes

In addition to the normal warranty as to the claims against the vendor, the purchaser will require the vendor to warrant that there are no claims or proceedings in relation to the fund, that none have been threatened and that they are not aware of any facts likely to give rise to claims.

Contributions

If the scheme is a money purchase fund, the vendor will be required to warrant that all contributions due to be made to the fund up to and including completion have been made.

Chapter 7

Taxation

INTRODUCTION

Taxation will frequently have a significant impact on the commercial merits of a transaction for both the purchaser and the vendor and should not be overlooked. However, it cannot be overstressed that taxation is only one aspect of a transaction and should not be allowed to cause either the purchaser or the vendor to lose sight of the prime commercial objectives. In the phrase much over-used by lawyers (but which is not always observed with the same frequency) the tax tail should not be allowed to wag the commercial dog.

Where a taxation issue arises, there is usually a conflict between the purchaser and the vendor and, depending on their respective negotiating strengths, an element of compromise is required from both parties. It is therefore important for the purchaser and the vendor to have a good understanding of each other's taxation considerations as well as their own. It should also be stressed that once a taxation issue has been identified it should then be quantified in order to determine its commercial significance in the overall context of the transaction. It is all too easy for both parties to become entrenched in a taxation issue without asking the basic commercial question of how much does the issue mean?

The main areas covered in this chapter are: purchaser's considerations; vendor's considerations; hive downs; stamp duty; apportionment of the consideration; VAT and inheritance tax.

Some taxation considerations are relevant to both the purchaser and the vendor and there will therefore be an element of repetition in this chapter. The purpose of this chapter is merely to make the reader aware of the common taxation issues and it is not intended as a substitute for reading the appropriate legislation.

PURCHASER'S CONSIDERATIONS

From a taxation point of view, a purchaser will normally prefer an asset sale to a share sale. The principal taxation advantage of an asset sale, as opposed to a share sale, is the ability to leave the tax history of the vendor company behind. The other main taxation advantages of an asset sale for the purchaser relate to:

(1) Roll-Over Relief.
(2) Base Cost.
(3) Capital Allowances.
(4) Trading Expenses.
(5) Stamp Duty (though this is not always an advantage).

Roll-over relief—TCGA 1992, s 152

The general rule

The sale of business assets will normally give rise to a chargeable gain either for the purpose of corporation tax for a vendor company or capital gains tax for an individual vendor. To ease the financial pressure of replacing assets, a purchaser who buys certain types of business assets, commonly called qualifying assets (described below) to replace other such qualifying assets may, if certain conditions are satisfied, claim relief in respect of the gain made on disposal. The relief is available for both individuals, whether they be sole traders or members of a partnership or trustees, and for companies. Under the Taxation of Chargeable Gains Act (TCGA) 1992, s 152, the purchaser may defer tax that would otherwise be payable on the gain made on a disposal of qualifying assets by rolling over and subtracting the gain from the acquisition cost of the new qualifying assets bought from the vendor. The purchaser is treated as having disposed of his old assets at such price as gives rise to neither a gain nor a loss on the disposal. The price paid for the new assets will be treated as having been reduced by the amount of the gain. Hence, where a purchaser is selling qualifying assets at the same time as the relevant acquisition from the vendor or within a prescribed time before or after such acquisition (see below), he will normally prefer to buy assets rather than shares in order to defer any capital gain arising on his own sale. This is only a means of deferring tax.

Conditions

Roll-over relief will only be available if the conditions of TCGA 1992, ss 152–155 are satisfied. The conditions relate principally to:

(i) the nature of the assets sold and bought;
(ii) the time period between buying and selling; and
(iii) the purpose for which the assets are used.

NATURE OF ASSETS—'QUALIFYING ASSETS'

Section 152 relief will only be available if both the assets sold and the replacement assets bought by the purchaser are qualifying assets as defined in TCGA 1992, s 155. The assets sold and the assets bought need not be of the same category. It is notable that the categories do not include shares. Hence, the relief is only available to the purchaser in an asset sale rather than a share sale. However, FA 1993, Schedule 7 enables gains made on the sale of shares in an unquoted trading company, in which the vendor has at least a five per cent interest, to be rolled over if the proceeds of the sale are reinvested in shares comprising not less than five per cent of another unquoted trading company within broadly the same time limits as apply to roll-over relief under TCGA 1992, s 152. Qualifying assets include the following categories:

    (a) any land and buildings both occupied *and* used for the purposes of the trade. If the trade is dealing in or developing land, relief will not be available in respect of any land if the profit from a disposal of that land would be treated as a trading profit;

    (b) fixed plant or machinery. In *Williams v Evans* 59 TC 509, Nourse J considered that the word 'fixed' applied to machinery as well as to plant;

    (c) goodwill;

    (e) ships, aircraft, hovercraft, satellites, and other more unusual items such as milk quotas and potato quotas.

TIME PERIOD BETWEEN BUYING AND SELLING

The replacement qualifying asset must be acquired or an unconditional contract for its acquisition must be entered into within 12 months before or three years after the sale of the original qualifying asset. The Inland Revenue have a discretion to extend the time limit where, in the circumstances, it was impossible to acquire the new asset within the time limit. The discretion will not be exercised where impossibility arises from delay on the part of the purchaser.

PURPOSE FOR WHICH THE ASSETS ARE USED

The asset sold is required to have been used solely for the purpose of the vendor's trade throughout the period of ownership. However, a tapering of the relief will apply if the asset was only used intermittently for the purpose of the trade during the period of ownership (see TCGA 1992, s 152(7)). Similarly, if only part of a building or structure was used for the purpose of the vendor's trade throughout the period of ownership, the relief will be applied as if that part was a separate asset (see TCGA 1992, s 152(6)). The asset acquired must be brought into use in the trade and must be used solely for the purpose of the trade. There is no statutory minimum period for which the asset acquired must continue to be used for the purpose of the trade.

As a general rule, under the provisions for rebasing assets to 31 March 1982, assets sold after 5 April 1988 but acquired before 31 March 1982 are treated as having been re-acquired at market value on 31 March 1982 when calculating the gain on disposal. Where rebasing applies any non-business use before 31 March 1982 is ignored for the purpose of roll-over relief.

There is no requirement that the new and old assets should be used in the same trade, so a new unrelated business bought within 12 months before or three years after the sale of a business will be appropriate where qualifying assets have been bought and sold.

Group companies

For the purpose of roll-over relief, the trades of all members of a 75 per cent group of companies are treated as one trade (see TCGA 1992, s 175(1)). On this basis the gains of any one group member can be rolled over against the acquisition costs of another group member provided, of course, that the conditions of TCGA 1992, s 152 are satisfied.

Considerable confusion and uncertainty as to the availability of roll-over relief within a group of companies has been caused by the recent case of *Campbell Connelly & Co Ltd v Barnett* [1992] STC 316. The case suggests that roll-over relief will not be available to one trading company in a group if the replacement asset was acquired by another trading member of the same group notwithstanding that they are treated by the legislation as carrying on a single trade. At the time of writing the case is under appeal. However, the Financial Secretary to the Treasury has sought to remove the uncertainty by making an announcement that 'the case is still under appeal but, in the light of Knox J's judgment it is clear that the Revenue's established practice in relation to roll-over relief in a group of companies is probably based on an incorrect understanding of the law. The Revenue's practice seems to me to be sensible and to reflect how commercial transactions are commonly organised. We will ensure that it continues to apply. What needs to be done will depend on the outcome of the appeal'. It is suggested that if the appeal upholds the original judgment in the *Campbell Connelly* case, it is highly likely that Parliament will act to rectify the position and bring the law into line with the Inland Revenue's practice.

Base cost

Except where roll-over relief applies, the purchase price as apportioned between the assets will form the purchaser's tax base cost for these assets. If, instead, the purchaser had bought shares he would effectively have acquired these assets at their written down value in the books of the target company which is probably less than the market value paid on the asset sale. The higher base cost will reduce any gain on a subsequent disposal by the purchaser and may increase the depreciation element in the purchaser's future corporation tax calculations.

Capital allowances

Capital allowances are the taxation equivalent of depreciation. They are allowances given in respect of certain capital assets and are allowed as a deduction from the income of a business for the purposes of calculating profit chargeable to corporation tax. The advantage of an asset sale for the purchaser is that the allowance will be calculated by reference to the purchaser's acquisition cost of the capital asset from the vendor which should be market value. If, instead, the purchaser had bought shares, the capital allowance would only be calculated by reference to the value of the capital asset as written down in the books of the target company. This is normally less than market value and hence the capital allowances would be less.

The precise details of capital allowances are extremely complex and require not only a thorough understanding of the legislation but also detailed knowledge of the assets being sold.

The significance of capital allowances has diminished in recent years largely due to the withdrawal by the Finance Act 1984 of both first year allowances of up to 100 per cent on plant and machinery and of initial allowances of up to 75 per cent on industrial buildings. Further reforms were enacted by the Finance Acts 1985 and 1986 and now all the reforms are consolidated in the Capital Allowances Act 1990. One of the few original 100 per cent allowances to be left unaffected by the reforms is that on scientific research. There are now two main types of allowance:

(a) plant and machinery; and
(b) industrial buildings.

Plant and machinery allowance

Plant and machinery is a rather loose label and includes not only plant and machinery as such, but also patents, know-how and certain other unusual assets. The plant and machinery capital allowance is a writing down allowance of 25 per cent of the balance of qualifying expenditure. Most items of plant and machinery qualifying for capital allowances are included in a single pool of assets. In any financial period the balance of qualifying expenditure for the pool is the balance of expenditure brought forward from the previous financial year plus any acquisitions during the period less any disposals which are brought in at the lower of cost or sales proceeds. Allowances in respect of some assets, such as cars costing over £8,000, have to be calculated separately outside the pool. FA 1993, s 115 contains provisions to implement the announcement made by the Chancellor in the March 1993 Budget to allow first year allowances of 40 per cent for expenditure incurred on plant and machinery between 1 November 1992 and 31 October 1993.

There are a considerable number of cases on precisely what constitutes plant. One guideline to follow is whether the asset is used and employed in the business. This is not conclusive as, for example, passive use of assets may qualify in certain circumstances so long as the asset is kept for permanent use in the business. Lindley J in *Yarmouth v France* (1887) 19 QBD said 'there is no definition of plant . . . . but, in its ordinary sense it includes whatever apparatus is used by a business man for carrying on his business'. He expanded on this to say that plant excludes stock in trade but includes all goods and chattels, fixed or movable, kept for permanent employment in a business.

Industrial buildings allowance

Industrial buildings allowances are given not only in respect of industrial buildings themselves, but also in respect of commercial buildings in enterprise zones and qualifying hotels. The allowance is a 25 year straight line writing down allowance of four per cent of the amount of the original qualifying expenditure and is given for each year at the end of which the building is in industrial use. Industrial buildings are required to be buildings of an industrial nature and either used in an industrial trade or located in an enterprise zone. Industrial building allowances cannot normally be claimed to the extent the acquisition cost exceeds the original cost of construction or in respect of a building which is more than 25 years old or more than 50 years old for a building constructed before 1961.

Trading expenses

The value of trading stock and work in progress bought by the purchaser will be a deductible expense for the purpose of corporation tax in the financial year of the acquisition.

Under the Income and Corporation Taxes Act (TA) 1988, s 100 when trading stock is transferred for valuable consideration to a purchaser who carries on (or will carry on) a trade in the United Kingdom and the cost of the stock constitutes a trading expense of that trade, the value of the trading stock purchased is taken to be the price agreed between the purchaser and the vendor. If these conditions are not satisfied the stock is treated as having been transferred at market value.

Stamp duty

There may be stamp duty savings for the purchaser depending on the nature of the assets bought and the apportionment of the consideration paid between the relevant assets. It should be remembered that whereas the stamp duty rate on assets is double that on the transfer of shares, stamp duty on an asset sale is not usually payable on the whole consideration but only on part. Stamp duty is discussed at page 131.

What is often seen as the main tax disadvantage of an asset sale for the purchaser is that it may prevent him from using any of the vendor's accumulated trading or capital losses and unrelieved advance corporation tax. However, if on a share sale there is any value available to the purchaser from these, the vendor will want some payment. On the other hand, a purchaser is not normally willing to pay for the losses or unrelieved advance corporation tax until such time as the purchaser has received the benefit of these, and the negotiation of appropriate provisions in a sale agreement can be complex. Also, it may still be possible for the purchaser to obtain the benefit of losses and unrelieved advance corporation tax by the vendor structuring the transaction as a hive down. Hive downs are discussed at page 127.

VENDOR'S CONSIDERATIONS

From a taxation point of view, a vendor will normally prefer a share sale to an asset sale. The main taxation considerations for a vendor on an asset sale relate to:

(1) Double tax charge if the vendor is a company.
(2) Balancing charges.
(3) Roll-over relief.
(4) Incorporation of a business.
(5) Retirement relief.

Double tax charge

The most frequent objection to asset sales by vendors is that there will be a double tax charge, particularly if the ultimate vendors are individuals. This is only relevant if the vendor is a company. The double charge arises in that the vendor company will face corporation tax on any gain made on the sale of chargeable assets. The chargeable gains arise in respect of the excess of the apportioned sale proceeds of capital assets over indexed March 1982 value or book value if greater. If the shareholders are individuals they will subsequently face a charge to tax when removing the net gain from the company.

It is suggested that a purchaser should not immediately accept the double tax charge argument at face value. The vendor should be required to consider and quantify the likely tax charges after taking account of all reliefs that may be available to the vendor and the benefit of indexation.

Balancing charges

If a vendor sells assets on which capital allowances have been claimed at a value greater than their tax written down value, a balancing charge may arise automatically under the Capital Allowances Act 1990. Where the asset sold had been pooled with similar assets, the lower of cost or the sale proceeds is deducted from the balance in the pool. A balancing charge is then only likely to occur where the asset is not replaced in the same basis period or, if replaced, where proceeds exceed the value brought forward in the pool. However, if the vendor has substantial trading losses, these will absorb either all or part of the balancing charge and the risk may therefore be insignificant.

Roll-Over Relief—TCGA 1992, s 152

Roll-over relief has been discussed at page 119. If the vendor wishes to carry on business or to resume a trade within three years of the sale, it may be able to roll over the gain on disposal of qualifying assets into the acquisition of new qualifying assets.

Incorporation of a business

Shares are not qualifying assets for the purpose of roll-over relief under TCGA 1992, s 152. As a result, roll-over relief under s 152 is not available to individuals whether as sole traders or partnerships who incorporate their businesses. Where the consideration paid for the transfer of the business is satisfied by the issue of shares to the purchaser, this may leave the individual in the particularly harsh position of facing a capital gains tax liability while not having received a readily realisable form of consideration.

However, TCGA 1992, s 162 provides a specific form of roll-over relief for individuals provided certain conditions are satisfied. The relief is mandatory and, contrary to s 152 relief, the vendor must claim for the relief. The conditions for s 162 relief are that:

(a) the vendor is a person or persons other than a company;

(b) the business is transferred as a going concern (as discussed in Chapter 5);

(c) all the assets of the business (with the optional exclusion of cash) are included in the transfer;

(d) the business is transferred wholly or partly in exchange for the issue of shares; and

(e) the shares are issued by the purchaser to the vendor.

Section 162 relief is not restricted to the incorporation of a business into a new shelf company. The purchaser may be a long established company merely using the issue of shares as consideration for taking over the business of a sole trader or partnership. However, in such circumstances vendors should be cautious if they already have an interest in the purchaser and should consider seeking prior confirmation from the Inland Revenue under TA 1988, s 707 that it will not serve a notice challenging the relief under s 703 of that Act.

Section 162 relief is only available to the extent that the vendor receives consideration in the form of newly issued shares. Vendors may prefer to take at least a small amount of the consideration in other forms, such as cash or loan accounts if only for the purpose of utilising their annual exemption. In those circumstances tapering of the relief will apply, being approximately the consideration satisfied by the issue of shares as a proportion of the total consideration. Normally the assumption by the purchaser of the vendor's business liabilities would be consideration. However, the Inland Revenue in *Extra Statutory Concessions Practice D32*, do not treat the transfer of liabilities as consideration for the purpose of s 162 relief.

Retirement relief

Retirement relief is available to individuals who make a material disposal of business assets if at the time of the disposal the individual is age 55 years or more or the individual has retired on the grounds of ill health before the age of 55. The ill health ground may be difficult to prove. Not only must the individual cease to be engaged in the business due to ill health but the individual must be likely to remain permanently incapable of resuming the business.

To qualify, the individual must make a material disposal of business assets. Amongst other things this includes:

(a) the disposal of the whole or part of a business by a sole trader;

(b) the disposal of an interest in a business by a member of a partnership; and

(c) the disposal of business assets following the termination of the business.

From a series of cases (the most recent being *Pepper v Daffurn* [1993] STC 466) it is clear that the requirement for the sale of at least part of a business, where the relevant business is continuing, would not be satisfied by the sale of selected assets. It is only where the business has been terminated that the proprietor can sell off individual business assets and still qualify for the relief (ie under (c) above). However, in such a situation it is important to ensure that the assets are only sold after the business has been terminated. In reality this may be difficult to achieve as a proprietor will normally wish to continue a failing business until the sale of any valuable assets such as land has been negotiated and a contract has been exchanged. On a strict interpretation the disposal of the selected assets would have taken place prior to termination of the business and retirement relief would not be available. Further, on termination of a business, the material disposal must take place within the following 12 months.

Retirement relief operates under a two-tier system. Assuming all the relevant conditions are satisfied, 100 per cent relief is available on the first £150,000 of gain and thereafter a reduced relief at the rate of 50 per cent is available up to a limit on gain of £600,000. Hence the maximum retirement relief available at present is £375,000. The limits are different for disposals made before 19 March 1991. There are fairly complex rules governing what gains can qualify for relief.

HIVE DOWNS

Hive downs (and hive across) are a structure of transaction designed to enable the purchaser to benefit from the vendor's accumulated losses, normally denied to a purchaser on an asset sale, but at the same time not requiring the purchaser to assume all of the vendor's liabilities as would be the case on a share sale. For these reasons hive downs are a popular method of receivership sales.

The hive down is relatively straightforward and comprises elements of both a share sale and an asset sale. To effect a hive down the vendor will first incorporate a new subsidiary and then transfer the assets to be bought by the purchaser into the new subsidiary. For hive downs to be effective the trade itself must be transferred and not merely the assets. The purchaser then buys the shares in the new subsidiary from the vendor. On a hive across, the parent company of the vendor will form a new subsidiary. The vendor will then transfer the assets to be bought by the purchaser to the parent's new subsidiary and the parent will sell the shares in the new subsidiary to the purchaser. For stamp duty saving purposes it is sometimes preferred to transfer certain assets such as land directly to the purchaser, though care must be taken to ensure this does not risk jeopardising the benefits of the hive down and for this reason goodwill is not normally excluded. In the case of excluded land this risk is averted by granting the new company a licence to occupy the property.

It is particularly important for both the purchaser and the vendor to have an understanding of the taxation considerations in each step of a hive down. The same considerations apply for a hive across. There are advantages and disadvantages for both the purchaser and vendor which will need to be evaluated. In general, the main advantages of a hive down lie with the vendor and a summary is provided at the end of this section.

The main tax considerations which are complex and tend to be interlinked are set out below.

No-gain no-loss transfer—TCGA 1992, s 171

Section 171 of TCGA 1992 represents the main advantage of hive downs to the vendor. Under this section, the transfer of the assets by the vendor to the new company will take place on a no-loss no-gain basis. As a result, the transfer will not crystallise any capital gains for corporation tax purposes in the vendor.

No capital allowances claw back—TA 1988, s 343

If TA 1988, s 343(2) is applied, the advantage for the vendor is that it will not suffer any claw back of capital allowances in respect of the qualifying assets transferred to the new company. The new company simply assumes the capital allowance position of the vendor. The disadvantage for the purchaser is that the new company will only be entitled to capital allowances on the qualifying assets at their written down value as opposed to any higher value allocated to them on an apportionment of asset sale consideration.

Restrictions on the carrying forward of losses

One of the main advantages to the purchaser is that, as a result of TA 1988, s 343(3), if the relevant conditions are satisfied, the vendor's unrelieved accumulated losses in respect of the trade transferred may be preserved for use by the new company. The losses of the trade acquired by the new company may only be set off against future profits of the company that arise from that trade. The use of the losses will be restricted if the new company does not assume all of the vendor's liabilities in relation to the trade transferred.

Even if a hive down is successfully effected, a purchaser cannot take it as guaranteed that the trading losses will be available to the new company and the purchaser should be made aware of TA 1988, s 768. The effect of this section is to disallow the carrying forward of the trading losses by the new company if:

(a) within three years before or after the sale of the shares in the new company to the purchaser there is a major change in the nature or conduct of the trade; or

(b) at the time of the sale of the new company to the purchaser, the new company's trade has become small or negligible and later revives.

TA 1988 does not define a major change but specifies that it includes a major change in the type of property dealt in or services or facilities provided or a major change in customer, outlets or markets. In *Inland Revenue Statement of Practice SP10/91*, the Inland Revenue has given some guidance as to what it considers to be a major change in the nature or conduct of a trade.

Purchasers should also be made aware that the Inland Revenue tends to give s 768 a wide interpretation and will examine carefully any claim for carrying forward of trading losses. If, therefore, the vendor has insisted that the purchaser pays for the trading losses, such payment should only be made once the losses have been utilised.

Further, the benefit of s 343 will be lost if, at the time of the hive down, the shares in the new company are not beneficially owned by the vendor. In *Wood Preservation Ltd v Prior* 45 TC 112 it was held that the vendor had ceased to be the beneficial owner of its shares in its subsidiary from the date of acceptance of a conditional offer for the shares. Hence, the asset transfer should take place before the share sale contract is exchanged.

Capital gains crystallisation

It has been seen that one of the advantages to the vendor of a hive down is that for the vendor's tax purposes the assets are treated as being transferred to the new company on a no-loss no-gain basis. This means no-gain crystallises in the vendor. The main concern for the purchaser arises from the fact that the new company then ceases to be a member of the vendor's group of companies by virtue of its shares being sold to the purchaser. As a result, TCGA 1992, ss 178 and 179 may apply in which event the new company will be treated as having, immediately after the hive down, sold and immediately repurchased the assets at market value. The new company will thereby be treated as having made a chargeable gain at the excess of market value at the time of the deemed disposal over the vendor's book value. In such circumstances the purchaser should seek an indemnity from the vendor against the resulting corporation tax.

Furniss v Dawson

Hive downs are a well established means of compromising the opposing tax considerations of the vendor and purchaser. However, there is always a danger that the scheme could be challenged under the principle laid down by Lord Brightman in *Furniss v Dawson* [1984] 1 All ER who said that:

Where there is a series of pre-ordained steps in a scheme that has no commercial purpose other than the avoidance or deferment of tax the courts are entitled to disregard those steps and consider the substance of the transaction.

The Inland Revenue have indicated to the Institute of Chartered Accountants in England and Wales that, in the situation of a receivership sale, it does not expect to use *Furniss v Dawson* to challenge the hive down of the whole or parts of a trade and related assets and liabilities. However, this indication only relates to a receivership sale. In a letter dated 20 September 1985, the Inland Revenue confirmed the uncertainty over whether *Furniss v Dawson* may apply to hive downs and suggested it may have some relevance where the purpose of a hive down is little more than hiving down tax losses. They indicated they would not normally expect the *Furniss v Dawson* approach to be relevant in cases where an entire trade or part of a trade together with its related assets and liabilities are hived down with a view to the trade being carried on in other hands.

Summary of hive downs

The main advantages to the vendor are no-gain crystallising on disposals and no balancing charge arising.

It is a little more complicated to summarise the purchaser's priorities. The main disadvantages to the purchaser are:

(1) Lower capital gains tax base values which in turn increase the gains on any subsequent disposal by the purchaser and reduces the effect of indexation. This assumes that no charge has arisen under TCGA 1992, ss 178 and 179 (see above).

(2) Lower capital allowance base value.

(3) Inability to apportion part of the purchase price as a trading expense.

(4) Inability to take advantage of roll-over relief if the purchaser has disposed of qualifying assets.

The main advantages to the purchaser are:
(1) Benefit of trading losses assuming all conditions are satisfied.
(2) Possible reduction in stamp duty if the vendor agrees to bear the stamp duty on the asset transfer.
(3) It is normal practice for the vendor to obtain any necessary novations or consents to the transfer of contracts.
(4) Buying a relatively clean company without historic liabilities thereby simplifying the warranties and indemnities a purchaser would otherwise wish to negotiate.

STAMP DUTY

What is stamp duty payable on?

The term stamp duty is used here to cover both transfer duty and ad valorem duty. Stamp duty is a duty payable by the purchaser at the rate of one per cent on the consideration (including the value of non-cash consideration such as shares) paid for assets transferred by document and on any liabilities assumed by the purchaser. Stamp duty is not payable on items which are transferred by delivery. These include loose plant and equipment, furniture, stocks and motor vehicles. If any assets comprise shares, stamp duty is payable at half of one per cent.

As a general rule stamp duty is normally payable at one per cent on the following items (see the Stamp Act 1891, ss 57 and 59):
(a) land and buildings;
(b) fixtures such as fixed plant and equipment;
(c) goodwill including where a payment for goodwill is disguised as payment for the vendor (or its senior management) by entering into restrictive covenants;
(d) debtors;
(e) the benefit of contracts;
(f) cash on deposit;
(g) liabilities assumed by the purchaser; and
(h) intellectual property rights including patents, trademarks and copyright (but not know-how).

The stamp duty is payable by the purchaser within 30 days of completion of the sale and the purchaser should present all documents transferring title together with a completed Stamps 22 Form, to the local Inland Revenue office. On the Stamps 22 Form, the purchaser is required to apportion the total purchase price between the categories of assets purchased. In view of the 30 days limit, it is suggested that the purchaser should include an apportionment in the sale contract.

Avoiding stamp duty

Execution of documents abroad

Stamp duty is often described as a voluntary tax. The explanation for this is that stamp duty is not an obligatory tax in itself but is instead a prerequisite if documents are to be used for certain purposes, ie documents can only be used for certain purposes if they have been stamped. For example, a document which is stampable cannot be used as evidence in civil court proceedings or relied on to prove title (such as a conveyance of land) unless the stamp duty on it has been paid. The change in ownership cannot be recorded on a UK title register unless the duly stamped document that transferred ownership is produced to the registrar. Therefore in practice it is necessary to stamp documents transferring land, shares and registrable intellectual property rights. The purchaser should also remember that where the consideration is the issue of shares in a limited company incorporated in England and Wales the provisions of CA 1985, s 88 make it obligatory to stamp either the sale agreement or Statutory Form 88(3) if the contract is not reduced to writing.

Where it is thought unlikely that a document will need to be used in the United Kingdom, it is common practice for the purchaser and vendor to execute the documents outside the United Kingdom and for it to be kept overseas. Under the Stamp Act 1891, s 15(3), no penalty will be payable on these documents provided they are stamped within 30 days after they are first brought back into the United Kingdom.

If documents are to be executed abroad for the purpose of saving stamp duty, the purchaser and vendor should enter into a separate agreement setting out the circumstances in which such documents will be brought back into the United Kingdom. Such circumstances normally cover the situation where the vendor needs to use the documents as evidence in proceedings and the person responsible for the proceedings has confirmed that certified copies are not sufficient. Other circumstances are where the vendor is under a legal obligation to produce the document in proceedings in the United Kingdom or the document is requested by the Inland Revenue or HM Customs and Excise in settling the vendor's tax position. In return, the vendor should undertake to use all reasonable endeavours to persuade people to rely on certified copies and not to cause documents to be brought back except in the specified circumstances he has agreed with the purchaser. If the vendor brings or causes the documents to be brought into the country other than in one of the specified circumstances the agreement should provide for the vendor to indemnify the purchaser against all duty including fines, penalties and interest. If the documents are to be retained by an independent third party, the vendor and purchaser should write a joint letter appointing such person as bailee specifying that the documents are only to be returned to the vendor if the vendor identifies a specified circumstance.

Excluding debtors and creditors

Both the value of debtors taken over by the purchaser and the amount of any liabilities to creditors assumed by the purchaser attract stamp duty. In the absence of a good reason why the purchaser should take over debtors and creditors, it is normal practice for the vendor to retain the debtors and use the monies received to satisfy the creditors. This is usually dealt with by the purchaser collecting debts and paying creditors as agent for the vendor (discussed in more detail in Chapter 4).

Unbolting machinery

Stamp duty will be payable on the consideration allocated to fixed plant but not loose plant. It is, therefore, common practice for equipment such as heavy plant and machinery to be unbolted temporarily on the day of completion. The purchaser should seek to arrange for a representative such as his accountant to be present at the vendor's premises in case the purchaser subsequently needs to prove certain equipment was not fixed at completion. However, it should be remembered (see page 119) that roll-over relief under TCGA 1992, s 152 is available on fixed plant but not loose plant. The benefit of roll-over relief may outweigh any stamp duty saved by unbolting the fixed plant.

Stamp duty on hive downs

In order to satisfy TA 1988, s 343 at the time of the transfer of assets to the new company, the vendor and the company should be members of the same group of companies. However, the relief from stamp duty under the Finance Act 1930, s 42 (as amended by the Finance Act 1967, s 27) for transfer between members of the same group will not be available if, at the time of transfer, arrangements are already in place for the new company to leave the vendor's group. If such arrangements are in place, stamp duty will be payable by the new company at one per cent on the assets transferred by document and liabilities assumed by the new company. Stamp duty will in any event be payable by the purchaser on the consideration paid for the shares in the new company but at the lower rate of half of one per cent.

To minimise the stamp duty where relief is not likely to be available under the Finance Act 1930, s 42 (as amended) it is normal to exclude from the transfer to the new company and sell directly to the purchaser as many assets as possible as would attract stamp duty. Although it attracts stamp duty, goodwill will not normally be excluded as this would jeopardise the application of the Transfer Regulations and the special provisions exempting value added tax.

Stamp duty on earlier documents

While the purchaser will wish to avoid stamp duty, he will at the same time wish to ensure that all documents by which the vendor derives title to the assets now being sold have been properly stamped. An appropriate warranty is included as warranty P2 in the standard sale agreement (see Appendix III).

APPORTIONMENT OF THE CONSIDERATION

The apportionment of the consideration between the assets is included in this chapter as it will have important corporation tax consequences for both the vendor and the purchaser and will also significantly affect the stamp duty payable by the purchaser. The interests of the vendor and the purchaser in apportioning the consideration conflict greatly. In order to avoid the possibility of a dispute after completion, it is normal and indeed sensible practice for the purchaser and the vendor to agree in the sale agreement the apportionment of the consideration between the various categories of assets sold. This is the purpose of the second column in Part I of Schedule 1 to the standard sale agreement (see Appendix III). It is not necessary to agree the apportionment between each asset within an individual category though it is normal to do so in the case of land.

As a result of the conflict, it is unusual for the Inland Revenue to substitute their own apportionment in considering either the purchaser's or vendor's tax liability as they will generally consider the vendor's and purchaser's apportionment to have been negotiated at arm's length. Similarly, the Inland Revenue will normally be willing to accept the purchaser's apportionment on the Stamps 22 Form to the extent that it corresponds with any apportionment of the consideration in the sale agreement.

The following are the areas in which the main conflicts between purchaser and vendor will arise.

Capital allowances

The purchaser will wish to maximise the apportionment of the consideration to those assets which attract capital allowances thereby maximising the capital allowances available. The purchaser's financiers will also wish to see as much consideration as possible allocated to these assets as they will be taking a charge as part of their security. On the other hand, the greater the apportionment to capital assets the greater the risk that the vendor will face a balancing charge on these assets. The vendor may instead prefer to allocate greater consideration to goodwill if it is concerned to maximise roll-over relief. Ideally the vendor would like to minimise the amounts apportioned to assets which have qualified for capital allowances on the basis that, if the apportioned consideration is less than the written down book value, the vendor may be entitled to a balancing allowance.

From a stamp duty point of view, within those assets which are subject to capital allowances, the purchaser will wish to minimise the apportionment to property and fixed plant and maximise the apportionment to loose plant.

Trading stock

The purchaser will wish to maximise the apportionment to trading stock as its acquisition is a deductible expense. On the other hand, consideration allocated to trading stock is treated as income in the hands of the vendor.

Roll-over relief

If either the purchaser or vendor are claiming roll-over relief under TCGA 1992, s 152 they will be concerned as to the apportionment in respect of qualifying assets.

Stamp duty

The purchaser, but not the vendor, will be concerned as to how the apportionment affects stamp duty. This is discussed above.

VALUE ADDED TAX

When is VAT payable, including VAT on land?

The main value added tax (VAT) issue to be addressed on any asset sale is whether or not VAT is payable. In most business sales it is normal to find that VAT is not payable on the basis that the statutory exemption under the Value Added Tax (Special Provisions) Order 1992 (SI 1992/3129) applies. This is discussed in detail below. But for this exception, as a general rule, the vendor will be liable to account for VAT on an asset sale as the sale of assets is usually the 'supply of goods or services' by the vendor 'in the United Kingdom in the course or furtherance of any business carried on by him' (Value Added Tax Act (VATA) 1983, s 2(1)). Further VATA 1983, s 47 provides that:

anything done in connection with the termination or intended termination of a business is treated as being done in the course or furtherance of that business.

The disposition of a business as a going concern, or of its assets or liabilities (whether or not in connection with its reorganisation or winding-up), is a supply made in the course or furtherance of the business

If VAT is payable on a sale, the VAT liability is the same as would normally apply to the sale of each item individually. In other words it is not necessarily appropriate to charge 17.5 per cent (the standard rate at the time of writing) on the total consideration paid. Each item would need to be considered individually to determine whether it is standard rated, zero rated or exempt. The disposal of current assets, such as trading stock, and capital assets such as plant and machinery, goodwill and cars is standard rated. The sale of land is normally exempt as is the sale of shares. The recovery by the purchaser of any VAT paid on the assets will depend on whether the assets are being used for making taxable or exempt supplies. The purchaser will only be able to recover its input VAT paid in respect of those assets to the extent that it subsequently uses them for taxable supplies. For purchasers not intending to make taxable supplies the risk of facing an additional cost of up to 17.5 per cent of the agreed consideration, rather than what would otherwise only be a cash flow cost if taxable supplies are made, is particularly significant. Such a purchaser should insist that confirmation from HM Customs and Excise that the VAT exemption is available be a condition precedent to completing the sale (see clause 4.1(e) of the standard sale agreement—Appendix III) and full disclosure of the relevant facts will need to be made to both the vendor's and the purchaser's VAT offices.

One of the areas that is particularly complicated is the question of whether and if so to what extent, VAT is payable on land and buildings.

The general principle provided in VATA 1983, Sched 6, Group 1 is that the grant or assignment of any interest (whether legal or equitable) or right over land or of any licence to occupy land is an exempt supply. Thus, rents in respect of land are generally exempt from VAT.

Certain supplies in relation to land are expressly excluded from this general principle and are standard-rated supplies. The most important of these exclusions is the sale of a freehold interest in a 'new' or 'uncompleted' commercial building. For this purpose, a building is 'completed' when certified as such by an architect or if earlier, when it is first fully occupied. A building is 'new' if it was completed less than three years before the relevant sale, and a building is a 'commercial building' if, broadly speaking, it is not intended for use solely for one of the residential or charitable purposes set out in VATA 1983, Sched 6.

The general principle that supplies in relation to land are exempt is further qualified by the fact that as a result of VATA 1983, Sched 5, Group 8 certain supplies in relation to land which are made in connection with the construction of non-commercial buildings are specifically treated as zero-rated supplies. Thus, the grant or assignment by a person constructing a non-commercial building, of a freehold or long leasehold interest in any part of the building or its site is zero-rated. So also is the supply in the course of the construction of such a building of any services other than the services of an architect, surveyor or any person acting as a consultant or in a supervisory capacity.

The dividing line between exempt and standard-rated supplies is further muddled by provisions which enable what would ordinarily be an exempt supply of land to be treated as a standard-rated supply. Where an election to waive exemption from VAT (otherwise known as an option to tax) has been made in respect of any land specified or described in the election, grants made in respect of that land by the person who made the election (or, if a company, any associate) become taxable rather than exempt supplies (VATA 1983, Sched 6A, para 2). The election, once made, applies to the whole of a building or planned building and all the land within its curtilage even where the election is expressed to be made in respect of part only of that building (VATA, Sched 6A, para 3(3)).

The election has effect from the beginning of the day on which it is made or any later day specified in the election. Once made, the election continues to bind the person by whom it was made until and including the occasion of the sale by the maker of his interest in the building (VATA 1983, Sched 6A, para 3(1)).

Where the election is made by a body corporate, the election will also bind:

(a) any company which was a member of the first company's VAT group at the time the election first took effect;

(b) any company which has since become a member of the first company's VAT group and at a time the first company still had an interest in the relevant land;

(c) if any company within (a) or (b) above obtains an interest in the relevant land, any other company which was a member of the VAT group at any time whilst the interest subsisted.

Where a grant in respect of a building has been zero-rated on the basis that it is a 'new' or uncompleted building which is intended for non-commercial use and, within ten years of the completion of the building its use is changed, a standard-rated supply is deemed to take place on the date of change of use so as to claw back the benefit of the zero-rated treatment previously allowed in respect of the building (VATA 1983, Sched 6A, para 1(4)). If, instead of the person who received the original zero-rated grant changing the use of the building, he grants, within the same period of ten years, an interest to another person who intends to use it for a commercial purpose, that later grant is treated as a standard-rated supply (VATA 1983, Sched 6A, para 1(2)).

The inter-action of stamp duty and VAT raises special problems in relation to land. On the sale of new commercial buildings which are standard-rated supplies for VAT purposes, stamp duty is charged on the VAT inclusive amount of the consideration. Transactions in respect of 'old' commercial buildings are generally exempt from VAT subject to the right of the vendor or lessor to waive the exemption. Where this election has been exercised, stamp duty is chargeable on the VAT inclusive consideration. If the election has not been exercised but is still capable of being exercised at the relevant time, stamp duty should be charged as if the election had been exercised (ie on the VAT inclusive consideration).

The special exemption provisions which apply where land forms part of the transfer of a business as a going concern are discussed below. However, if the exemption does not apply (and it is unusual for it not to apply) the purchaser should concentrate on two main concerns.

Firstly, if one of the assets being acquired is a commercial building, the purchaser will wish to know when the building was completed in case it is a 'new' building to ensure there is no risk of a charge arising on change of use. The second concern relates to the post-acquisition effect. Where the purchaser is a trader who makes both taxable and exempt supplies and the cost of the land exceeded £250,000, the input tax credit to which the purchaser is entitled on acquisition is subject to adjustment over a period of ten years in the case of freehold land and leases with more than ten years unexpired (and five years in respect of other leases). The input tax credit allowed on acquisition will require adjustment if the extent to which the land is used for taxable supplies changes during the period from the extent of such use in the year of acquisition (Value Added Tax (General) Regulations 1985 (SI 1985/886) Part VA). It is worth noting that the obligation to review annually applies not only to land and buildings but also to computers and items of computer equipment acquired on or after 1 April 1990 for a VAT exclusive value of £50,000 or more.

In summary, it is prudent for a purchaser before acquiring land and buildings for £250,000 or more and computers and computer equipment for £50,000 or more to establish:

(a) the date of acquisition;
(b) the number of remaining years in the adjustment period;
(c) the total VAT incurred on the acquisition of the asset by the vendor;
(d) the percentage of the VAT originally claimed on the item in the first period.

The exemption—transfer of a going concern

Contrary to the general rule, no VAT will be payable if all of the conditions of art 5 of the VAT (Special Provisions) Order 1992, SI 1992/3129 apply (see Appendix V for the text of art 5). The art 5 exemption is often loosely described as the transfer as a going concern exemption. Whether a sale is a transfer as a going concern is a question of fact in all the circumstances and is discussed in more detail in Chapter 5. It should be stressed that the transfer of a business as a going concern is only one of the five conditions of the exemption that need to be satisfied. The purchaser, but more particularly the vendor, should satisfy itself that every condition in art 5 has been satisfied and not merely the going concern condition. Indeed HM Customs and Excise will look to see if all other conditions are satisfied before considering the going concern condition. The Commissioners have produced a helpful guide to the conditions in the form of Leaflet 700/9/87.

The conditions that need to be satisfied for art 5 to apply are that:

(a) the assets are supplied to the purchaser;
(b) the assets are to be used by the purchaser in carrying on the same kind of business either as a new business or as an expansion of a separate business;
(c) if only part of the vendor's business is being transferred, it is capable of separate operation, although it is not necessary for it actually to be operated as a separate business after completion but merely for it to be capable of such operation;
(d) the business or part of the business is transferred as a going concern;
(e) if the vendor is a taxable person for VAT purposes the purchaser must be registered for VAT either before the sale or immediately following the sale.

VAT tribunals have recently given a generous interpretation to the condition that the assets are to be used by the purchaser in carrying on the same kind of business as that carried on by the vendor prior to the acquisition. For example, in *Brooke Saddler Limited* [1992] STI 1038, although the purchaser changed the business from wholesale to retail in emphasis, the tribunal held that this was the same business after transfer as before. In *Augusta Extrusions Limited* [1992] STI 1043 the VAT exemption was available even though the purchaser acquired the constituent parts of the business from different vendors.

An area that is often easy to overlook during negotiations is to ensure that the purchaser is registered for VAT preferably before exchange of contract. This is particularly important where the purchaser is a shelf company or a relatively new company as is usually the case in management buy-outs, joint ventures and hive downs.

As a result of the VAT (Special Provisions) (Amendments) Order 1991 (SI 1991/2503), art 5 of the VAT (Special Provisions) Order 1992 provides that a supply of assets shall not be treated as a transfer of a business as a going concern and potentially exempt from VAT *'to the extent that'* it consists of a grant in respect of:

(1) Land in respect of which the vendor has decided to waive the exemption from tax unless the purchaser has agreed to adopt the same treatment for the land.

(2) A new or unfinished freehold commercial building or civil engineering works (which is normally standard-rated) unless the purchaser has opted to tax.

In summary, the principal change is to exclude supplies of property subject to VAT from being treated as a transfer of a going concern unless, in addition to meeting the conditions in para 1 of art 5 (see Appendix V), the purchaser has:

(1) Elected to waive exemption in relation to the property.

(2) Given written notification of the election to HM Customs and Excise before the date on which the grant of the property would have been treated as having been made or, if there is more than one such date, the earliest of them.

In the case of hive downs, it is important to ensure that the assets are used by the new company for a period and are not transferred straight out to the purchaser which is its new parent or to another subsidiary of the purchaser.

If the transfer of assets is part of a group reorganisation and the vendor and purchaser are both members of the same VAT group no VAT is charged.

Is VAT a purchaser or vendor issue?

The issue of whether VAT is payable primarily concerns the vendor as it is the vendor's responsibility to get the VAT treatment of the sale correct and to collect and account for VAT if any is payable. Under

VATA 1983, s 10(2) if the sale agreement is silent as to VAT it will be assumed that if VAT is chargeable, the sale price is inclusive of VAT and the vendor will pay the VAT out of the agreed sale price. As a result it is normal practice for the vendor to stipulate in the sale agreement (see clause 3.3 of the standard sale agreement—Appendix III) that the price is exclusive of VAT if any VAT is chargeable. The availability of the art 5 exemption depends on the use to which the purchaser puts the assets. Therefore, it is normally considered reasonable for the contract price to be exclusive of VAT if both the purchaser and vendor state in the contract that they consider art 5 applies. Whether or not the purchaser is willing to accept the price as being exclusive will, of course, also depend on the extent to which the purchaser considers it can recover any VAT and any understanding reached with the vendor in relation to VAT at the outset of negotiations.

A purchaser should strongly resist the vendor charging VAT on the sale price at completion unless the vendor can prove that it is correctly charged. If the VAT was incorrectly charged the vendor will still need to account for the VAT collected but the purchaser is not entitled to recover it.

Purchasers need to pay particular care and attention while they are a member of a partially exempt VAT group of companies and specialist VAT advice must be sought. The general position is that where the business is transferred as a going concern to a partially exempt VAT group, the representative member of the purchaser's VAT group is deemed to have acquired and immediately disposed of the business for VAT purposes. The effect of this is that the representative member may have to account for output VAT on the deemed disposal without obtaining any corresponding credit.

VAT records and registration number

The purchaser should seek to take over the vendor's VAT records for the last six years (VATA 1983, s 33(1)(b)) but at the same time be prepared to grant the vendor a right of access (see clause 3.6 of the standard sale agreement—Appendix III). A vendor may only retain the VAT records in relation to a business transferred as a going concern if, at the vendor's request, HM Customs and Excise have consented to him so doing. The vendor is most likely to want to make such an application where it is only transferring part of a business. Whether the vendor or the purchaser keep the records, the other party should reserve a right to inspect and take copies of the records (see clause 3.6 of the standard sale agreement—Appendix III) and require the other party to keep the records for a minimum period of six years after completion as this is the statutory period within which earlier VAT treatment can be challenged. In return, the party granted the right of access should undertake to the other party not to apply to HM Customs and Excise for an order that the VAT records be delivered up (see clause 3.5 of the standard sale agreement— Appendix III).

A vendor may suggest it would be simple for the purchaser to take on the vendor's VAT registration and thereby avoid the reprinting of invoices and perhaps the need to register. However, on re-registration the purchaser will assume all the vendor's VAT liabilities including unpaid VAT and the vendor's compliance record (see *Ponsonby v HM Customs and Excise* [1988] STC 28) and the purchaser should reject such a suggestion outright unless it is confident that it has full details of the vendor's registration history and knows about all liabilities. If, despite this, a purchaser is willing to take over the vendor's registration number a purchaser should ensure that he has a thorough understanding of the cumulative nature of VAT penalties. Re-registration will require a joint application to HM Customs and Excise on Form VAT 68 and the purchaser will also need to submit Form VAT 1 or Form VAT 2.

VAT warranties

The VAT warranties in the standard sale agreement (see Appendix III) assume that the purchaser is not taking over the vendor's VAT number and their prime purpose is information seeking rather than establishing a means of redress. If the vendor's VAT number is to be taken over, a purchaser should seek a full indemnity from the vendor for any VAT interest and penalties relating to the period prior to the transfer date.

The purchaser will be particularly interested to identify whether there are any special agreements relating to the business between HM Customs and Excise and the vendor and whether the vendor has been required to give security. As regards the former, the purchaser will wish to consider whether such agreements are advantageous and should be continued if possible. As regards security, the purchaser will wish to establish whether security was requested due to the nature of the business or the financial status of the vendor. If the purchaser is to be required to provide security this will affect his cashflow.

As the purchaser normally takes over the VAT records for the previous six years, the vendor should be required to warrant the good state and completeness of all records for that period.

Lastly but perhaps most importantly, the purchaser will normally seek a warranty that in conducting the business the vendor has not made exempt supplies as this is likely to mean that the purchaser will also make exempt supplies and will not be able to obtain a full credit for input tax.

CAPITAL TRANSFER AND INHERITANCE TAX

Capital transfer and inheritance tax is only of minor interest on an asset sale and the two main points are addressed in warranties P.5 (a) and P.5 (b) of the standard sale agreement (see Appendix III).

The first concern (warranty P.5 (a)) is that as a result of the Inheritance Tax Act 1984, s 212 a person who is liable for inheritance tax attributable to the value of any property is given the power to raise the tax payable, or to recover the tax he has already paid by the sale or mortgage of, or a terminal charge on, that property or any part of it. The concern for the purchaser is that where one person, X, has given property to another person Y, who then gave the property to the vendor, if X could or would not pay the capital transfer tax in respect of the first transfer the Inland Revenue may proceed against Y in respect of the first transfer and Y may be able to raise the amount of the tax by selling the property.

The second concern (see warranty P.5 (b)) is that the Inland Revenue has a charge on property where the transfer of that property has given rise to an inheritance tax liability. It is normal practice for a purchaser to seek an express warranty to ensure that none of the assets sold are the subject of a capital transfer tax charge. This is in addition to the general warranty that all purchasers will include that none of the assets sold is subject to any charge, mortgage or other encumbrance (see warranty A.1(a) in the Standard Sale Agreement—Appendix III).

Chapter 8

Intellectual Property

INTRODUCTION

Intellectual property rights are intangible assets of the business and as such are often overlooked by a purchaser. Purchasers should remember that every business uses or owns some intellectual property though it varies as to whether the intellectual property in any instance forms a material part of the business being sold.

A purchaser will have two general concerns. Firstly, does the vendor of the business either own or have the transferable right to use sufficient intellectual property to enable it to conduct the business in the manner in which it is currently conducted? Secondly, does the vendor have sufficient intellectual property rights to be able to prevent competitors from copying the unique or most valuable elements of the business?

To be able to answer these concerns a purchaser will need an understanding of the following:

(1) What different types of intellectual property are there?
(2) What intellectual property is material to the vendor's business?
(3) How do you transfer intellectual property rights?
(4) What should the warranties cover?

DIFFERENT TYPES OF INTELLECTUAL PROPERTY RIGHTS

Intellectual property rights can be categorised according to whether or not a right is registered or registrable. Registrable intellectual property rights include patents, trade marks and certain design rights. In an asset sale, registrable intellectual property rights tend to be easier to deal with by virtue of the fact that their registration is a means of identification and ownership. Non-registrable intellectual property rights can be more difficult to identify and protect and include copyright, design rights (to the extent these are not registrable), know-how and moral rights. There are other more esoteric rights outside the scope of this book.

A further distinction a purchaser should appreciate is that intellectual property rights are territorial. Registrable intellectual property rights are likely to be registered in each country in which they are used.

Patents

A patent comprises an exclusive right issued by a state regulatory authority to the applicant for a limited period to utilise a specific invention. In the United Kingdom and in most of Europe, the limited period of protection is 20 years from the filing of the patent application. The applicant will need to provide full details of its invention to the appropriate regulatory authority by submitting what is described as the specification. The specification comprises technical drawings, a written description of the invention and at the end of the description a section known as the claims, namely a narrative defining the nature and extent of the invention. The claims are the key to assessing the extent of the patent's monopoly. In return for the limited period of exclusivity, the applicant discloses full details of its invention to the public in the published application and subsequently the granted patent becomes a public record.

A patent protects the proprietor against anyone within the territory who makes unauthorised use of the invention. However, a competitor is unlikely to have made an exact copy and enforcement of a patent will often involve complex technical argument. Independent creation of an invention without consciously copying one that has already been registered as a patent is no defence to a claim that the registered patent has been infringed.

After the fourth anniversary of the patent application a patent must be renewed annually by payment of a fee. The patent lapses automatically if the fee is not paid within the appropriate period but may be restored if a further fee is paid within six months.

Purchasers should be aware that, although the proprietor of a patent generally has a discretion whether or not to grant licences to third parties, in certain circumstances a compulsory licence may be ordered, or licences may be available as of right.

Trade marks

A trade mark may be a word, a logo, or a combination of the two. Its function is to identify the trade origin of particular goods or services. Trade marks are closely bound up with the goodwill or reputation of a business.

Trade marks may be applied for and registered but need not be. Trade marks are granted for an initial period of seven years and can be extended for an indefinite period but will expire if the appropriate renewal fees are not paid, or if an objection is raised that the applicant has ceased to use them for a continuous period in excess of five years. Trade marks are only granted in relation to specific products or services and for use within specific classes. The trade mark registration cannot be used by the proprietor to prevent a person using the exact same mark, either in relation to goods and services or within a class not covered by the proprietor's registration. However, a separeate action may be available under passing-off or competition laws, whether the trade mark is registered or not.

Great care must be exercised if the sale of a business involves separating the trade marks used in the business from the goodwill, or if only part of the business and some of the trade marks are transferred, or if the same trade mark in different countries is sold to different entities.

Industrial designs

Industrial designs were until 1989 largely protected by copyright. Since then, registered design protection has been enhanced and there is a new unregistered design right. Registered design rights are similar to patents whereas unregistered design rights are comparable with copyright. Protection for both is for a limited period. In the United Kingdom this is 25 years for registered designs subject to payment of renewal fees every five years. For unregistered design rights the period is ten years from the first marketing of articles made from the design subject to a maximum period of 15 years from creation of the design if there is a delay between design and marketing (see the Copyright, Designs and Patents Act (CDPA) 1988, s 216). Purchasers should be aware that licences are available as of right in all cases in the last five years of the unregistered design right (CDPA 1988, s 237) and if the parties cannot agree terms for the licence, they will be settled by the Comptroller of Patents. Licences as of right are available for both registered and unregistered design rights if a Monopolies and Mergers Commission report concludes that the design right is being used against the public interest.

Copyrights

Copyright is essentially the right of the creator not to have its work copied or adapted, intentionally. Unlike registered designs and patents, wholly independent creation without copying is a defence. Copyright arises automatically on creation and is not capable of protection by registration. The law of copyright is governed by the Copyright, Designs and Patents Act 1988 which replaces the Copyright Act 1956.

Section 1 of CDPA 1988 defines what is protected by copyright. The main categories include:

(1) Original literary, dramatic, musical or artistic works (CDPA, 1988 s 3). Literary works include computer programs (ie. software) and tables of data. Artistic works include graphic work such as drawings, plans, diagrams and prints and photographs.

(2) Sound recordings, films, broadcasts or cable programs.

(3) Typographical arrangements of published editions.

Copyright is for a restricted, albeit a long period. In the United Kingdom the period is generally limited to the life of the creator plus 50 years.

Under CDPA 1988, s 9 the first owner of copyright is the author of the work or the person who created the work. Where a work capable of forming copyright is created by an employee in the course of employment, the employer owns the copyright unless agreed otherwise with the employee (see CDPA 1988, s 11).

The precise period of protection for copyright depends on the work being protected and is governed by the provisions of the CDPA 1988. For example, under s 12 of the Act, literary, dramatic, musical and artistic works are protected for the life of the author plus fifty years after the end of the year in which the author died, whether or not the work is published. There are special provisions where the identity of the author is not known. As indicated above, copyright was formerly an important right for the protection of industrial designs but this importance has been virtually extinguished by CDPA 1988.

One of the main areas of copyright present in virtually all businesses is computer software. Software is considered a literary work and it cannot be reproduced nor can the right to use it usually be assigned without the consent of the copyright owner. If the vendor uses software under a licence from a third party supplier such licences are frequently non-assignable.

Know-how

In a business sale the know-how of the vendor comprises the trade secrets and confidential information used by the vendor to give its business a competitive edge. Know-how is not capable of registration. Further, it is difficult to identify and therefore difficult to protect, yet without the know-how the business may well be unattractive to the purchaser. Know-how is often stored in the memories and experiences of the vendor's employees. This factor should cause the vendor to consider carefully the implications of any redundancy proposals or alternatively, the need for specific employees to enter new contracts of employment as a condition precedent to completing the purchase.

The vendor will also be conscious of the value of its know-how. The vendor should ensure the purchaser enters a confidentiality agreement at the outset of negotiations (see Chapter 1, page 14) as the purchaser's due diligence exercise will inevitably reveal some or all of the vendor's know-how. If the sale is not completed it is important that the purchaser returns all printed confidential information provided by the vendor together with any copies it made subsequently, and has agreed not to use any information about the vendor's business which has been disclosed. This is not an absolute means of protecting the vendor against the purchaser setting up in competition but should be a means of preventing the purchaser from making unauthorised use of the vendor's know-how. A standard form of confidentiality agreement is provided in Appendix I.

Moral rights

Moral rights were introduced by CDPA 1988. They give the authors of literary, dramatic, musical and artistic works and directors of films the right to be identified as the author (CDPA 1988, s 77) and the right to object to derogatory treatment of the work (CDPA 1988, s 80). The right to be identified as the author only comes into being if expressly asserted by the author. These rights vest in individuals only and cannot be assigned. However, if copyright forms an important part of the vendor's business, the purchaser should consider whether it is necessary to obtain a waiver of moral rights.

WHAT INTELLECTUAL PROPERTY IS MATERIAL TO THE VENDOR'S BUSINESS?

The purchaser not only needs to consider what intellectual property is relevant in the vendor's business but more importantly needs to identify what is material. Against the need to make thorough enquiries and investigations the purchaser needs to balance the costs it will incur together with the value of any warranties the vendor may give. As a general guide, the more significant the intellectual property in relation to the vendor's business as a whole, the more thorough the purchaser's investigations should be. The responses to the information questionnaire (see Appendix II) will be a helpful starting point. However, the purchaser should also consider what intellectual property rights would normally be relevant to the general nature of the vendor's business. This requires a basic understanding of the vendor's business. Then the purchaser should consider in detail precisely what rights does the vendor require in order to conduct the business in its present form. The responses to the questionnaire are unlikely to provide the level of detail or assurance sought and the purchaser will need a more thorough understanding of how the vendor's business operates.

Intellectual property can usefully be looked at in two ways. Firstly, what intellectual property rights does the vendor benefit from in order to conduct the business? Examples of these include software licences used by the vendor to operate its computers. Secondly, what intellectual property rights does the vendor possess that are valuable to its customers? For example, does the vendor create software and licence this out to customers? Registered rights are simpler to investigate than unregistered ones. In the United Kingdom, the Department of Trade and Industry is the regulatory authority and searches should be made at the Patent Office, Trade Marks Registry and the Designs Registry as appropriate. Searches should also be made in any other country in which the vendor operates its business. Precisely what searches need to be made and what information the purchaser will wish to obtain from such searches will vary from case to case and it is wise to seek professional advice.

HOW TO TRANSFER INTELLECTUAL PROPERTY RIGHTS

The appropriate method depends on the rights being transferred. It is normal for separate transfer documents to be executed for each type of intellectual property right rather than one global transfer, particularly for registered rights, as the document will need to be presented to each appropriate registry. It will also be preferable to execute separate assignments for each country in which the rights are registered. The UK registries will require evidence that stamp duty has been paid or is not due, and this should be considered in the context of tax planning for the transaction as a whole.

Patents

Patents, applications for patents and rights under patents are all transferable under the Patents Act 1977, s 30. The assignment must be in writing and must be signed by both the vendor and the purchaser.

In addition to the main sale agreement, it is normal for the vendor and purchaser to execute a separate form of patent assignment as this will need to be stamped and registered with the Patent Office in the United Kingdom and perhaps with registries outside the United Kingdom.

One form of assignment can be used to encompass existing patents, applications for patents and rights under patents. However, there are some basic terms to incorporate in every assignment. The assignment of an application must include an assignment of the rights to be registered as the owner of the patent. Also an assignment should expressly include the right to sue for previous infringements and to recover all remedies. Lastly, the purchaser should insist on the vendor giving a further assurance undertaking as it is common for the purchaser to require assistance in providing further information or executing further documents for submission to the Patent Office. In addition, the purchaser cannot sue for infringement until it has been registered as the new owner and in the interim will require the vendor to commence and pursue the infringement action on the purchaser's behalf.

It is important for the purchaser to register the assignment as quickly as possible for a number of reasons. For example, a subsequent purchaser from the vendor of the same patent rights will not necessarily be bound by the sale to the original purchaser if he had no actual knowledge of the first assignment or if no application had been made to register the first assignment at the time of the second sale. The application to register the assignment should be made immediately after the sale once the stamp duty has been paid, although it is possible to apply even before the duty has been paid, to become effective after payment. If an infringement occurs after transfer of title, damages cannot be given for the period before the assignment is registered unless the assignment is registered within six months or the court is satisfied that registration was not practicable within that time (see the Patents Act 1977, s 68).

Trade marks

The assignment of trade marks is complex due to the fact that historically, trade marks represented and were inextricably linked with the goodwill of the business and were not considered to be a separate right. The trade mark was considered as representing the trading source of the goods or services. To allow unrestricted assignment of trade marks was thought to cause consumer confusion and, as a safeguard, before 1938 trade marks whether registered or not could only be transferred if sold with the goodwill of the business concerned.

However, under the Trade Mark Act 1938, s 22 registered trade marks may now be assigned either with or without goodwill and either in respect of all or only some of the goods for which the mark is registered. An assignment without goodwill must follow the procedure under the Patents Act 1938, s 22(7) and includes the need to issue an advertisement so giving third parties a right to object before the assignment can be registered. The underlying theme in the legislation is the protection of the consumer and any assignment which results in more than one person owning trade marks that are confusingly similar will be invalid. Assignments must be in writing but need only be signed by the vendor/proprietor, not by both parties. Care must be exercised if trade marks are 'associated'. All associated marks must be assigned together, unless the Registry can be persuaded to dissolve the association.

Unregistered trade marks are assignable either together with and at the same time as registered trade marks or separate from the registered trade marks provided that they are assigned with the goodwill of the business as required by the pre-1938 law. Examples of unregistered trade marks might include a company's trading name. Although it is feasible, the splitting of the assignments of goodwill and registered and unregistered trade marks is a highly complex area and is outside the scope of this book.

Industrial designs

Registered designs are assigned in writing and the assignment needs to be signed by the vendor. Under the Registered Designs Act 1949 only the registered owner can sue for infringement and therefore the purchaser should ensure the assignment is registered. In addition, an assignment must first be registered if it is to be used as proof of title.

Section 224 of CDPA 1988 and s 19(3B) of the Registered Designs Act 1949 (as amended) provide that any assignment of a registered design is deemed automatically to assign the associated design right unless expressly excluded in the form of assignment. Despite this ability to exclude the design right, it is commonly considered that the Registered Designs Act 1949, s 19(3A) provides that an interest in the registered design will not be registered unless the person entitled to that interest is also entitled to a corresponding interest in the design right. The effect of this interpretation is that as a practical matter, the design right probably cannot be separated from the associated registered design. Design rights must be assigned in writing, signed by the vendor (CDPA 1988, s 222).

Copyright

As a result of CDPA 1988, s 90 an assignment of copyright is only effective if it is in writing. Contrary to the position with patents, the assignment of copyright need only be signed by the vendor and not the purchaser. The unusual feature of copyright (and design right) when compared to other intellectual property is that it is divisible. For example, the author of a book may assign separately the right to copy the book as a cinema film, video film or as a musical or theatre production.

It is desirable for a purchaser to obtain a formal assignment of copyright. Purchasers sometimes rely on the agreement to transfer provisions in the main sale agreement together with a further assurance clause in order to ask for a separate assignment, if needed at a later stage, but the willingness of the vendor to co-operate is likely to decrease as time goes by. For a separate assignment to be executed at completion, the main point to address in the assignment is identifying the copyright. The purchaser will usually prefer a general assignment of all of the vendor's copyright which also identifies specific known examples. The vendor will be concerned in case this catches by accident any copyright the vendor needs for his remaining business.

Know-how

In the United Kingdom, know-how is not strictly speaking capable of assignment as it is not a property right, but is the accumulated experience of the vendor and its employees in relation to a particular business. As know-how cannot be formally assigned, a purchaser will seek to obtain the exclusive benefit of the know-how by preventing others from using it and ensuring that all tangible records are within its possession. These obligations are often contained in a form of 'assignment'. The main protection for the purchaser will be restrictive covenants by the vendor not to solicit customers or employees, and not to compete with the business or use confidential information (see Chapter 3, page 70). In addition, as has been discussed at page 147, the purchaser should identify and ensure he has retained and does not immediately dismiss key employees. Finally, the purchaser should ensure that he takes possesison of all books and records relating to the business.

Moral rights

Moral rights are personal in nature and cannot be assigned. Instead the purchaser should seek a waiver from the author or his estate of his moral rights (either in whole or in part) which should include an acknowledgment of non-objection to use of his works before assignment of the relevant copyright. Any existing waivers are presumed to apply in favour of the vendor's successor in title unless limited to exclude such a presumption.

WHAT SHOULD THE WARRANTIES COVER?

Intellectual property tends to be an area in which warranties are more useful for the disclosures they provoke rather than the protection they give. The following are the main areas the vendor will be asked to warrant and are covered in the standard sale agreement, (see Appendix III) though not in the same order.

Identification

The vendor should be prepared to warrant that details of all intellectual property registrations and applications used or required by the business are set out either in a schedule to the agreement or in the disclosure letter. The vendor should also disclose full copies of all patent specifications. The purchaser will also want the vendor to warrant that it has provided details of specific material unregistered rights.

In any event, the vendor should be prepared to warrant that it has disclosed full details of all intellectual property licences granted by and to the vendor in relation to the business.

Title

The vendor should be asked to warrant that it owns or has the unrestricted right to use all the intellectual property rights that it needs to conduct the business or alternatively, those disclosed in response to the identification warranty above. The vendor will be unwilling to provide an absolute warranty in respect of unregistered rights and licences.

Assignment

The purchaser will start by asking the vendor to warrant that it does not need the consent of any third party to assign the intellectual property to the purchaser. This is unrealistic and a purchaser should be suspicious if the vendor gives this warranty with apparent ease as it is invariably untrue. The most common example is where a consent is usually needed is for the assignment of a software licence. The purpose of the warranty is to encourage the vendor to identify those items which do require consent. The purchaser will then consider which of these are material to the business and decide how best to address the issue. Whether or not the vendor should be required to seek a novation of any such licences is a matter of negotiation and the issues raised in Chapter 4 should be considered.

Validity

It is unreasonable of the purchaser to insist on a warranty that all intellectual property rights are valid and enforceable. Instead a vendor should be prepared to warrant that all registrable intellectual property has been duly registered and that the vendor knows of no reason why these should be invalid and has not received any notice of an adverse claim. Due to their nature and complexity, patents in particular are often open to challenge for invalidity.

Infringement and litigation

The vendor is unlikely to, and indeed should not, warrant in absolute terms that it has not infringed the intellectual property rights of any third party and that no infringement of the vendor's rights has taken place. However, at the very least the vendor should warrant that there is no current litigation either by or against the vendor and the vendor knows of no circumstances that may give rise to any claim of infringement.

Fees

The vendor will be required to warrant that all fees including annual renewal fees for registered intellectual property rights have been paid.

Employees

The purchaser will expect the vendor to warrant that neither the vendor nor any other company in its group has any liability to pay compensation under the Patents Act 1977, ss 40 and 41. These are the provisions that provide for compensation to be paid to employees if they make inventions which are of outstanding benefit to their employer or if the invention has been transferred to the employer.

Know-how and confidential information

The vendor will be required to warrant that neither it nor any other company in its group has disclosed know-how, trade secrets, or confidential information to any person other than the purchaser nor has it entered into any agreement to disclose any such information.

Appendix I

CONFIDENTIALITY AGREEMENT

Vendor's letterhead

[name and address
of Purchaser]

Dear Sirs   [   ] 19[   ]

Confidentiality Agreement

We refer to your proposed acquisition of [   ] ('the Business') and
your request for information relating to the Business.

In order that you may investigate and evaluate the Business for the purpose of
the proposed acquisition we have agreed to disclose to you information
relating to the Business [and other business in our group] ('Confidential
Information') on the basis that in consideration of our disclosing the
Confidential Information you hereby undertake:

(1) To treat the Confidential Information as confidential and keep it
    confidential.

(2) To use the Confidential Information for no purpose other than
    assessing your proposed acquisition of the Business.

(3) Not to disclose the Confidential Information to any person other than
    [your employees] [specific named employees] and professional advisers
    without our prior written consent.

(4) To ensure that each employee and professional adviser only receives
    Confidential Information after being made aware of and agreeing [with
    us in writing] to comply with the terms of this letter.

(5) Not to disclose the existence of the negotiations to acquire the Business
    or your investigations of the Business to any one even if the proposed
    acquisition does not complete.

(6) To return to us forthwith on demand all Confidential Information together with all copies you have made, including copies stored on tape or disc or produce a declaration to our satisfaction signed by a duly authorised officer certifying that the same has been destroyed.

SAVE THAT your undertaking shall not prevent you from disclosing the Confidential Information if you are required to do so by an order of a court of competent jurisdiction and have made available to the court a copy of this letter or in order to comply with the rules of a stock exchange [name stock exchange if possible] or which comes into the public domain through no fault of your own.

Without limiting in any way any other rights and remedies available to us, you hereby acknowledge that on a breach by you of the terms of this agreement we shall be entitled to apply to the courts for an injunction preventing you from using or passing on any Confidential Information to any other person, either directly or indirectly.

This agreement shall be governed by and construed in accordance with the laws of England.

Please acknowledge your undertaking by signing and returning the enclosed copy of this letter.

Yours faithfully

for and on behalf
of [Vendor]

We hereby agree with and agree to be bound by our undertaking on the basis set out above in this letter.

_____ Dated [   ] 199[   ]
for and on behalf of
[Purchaser]

Appendix II

INFORMATION QUESTIONNAIRE

This questionnaire addresses information needed by [name of the Purchaser] to assess its proposed purchase of the [entire] business, assets and undertaking of [name of Vendor] carried on under the name of [   ] ('the Business').

Please supply responses as and when the information is available rather than waiting until all the information has been collected.

The questionnaire is to be interpreted as covering not only [name of Vendor] but all other members of the Vendor's group involved in the Business.

Please provide the following information:

A Vendor's group structure

(1) Brief description of the Business and the function and location of each place where the Business operates from including locations overseas.

(2) Explain how the Business can be identified against other businesses of the Vendor and businesses of other companies in the Vendor's group.

(3) Memorandum and articles of association of [name of the Vendor] and all other members of the Vendor's group involved in the Business.

(4) Details of all shares owned by Vendor identifying those owned in relation to the Business and details of all other shareholders and their shareholding in such companies.

(5) Names of all directors and senior managers of the Vendor and any directors or managers of other group companies involved in the Business.

(6) Particulars of the involvement or interests of the persons in question 5 above in any business other than the Business and in transactions with the Business.

B Accounts and finance

(1) Audited accounts of [the Vendor] for the last three years and audited accounts for the last three years of each company in [the Vendor's] group involved in the Business.

(2) Management accounts for the Business.

(3) Business plan for the Business for current and next financial year.

(4) If appropriate divisional accounts of the Vendor in relation to the Business.

(5) Details of all bank accounts operated by or on behalf of the Business and in particular:
(a) details of all pooled banking arrangements;
(b) details of agreed overdraft limits and actual overdraft.

(6) Details and copies of all mortgages, charges, guarantees, indemnities and other financial commitments undertaken by or in respect of the Business including arrangements within [the Vendor's] group

(7) Details and copies of all loans made *to* the Business including inter group loans and staff loans.

(8) Details of the basis on which the cost of common group services are apportioned to the Business; eg:
(a) insurance;
(b) rental;
(c) accounting department;
(d) motor vehicles;
(e) marketing;
(f) research and development;
(g) computer time.

C Consents

(1) Details of all consents needed by [the Vendor] to transfer the Business; eg consents under:
(a) articles of association of [the Vendor] and its holding company and subsidiaries;
(b) shareholder's agreement governing the conduct of [the Vendor] and its holding company and subsidiaries;
(c) finance arrangements including, mortgages, loan notes, term debt and leasing contracts;
(d) stock exchange;
(e) regulatory authorities;
(f) trade contracts;
(g) software licences;
(h) leases.

D Contracts and trade

(1) Copies of all [material] contracts relating to the Business with customers and suppliers including:
(a) all contracts which require consent to assign;

    (b) licences;
    (c) agency agreements;
    (d) long term contracts;
    (e) franchise arrangements;
    (f) hire purchase;
    (g) credit sale;
    (h) lease agreements;
    (i) rental agreements.
(2) A schedule identifying all customers and the percentage of turnover they represent.
(3) Copies of all standard forms of contract used.
(4) A schedule itemising current debtors, period of debt and amount.
(5) Details of all trade within [the Vendor's] group indicating where and on what basis rates charged are discounted.
(6) Details of any restrictions on the Business to conduct business in any part of the world.

E Employees

(1) A schedule or print out containing in respect of all persons employed in the Business:
    (a) full name;
    (b) name of employee, and sex;
    (c) date of birth;
    (d) date of commencement of employment;
    (e) job description;
    (f) salary and next review date;
    (g) bonus entitlement including profit shares;
    (h) pension entitlement;
    (i) insurance cover, eg sickness and disability;
    (j) notice period;
    (k) holiday entitlement.
(2) Name the key personnel for the operation and management of the Business.
(3) Copies of standard terms of employment and any contracts of employment not on standard terms.
(4) Details of any persons engaged in the Business as an independent contractor.
(5) Details of any recognised trade unions and any relevant agreements with the unions.
(6) Details of any disputes with employees or contractors in the last four years.

F Pensions

(1) Details of every pension and life assurance scheme operated by or for the Business, including:
    (a) copies of the deeds and rules and all amendments;

(b) copy of the latest and preceding actuarial valuation and any investment report;
(c) copies of the latest accounts and trustees report;
(d) copies of all scheme booklets;
(e) copy of the contracting out certificate;
(f) copy of the Inland Revenue approval;
(g) copy of the memorandum and articles of association of any trustee company;
(h) names of current trustees;
(i) details of any insurance policies;
(j) details of active members;
(k) details of current pensioners;
(l) details of deferred pensions;
(m) details of employer's and employees contribution rates in the last four years;
(n) details of any discretionary practices;
(o) details of any paid up and closed schemes relevant to the Business.

G Insurance

(1) Details of all insurances taken out by or operated for the benefit of the Business.
(2) Details of all insurance claims in the last four years.

H Litigation/claims

(1) Details of all litigation including arbitration and alternative dispute resolution in which:
    (a) the Business has been involved in the last four years;
    (b) the Business is involved or which is currently threatened.
(2) Details of any regulatory investigations of the Business or any known investigations of its competitors in the last four years.

I Land

(1) Details of all freehold property owned by the Business including copies of title deeds.
(2) Details of all leasehold properties occupied or owned by the Business including:
    (a) copies of leases;
    (b) current rent and state of rent review negotiations if any;
    (c) title number if registered.
(3) Details and copies of all licences and leases granted to or by the Business including:
    (a) name of current tenant and landlord;
    (b) current rent.
(4) Details of current state of dilapidations of the properties including when liabilities will crystallise.

J   Tangible assets

   (1) Details of all plant and machinery and a copy of the plant register.
   (2) Details of all motor vehicles owned or used by the Business.

K   Intellectual property

   (1) Details of all patents owned by or used in relation to the Business including copies of all registrations and applications.
   (2) Details of all Trade Marks and registered designs owned by or used in relation to the Business and copies of all registrations, applications licence etc. including details of actual use in the last three years.
   (3) Details of all copyright including software owned by or used in relation to the Business including copies of all licences.
   (4) Details of all design rights owned by or used in relation to the Business.
   (5) Details including copies of all business names and logos used in the Business.
   (6) Details of any confidential know-how used in relation to the Business.
   (7) Copies of any confidentiality agreements entered into by the Business.
   (8) Details of any overlap between the intellectual property above and that used in the business retained by [the Vendor].
   (9) Details of any claims by any present or past employees in relation to title to intellectual property used in or by the Business.
   (10) Details of any known infringements by or against the Business.

                                        Dated [   ] 199[   ]

Appendix III

STANDARD SALE AGREEMENT

Contents

Documents in the Agreed Terms [To be listed]
[Deed of Release]
[Assignment of Intellectual Property Rights]
[Registered User Agreements]
[Name Change Special Resolution]

STANDARD SALE AGREEMENT

THIS AGREEMENT is made on [   ] 199[   ]

BETWEEN:

(1) [   ] [limited/plc] a company registered in England with
    registered number [   ] whose registered office is at
    [   ] ('the Vendor'); and
(2) [   ] [limited/plc] a company registered in England with
registered number [   ] whose registered office is at
[   ] ('the Purchaser');

WHEREAS:
The Vendor has agreed to sell the Assets (defined below) and to transfer the
Business (defined below) as a going concern to the Purchaser on the terms of
this Agreement.

IT IS AGREED THAT:

1   INTERPRETATION
1.1 In this Agreement the following words and expressions shall have the
    following meanings respectively:
    'Accounts'   the audited profit and loss account of the
                                  Vendor for the accounting period ending on
                                  the Accounting Date and the audited
                                  balance sheet of the Vendor as at the
                                  Accounting Date (including the notes,
                                  reports and statements thereto) and in rela-
                                  tion to the Vendor's Group the audited
                                  consolidated profit and loss account for the
                                  period ended on the Accounting Date and

'Accounts'—*contd*   the consolidated balance sheet of the Vendor and its Group Companies as at the Accounting Date (including the notes, reports and statements thereto), copies of which are annexed to the Disclosure Letter;

'Agreed Terms'   a document in terms agreed between the Vendor and the Purchaser and for the purposes of identification signed by the Vendor or the Vendor's Solicitors and by the Purchaser or the Purchaser's Solicitors;

'Assets'   the assets named in column (1) of Part I of Schedule 1 being all the assets to be sold and purchased under this Agreement;

'Accounting Date'   [31/30][   ] 19[   ]

'Business'   the business of [   ] as carried on by the Vendor at the Transfer Date under the name(s) [   ];

'Completion'   the Completion of the sale and purchase of the Business and Assets in pursuance of this Agreement;

'Completion Date'   [the date of this Agreement;] or [the date set for Completion in accordance with Clause 6.1 as subsequently revised under sub-Clause 4.3(b) if appropriate;]

'Completion Statement'   means the statement of the value of the Assets and the Liabilities as at the Transfer Date to be prepared and agreed pursuant to Schedule 1;

'Consideration'   the total purchase price for the Assets payable under Clause 3;

'Contracts'   all contracts, which have been entered into or undertaken by the Vendor in the ordinary and proper course of the Business (but excluding contracts for employment of the Employees or any contract forming part of the Excluded Assets) [being those listed in] [including without limitation those listed in] Schedule 4;

'Deed of Release'   the deed of release in the agreed terms by [name of bank] confirming that the Assets have been released from the fixed charge given by [the Vendor] dated [   ] 19[   ];

'Designated Account'   the bank account to be established by the Purchaser after Completion under Clause 12.1(a);

'Disclosure Letter'   the letter of today's date from the Vendor or the Vendor's Solicitors to the Purchaser;

'Employees'   those persons who are employed by the
                            Vendor in the Business on the Completion
                            Date and who are named in Column 1 of
                            Schedule 3;

'Excluded Assets'   the assets named in Part II of Schedule 1
                            which are excluded from the sale;

'Fixed Plant and Equip-   such of the Plant and Equipment as is
ment'   annexed to and forms part of the Properties
                            at Completion;

'Freehold Properties'   the freehold premises described in Part 1 of
                            Schedule 5;

'Goodwill'   the goodwill of the Business and the exclusive
                            right (to the extent the Vendor can grant the
                            same) for the Purchaser to use the name(s) of
                            [   ] and [   ] and to
                            represent itself as carrying on the Business in
                            succession to the Vendor;

'Group Company'   in relation to a party any holding company of
                            that party and any subsidiary (direct or
                            indirect) or subsidiary undertaking of any
                            such holding company and 'Group' means
                            the relevant party and each of its Group
                            Companies;

'Intellectual Property   patents, trade marks, service marks, designs,
Rights'   design rights, copyright (including all copy-
                            right in any designs and computer software),
                            inventions, trade secrets, know-how, confi-
                            dential information, registrable business
                            names and all other intellectual property
                            rights and rights of a similar character in any
                            part of the world which, or the subject matter
                            of which, are used for the purpose of the
                            Business (whether or not the same are
                            registered or capable of registration), and all
                            applications and rights to apply for protec-
                            tion of any of the same;

'Leasehold Properties'   the leasehold premises described in Part II of
                            Schedule 5;

'the Liabilities'   the amounts owing by the Vendor (whether
                            or not yet due and payable) to trade creditors
                            and other persons arising in the ordinary
                            course of the Business as at the Transfer
                            Date;

'Loose Plant and Equip-   the Plant and Equipment which is not Fixed
ment'   Plant and Equipment;

'Management   the management accounts of the Vendor for
Accounts'   the period ended [   ] a copy of which
                            is attached to the Disclosure Letter;

'Motor Vehicles'	the motor vehicles owned or used by the Vendor in connection with the Business details of which are set out in Schedule 7;
'Net Asset Value of the Business'	the total value of the Assets less the total value of Liabilities as determined in the Completion Statement;
'Plant and Equipment'	collectively all the plant, machinery, equipment, tools, furniture, fixtures and fittings owned by the Vendor at the Transfer Date in connection with the Business;
'Properties'	collectively the Freehold Properties and the Leasehold Properties;
'Purchaser's Accountants'	[ ] of [ ];
'Purchaser's Solicitors'	[Messrs] of [ ];
'Records'	the VAT Records and all other records relating to the Business which are required by the Purchaser to enable it to carry on the Business including accounting records, lists of customers, suppliers, agents and distributors, and all records relating to the Employees;
'Restricted Area'	the area comprising [ ];
'Restricted Business'	any business consisting of [ ] substantially similar to and competing with any of those of the Business;
'Restricted Period'	the inclusive period beginning on the Completion Date and ending on [ ];
'SSAP'	a Statement of Standard Accounting Practice issued by the Institute of Chartered Accountants in England and Wales as replaced from time to time by Financial Reporting Standards issued by the Accounting Standards Board Limited;
'Stocks'	all goods purchased or agreed to be purchased for resale, consumable stores, raw materials and components for incorporation into products for sale, products and services in the course of production, finished goods and other assts of the Vendor on the Transfer Date for use or resale in the ordinary course of the Business;
'Trade Debts'	all trade debts due and payable to the Vendor in respect of the Business up to and including the Transfer Date as shown in the Completion Statement;
'Transfer Date'	[the date on which the Completion takes place] [*other date if different from completion date*];

'Transfer Regulations'	the Transfer of Undertakings (Protection of Employment) Regulations 1981;
'VAT'	value added tax;
'VATA'	the Value Added Tax Act 1983;
'VAT Records'	all records relating to the Business referred to in Section 33 of and Schedule 7 to the VATA;
'VAT Regulations'	the Value Added Tax (General) Regulations 1985;
'Vendor's Accountants'	[ ];
'Vendor's Scheme'	the pension scheme of the Vendor full and accurate details of which are attached to the Disclosure Letter;
'Vendor's Solicitors'	[ ];
'Warranties'	the warranties, representations and undertakings set out in Schedule 2;
'Working Day'	any day except Saturdays and Sundays on which banks in the City of London are open for business.

1.2 Any references, to a statutory provision shall include that provision as from time to time modified, re-enacted, consolidated or replaced whether before or after today's date and shall include subordinate legislation made under any such provision.

1.3 Words and phrases defined in the Companies Act 1985 as amended shall have the same meanings in this Agreement unless otherwise defined.

1.4 The Interpretation Act 1978 shall apply to this Agreement in the same way as it applies to an enactment.

2 AGREEMENT FOR SALE AND PURCHASE OF BUSINESS

2.1 On and subject to the terms of this Agreement and in order that the Business is transferred as a going concern, the Vendor shall sell as beneficial owner free from all charges, liens, equities, encumbrances and other third party rights of any nature whatsoever and the Purchaser shall purchase as a going concern with effect from the [close]/[open] of business on the Transfer Date the Business and the Assets.

2.2 The Excluded Assets are excluded from this sale and purchase.

3 CONSIDERATION, PAYMENT AND VAT

3.1 The Consideration shall be the sum of:
   (a) £[   ]; and
   (b) an amount equal to the Net Asset Value of the Business.

3.2 The Consideration shall be allocated amongst the Assets in the manner set out in column 2 Part I of Schedule 1 and shall be payable in the manner set out in Part V of Schedule 1.

3.3 The Vendor shall use all reasonable endeavours to obtain as soon as possible confirmation from HM Customs and Excise that Article 5 of the Value Added Tax (Special Provisions) Order 1992 applies to the transfer under this Agreement. If such confirmation is obtained then the Consideration shall be inclusive of VAT. If such confirmation is refused or is not obtained the Consideration shall be subject to the addition of any VAT properly payable thereon. The Vendor shall immediately repay to the Purchaser any VAT paid by the Purchaser to the extent it is in due course determined that such VAT was not chargeable.

3.4 The parties consider that the transfer provided for by this Agreement is a transfer of the Business as a going concern and the Vendor and the Purchaser shall give notice of such transfer to HM Customs and Excise as required by paragraph 7 of Schedule 1 to the VATA or by paragraph 4 of the VAT Regulations.

3.5 The Vendor undertakes to the Purchaser that after Completion it shall not make any request to HM Customs and Excise for the VAT Records to be taken out of the custody of the Purchaser.

3.6 The Purchaser hereby undertakes to preserve the VAT Records for such periods as are required by law and, upon reasonable notice but only during normal business hours, to permit the Vendor or its duly authorised representatives to inspect and at the Vendor's cost to make copies of the VAT Records.

4   CONDITIONS PRECEDENT

4.1 Completion of this Agreement is conditional upon the performance of the following conditions:

(a) the passing at a duly convened general meeting of the Vendor of an ordinary resolution approving the sale of the Assets and the transfer of the Business pursuant to this Agreement;

EITHER

(b) the receipt by the Purchaser of confirmation from the Office of Fair Trading indicating in terms satisfactory to the Purchaser that, on the facts available to it, it is not the intention of the Secretary of State for Trade and Industry to refer the proposed acquisition of the Assets and transfer of the Business to the Monopolies and Mergers Commission.

OR

(b) the receipt by the Purchaser of written confirmation from the Commission of the European Communities that, based on the facts available to it, it does not consider that the sale of the Assets and transfer of the Business under this Agreement contravenes Article 86 Treaty of Rome;

(c) the Vendor procuring the delivery to the Purchaser of a certificate of non-crystallisation or release in the agreed form in respect of any charge affecting the Assets;

(d) the Purchaser being satisfied that the Vendor has complied with all its obligations under Clauses 5.1 and 5.2 and the Purchaser not becoming aware of any fact or event which in its reasonable opinion is or would at Completion be a breach of any of the Warranties;

[(e) the receipt by the Vendor of confirmation in terms satisfactory to the Purchaser that Article 5 of the Value Added Tax (Special Provisions) Order 1992 applies to the transfer under this Agreement;]

(f) [*Note*: any other important consents should be listed, eg:

      (i)   landlords' consents to assignment of Leasehold Properties;

      (ii) satisfactory surveyors' reports regarding the Properties;

      (iii) novation of Contracts;

      (iv) EC merger clearance.]

4.2 The Vendor shall use all reasonable endeavours to ensure that the conditions specified in Clauses [   ] and the Purchaser shall use all reasonable endeavours to ensure that the conditions specified in Clauses [   ] are fulfilled as soon as possible and in any event before the Completion Date.

4.3 If all the conditions specified in Clause 4.1 have not been satisfied by 6pm on the last Working Day before the Completion Date the Purchaser may at its option, in its absolute discretion and without prejudice to any other remedies it may have, elect by written notice to the Vendor to

    (a) waive the conditions in Clause 4.1 that have not been satisfied and proceed to Completion; or

    (b) delay Completion to a date not more than 20 Working Days after the date set in Clause 6.1 or such previously revised pursuant to this Clause; or

    (c) rescind this Agreement.

5   PRE-COMPLETION MATTERS

5.1 Until Completion,

    (a) the Vendor shall carry on the Business in the same manner as before the date of this Agreement in its ordinary and usual course so as to maintain it as a going concern; and

    (b) the Vendor shall ensure that no transaction outside the ordinary course of trading nor any material or significant transaction within the ordinary course of trade will be carried out without the prior written consent of the Purchaser, which the Purchaser shall not unreasonably withhold or delay.

[*Note*: An alternative to Clause 5.1(b) is to develop a list of specific matters that require the Purchaser's written consent eg charging or selling any of the Assets, dismissing an Employee, terminating major customer contracts, acquiring new assets, etc.]

5.2 Prior to Completion the Purchaser and its advisers shall be given full access to the Properties and to all books and records of the Business including the right to take copies and the Vendor will instruct the Employees and its officers to give to the Purchaser all such information in relation to the Business and the Assets and Liabilities as the Purchaser may reasonably request.

6   COMPLETION

6.1 Completion shall take place on [   ] 19[   ] at the offices of the Purchaser's Solicitors or such later date designated by the Purchaser pursuant to Clause 4.3(b).

6.2 Immediately prior to Completion, the Vendor shall ensure that all fastenings attaching any of the Plant and Equipment to land which can safely be undone shall be undone so that such Plant and Equipment are in a state of severance from the land at the time of Completion.

6.3 At Completion:

(a) the Vendor shall place the Purchaser in effective possession and control of the Business and shall deliver to the Purchaser:

    (i) all the Assets which are capable of passing by delivery, together with all relative documents of title;

    (ii) such duly executed conveyances, transfers, assignments, licences, consents and deeds of title as are necessary to complete the transfer of the Properties in accordance with Schedule 5;

    (iii) a duly executed assignment of the Goodwill in the agreed terms;

    (iv) duly executed [assignments] [registered user agreements] in respect of the Intellectual Property Rights in the agreed terms;

    (v) the duly executed Deed of Release and a letter of non-crystallisation from [   ] in terms satisfactory to the Purchaser;

    (vi) a special resolution in agreed terms changing the name of the Vendor which the Purchaser hereby undertakes to deliver to the Registrar of Companies with the appropriate fee within five Working Days of Completion;

    (vii) the Records;

    (viii) all the Motor Vehicle registration documents, together with all current test certificates and road fund licences;

(b) if the Vendor has performed all the provisions of Clause 6.3(a) the Purchaser shall [deliver to the Vendor a banker's draft for £[   ] in favour of the Vendor] [procure that a bank transfer (same day funds) for £[   ] is made to [   ] Bank plc Sort Code [/ /   ] account number [   ]] on account of the Consideration **PROVIDED THAT** the Purchaser shall be under no obligation to comply with this sub-clause unless all of the Assets are sold simultaneously in accordance with this Agreement.

6.4 On Completion the risk of loss or damage to the property in the Assets shall pass to the Purchaser with effect from the Transfer Date.

6.5 Immediately after Completion the Purchaser and the Vendor shall jointly instruct the Vendor's insurers to record, with effect from Completion, the interest of the Purchaser as the insured thereunder in the Vendor's existing insurance policies which are to be transferred under this Agreement.

7 APPORTIONMENT OF BUSINESS RESPONSIBILITY

7.1 Except as otherwise provided in this Agreement, the profit or loss of the Business from the Transfer Date shall be for the account of the Purchaser, and:

(a) the Vendor shall remain solely responsible for all debts and liabilities of the Business of any nature whatsoever resulting from any act, omission, default, transaction or circumstance occurring on or before the Transfer Date and the Vendor shall indemnify the Purchaser accordingly;

(b) the Purchaser shall be solely responsible for all debts and liabilities of the Business resulting from any act, omission, default, transaction or circumstance occurring after the Transfer Date and the Purchaser shall indemnify the Vendor accordingly.

7.2 All charges, or costs and income in respect of the Business which is of a periodic nature and which cannot be attributed to a specific time, shall be apportioned on a time basis so that such part of the relevant charge, income or payment attributable to the period ended on the Transfer Date shall be borne or received by the Vendor and such part of the relevant charge, income or payment attributable to the period commencing on the day following the Transfer Date shall be borne or received by the Purchaser.

7.3 Each party shall pay to the other sums to which it is entitled under the apportionments under Clause 7.2 within four Working Days of the sum being ascertained.

8   CONTRACTS

8.1 Subject to Clauses 7.1, 8.2 and 8.3, with effect from the Transfer Date the Purchaser shall to the extent they have not been fully performed assume the obligations of and become entitled to the benefits of the Vendor under the Contracts.

8.2 If consent to the assignment or novation of any of the Contracts is needed from any person, until such consent is obtained,
(a) the Vendor shall hold the benefits of such Contract on trust for the Purchaser and shall immediately upon receipt pay to the Purchaser any sums received by it under such Contract; and
(b) the Purchaser shall, at its own cost and for its own benefit, perform the Vendor's obligations under such Contract to the extent such obligations have been disclosed to the Purchaser and to the extent that the performance by the Purchaser is not a breach of such contract;
(c) the Vendor shall take such action as the Purchaser may reasonably require to obtain the necessary consents.

8.3 Upon the earlier of the person whose consent is required under Clause 8.2 refusing consent or the expiry of 45 Working Days after the Completion Date without the necessary consent having been obtained the Purchaser may elect no longer to assume or perform the obligations under that Contract and the Vendor shall indemnify the Purchaser against any liability in respect of such Contract and the provisions of Clause 7.1(b) shall be deemed never to have applied to such Contract.

8.4 The Vendor will at the Purchaser's request give to the Purchaser all assistance in its power to enable the Purchaser to enjoy the benefits of and to enforce the Contracts against the other contracting parties and the Purchaser shall reimburse to the Vendor any costs properly incurred by the Vendor in providing such assistance.

9   EMPLOYEES

9.1 The parties declare that they each consider the transaction contemplated by this Agreement to constitute the transfer of an undertaking for the purposes of the Transfer Regulations and agree that except in respect of pension arrangements the contracts of employment of the Employees will have effect from Completion as if originally made between the Purchaser and the Employees.

9.2 The Vendor shall indemnify and keep indemnified the Purchaser against all liabilities, damages, costs, claims, awards and expenses arising out of or relating to:

(a) any act or omission relating to the Employees occurring before the Transfer Date for which the Purchaser is or becomes liable under the Transfer Regulations;

(b) the Purchaser becoming responsible as a result of the Transfer Regulations for any person who was an employee of the Vendor but was not named in Schedule 3.

9.3 The Vendor undertakes to the Purchaser at the request of the Purchaser to waive irrevocably and unconditionally or assign to the Purchaser any rights against the Employees which the Vendor may have in respect of information supplied to the Vendor or omitted to be supplied to the Vendor by the Employees in respect of the Warranties and the preparation of the Disclosure Letter.

10 PROPERTIES
The provisions of Schedule 5 shall apply in relation to the Properties.

11 PENSIONS
The provisions of Schedule 6 shall apply in relation to pension arrangements.

12 COLLECTION OF TRADE DEBTS
[*Note*: Clause 12 only required if Trade Debts are Excluded Assets.]

12.1 The Purchaser, acting as agent for the Vendor, shall during the period from Completion up to [60] Working Days after Completion:

(a) use all reasonable endeavours to collect the Trade Debts and shall keep all money collected in a separate designated account on trust for the Vendor; and

(b) from time to time apply such moneys as are available in the Designated Account in discharging the Vendor's liabilities in relation to the Business; and

(c) on a two weekly basis provide the Vendor with details of all moneys paid into and out of the Designated Account.

12.2 On the 6th Working Day after Completion the Purchaser shall pay to the Vendor the balance of all moneys held in the Designated Account and shall thereafter account to the Vendor on a monthly basis for all money received by the Purchaser in payment of the Trade Debts.

12.3 The Purchaser shall not be under any obligation to commence legal proceedings to recover any of the Trade Debts and no such proceedings shall be commenced by the Purchaser against any person who is or remains a customer of the Business or was a significant customer of the Business in the year before Completion without the prior written consent of the Purchaser.

12.4 The Purchaser shall not be under any obligation to use funds from any source other than the Designated Account in discharging the Vendor's liabilities in relation to the Business.

13 WARRANTIES

13.1 The Vendor hereby represents, warrants and undertakes to the Purchaser that each of the Warranties is true and accurate in all respects and is not misleading at today's date and will continue to be so on the Completion Date as if repeated on such date.

13.2 The Vendor acknowledges that the Purchaser has been induced to enter into this Agreement by and in doing so has relied on the representations made in the terms of the Warranties.

13.3 Without limiting the rights of the Purchaser to claim damages on any other basis available to it, if any of the Warranties is found to be untrue or misleading (and without limiting the right of rescission in Clause 3.8) the Vendor shall on demand by the Purchaser at the Purchaser's option pay to the Purchaser:

(a) either
  (i) an amount equal to any depletion of the Assets or increase in the Liabilities arising from the breach of Warranty; or
  (ii) an amount equal to the amount by which the value of the Business is less than it would have been had the Warranties been true and correct;
(b) and in any event shall pay to the Purchaser all costs and expenses incurred by the Purchaser as a result of such breach.

13.4 The Warranties are given subject to the matters disclosed in the Disclosure Letter and in the documents annexed thereto but only to the extent such matters are fully and fairly disclosed. No other information of which the Purchaser may have actual or constructive knowledge shall reduce the amount recoverable in respect of any breach of Warranty.

13.5 Each of the Warranties is separate and independent and unless expressly provided is not limited by reference to anything in this Agreement including any of the other Warranties.

13.6 Where any statement set out in the Warranties is expressed to be given or made to the best of the Vendor's knowledge or is qualified in some other manner having a similar effect, such statement shall be deemed to be qualified by the additional statement that the Vendor has made full and proper enquiries in relation to such matter prior to the date or dates at which the Warranties are made.

13.7 The Vendor undertakes to the Purchaser that immediately upon it becoming aware of the actual, impending or threatened occurrence of any event after the date of this Agreement but before Completion which can reasonably be expected to cause or constitute a breach of any of the Warranties (when repeated at Completion) it will give the Purchaser written notice of such event.

13.8 If it becomes apparent to the Purchaser [before but not after Completion] that the Vendor is in breach of any of the Warranties or any other term of this Agreement, in addition to and without prejudice to all other remedies available to the Purchaser under this Agreement, the Purchaser shall be entitled to rescind this Agreement. Failure by the Purchaser to exercise a right of rescission shall not constitute a waiver by the Purchaser of any other right or remedy available to it in respect of such breach.

14 LIMITATION ON WARRANTY AND INDEMNITY CLAIMS

14.1 The Vendor shall be under no liability whatsoever in respect of any breach or non-fulfilment of any of the Warranties unless the Purchaser has served on the Vendor a written notice on or before the [third] anniversary of the Completion Date giving reasonable details of the claim except that this time limit shall not apply in respect of claims arising from fraud or wilful misconduct or wilful concealment by the Vendor or any of its officers or employees.

14.2 No claim shall be made in respect of any breach or non-fulfilment of any of the Warranties unless the total amount of all such claims exceeds £[   ] but if such amount is exceeded, the Vendor's liability shall be for the total amount of the claims and shall not be limited to the excess.

14.3 The Vendor's total liability in respect of any breach or non-fulfilment of the Warranties shall not exceed £[   ].

15 PROTECTION OF GOODWILL

15.1 The Vendor undertakes with the Purchaser that, except with the prior written consent of the Purchaser, the Vendor shall not and shall procure that its Group Companies shall not, in any capacity:

(a) at any time during the Restricted Period be interested in any business competing with the Restricted Business within the Restricted Area other than as a holder of less than five per cent of any class of shares listed on a stock exchange;

(b) at any time during the Restricted Period accept orders for the supply of any goods or services in competition with those supplied in the normal course of the Restricted Business from any person who has been a customer of the Business during the twelve months preceding the Completion Date;

(c) at any time during the Restricted Period do anything knowingly to assist any competitor of the Vendor in any material way in carrying on or developing any Restricted Business in the Restricted Area;

(d) at any time during the Restricted Period knowingly encourage any Employee to leave the employment of the Purchaser or employ or use the services of any such person in any other capacity;

(e) at any time after Completion use in connection with any activity whatsoever the name of [   ] or any name likely to cause confusion with such name;

(f) at any time after Completion make use of or disclose to any third party confidential information relating to and/or used for the purpose of the Business, except to the extent that such disclosure is required by law;

(g) at any time after Completion represent itself or permit itself to be held out as being in any way connected with or interested in the Business.

15.2 It is the Vendor's intention that each of the undertakings contained in the preceding Clause 15.1 shall be construed independently of the other undertakings and shall constitute entirely independent and separate restrictions on the Vendor.

15.3 It is agreed by the parties that although each of the undertakings contained in Clause 15.1 is considered, both separately and taken together, to be reasonable in all the circumstances. If any of the restrictions should be held invalid for any reason but would have been valid if part of the wording of or terms used in such undertaking had been deleted or modified, such undertaking shall apply with such modifications as may be necessary to make it valid and enforceable.

16 GENERAL PROVISIONS
Announcements

16.1 No announcement or communications concerning the terms or conditions of this Agreement shall be made or authorised by any of the parties to this Agreement before or after Completion without the prior written consent of the other parties except to the extent any statement or disclosure may be required by law [*Note*: insert stock exchange on which Vendor or Purchaser is quoted if appropriate.]
Further Assurance

16.2 The Vendor at its sole expense shall perform such acts and execute such documents as may be reasonably required after Completion by the Purchaser for securing to or vesting in the Purchaser the legal and beneficial ownership of the Assets and the rights granted to it under this Agreement.

16.3 The Vendor will after Completion refer to the Purchaser promptly any enquiries or orders it receives from actual or prospective customers of the Business.
Interest

16.4 If any party does not make a payment due under this Agreement on its due date such party shall in addition pay interest to the recipient party on the amount for the time being outstanding at the rate of [three per cent] per annum above the base rate of [   ] Bank plc in force on such due date from the due date for payment until payment in full (after as well as before judgment).
Continuing obligations and assignment

16.5 Each of the obligations, warranties, indemnities and undertakings accepted or given under this Agreement which has not been fully performed at Completion shall continue in full force and effect notwithstanding Completion.
Assignment

16.6 None of the benefits of the obligations, warranties, indemnities and undertakings accepted or given under this Agreement is assignable other than to a purchaser of the Business provided that such purchaser undertakes to the Vendor to be bound by the Purchaser's obligations under this Agreement.

Costs

16.7 Each party to this Agreement shall pay its own costs, charges and expenses incurred in the preparation, completion and implementation of this Agreement (and the documents referred to herein) unless the Purchaser shall lawfully exercise any right to rescind or terminate this Agreement when the Vendor shall indemnify the Purchaser against all costs and expenses incurred by the Purchaser in investigating the Business and in the preparing and negotiating of this Agreement and all related matters.

Notices

16.8 Any notice or other communication to be given under this Agreement shall either be delivered personally or sent by first class post or telex or facsimile transmission to the registered office of the party in question or such other address in England as the party to be served may have previously notified to the other parties.

16.9 Any notice personally delivered shall be deemed to have been served at the time of delivery. Any notice posted shall be deemed to have been served at the expiration of 72 hours after the envelope containing the notice was delivered into the custody of the postal authorities. Any notice sent by telex or facsimile transmission shall be deemed to have been served at the time of transmission.

Severability and suspension of restrictions

16.10 If any provision or provisions of this Agreement (or of any document referred to herein) is or at any time becomes illegal, invalid or unenforceable in any respect, the legality, validity and enforceability of the remaining provisions of this Agreement (or such document) shall not in any way be affected or impaired thereby.

16.11 No provisions of this Agreement or any agreement or arrangement of which it forms part by virtue of which this Agreement or any such agreement or arrangement is subject to registration under the Restrictive Trade Practices Acts 1976 and 1977 shall take effect until the day after particulars of this Agreement and any agreement or arrangement of which it forms part have been furnished to the Director General of Fair Trading pursuant to section 24 of the Restrictive Trade Practices Act 1976.

Entire agreement and variation

16.12 This Agreement (together with the documents referred to herein) constitutes the entire agreement between the parties in relation to the transactions referred to herein.

16.13 No variation of any of the terms of this Agreement or of any other documents referred to herein shall be effective unless it is in writing and signed by or on behalf of each of the parties hereto or thereto.

17 GOVERNING LAW AND JURISDICTION

17.1 This Agreement and all documents referred to in it shall be governed by and construed in accordance with English law and each of the parties hereto hereby submits to the non-exclusive jurisdiction of the High Court of England.

AS WITNESS the hands of the parties hereto or of their duly authorised representatives the day and year first before written.

SCHEDULE 1   THE CONSIDERATION

PART I—THE ASSETS AND ALLOCATION OF THE CONSIDERATION

(1) THE ASSETS	(2) PRICE ALLOCATION (£)
the Goodwill	£[ ]
the Intellectual Property Rights	£[ ]
the Stocks	
the benefit of the Contracts	the burden of the respective Contract
the Plant and Equipment comprising	
—Fixed Plant and Equipment	£[ ]
—Loose Plant and Equipment	£[ ]
Leasehold Properties	£[ ]
Freehold Properties	£[ ]
the Motor Vehicles	net book value as shown in the Completion Statement
[the shares in the Subsidiaries]	£[ ]
[the benefit of all debts owed by the Vendor's Group Companies to the Vendor at the Transfer Date]	
all the Vendor's rights against third parties or insurers which relate to the Business	
all other assets and property owned by the Vendor and used in the ordinary course of the Business	

PART II—THE EXCLUDED ASSETS

(1) All cash in hand or at bank.
(2) Any amounts repayable by or recoverable from the Inland Revenue or HM Customs and Excise (including VAT) attributable to a period ending on or before the Transfer Date.
(3) The benefit of any insurance or insurance claim attributable to any event occurring before the close of business on the Transfer Date which does not relate to the Assets or to the liabilities to be assumed by the Purchaser under this Agreement.

(4) The Trade Debts.

(5) [Any [other] shares or securities owned by the Vendor.]

PART III—AGREEING THE COMPLETION STATEMENT

(1) As soon as possible after Completion and in any event by not later than the 20th Working Day after Completion the Vendor shall procure that the Vendor's Accountants prepare and deliver to the Purchaser's Accountants:

    (a) the draft Completion Statement prepared in accordance with part IV of Schedule 1 specifying the Net Asset Value of the Business;

    (b) a written statement that in their opinion the draft Completion Statement has been prepared in accordance with this Agreement and gives a true and fair view of the state of affairs of the Business as at the Transfer Date;

    (c) the originals or copies of their working papers;

    (d) the apportionment between each category of the Assets necessary to complete column 2 of Part I of Schedule 1;

    (e) a statement of the apportionments to be made pursuant to Clause [7.2] and the dates on which such payments are due.

(2) The Purchaser shall procure that the Purchaser's Accountants shall as soon as possible review the draft Completion Statement (and within 20 Working Days of receipt) confirm to the Vendor's Accounts whether or not they agree with the draft Completion Statement.

(3) If the Vendor's Accountants do confirm their agreement with the draft Completion Statement they shall notify this to the Purchaser and the Vendor in writing and it shall constitute the Completion Statement for the purposes of this Agreement.

(4) If the Purchaser's Accountants are unable to agree with part or all of the draft Completion Statement the items in dispute shall be referred to and determined conclusively by an independent firm of accountants (acting as experts and not as arbitrators) agreed by the Purchaser and the Vendor or if such firm has not been agreed upon within five Working Days, by an independent firm of chartered accountants appointed by the President for the time being of the Institute of Chartered Accountants in England and Wales on the application of either the Vendor or the Purchaser. The fees of the independent accountant shall be shared equally by the Purchaser and the Vendor unless he shall determine otherwise.

(5) The Purchaser shall ensure that the Vendor's Accountants shall be given access to or copies of such records and such of the Employees as are necessary to enable the Vendor's Accountants to perform paragraph 1.

PART IV—THE COMPLETION STATEMENT

(1) The Completion Statement shall be a draft balance sheet of the Business as at the Transfer Date and shall be prepared on the following basis and in the following order of priority, namely on the basis that:

    (a) it presents a true and fair view of the Net Asset Value of the Business;

    (b) it is in accordance with the SSAPs;

    (c) it is consistent with and uses the same accounting principles, policies and practices as are used in the Accounts;

(d) the Warranties are true and correct in so far as they are applicable;

(e) all Assets are valued at net book value;

(f) the value of the Stocks is determined by a physical stock take carried out by the Vendor in the presence of and agreed with the Purchaser or the Purchaser's Accountant on the first Working Day following Completion;

(g) is consistent with the adjustments set out in the letter in the agreed form from the Purchaser's Accountants to the Vendor's Accountants.

PART V—PAYMENT

The consideration shall be payable as follows:

(a) on the Completion Date the amount of £[   ];

(b) if the Purchaser's Accountants have confirmed their agreement with the draft Completion Statement within five Working Days of such confirmation an amount equal to the Net Asset Value of the Business;

(c) if the Purchaser's Accountants are unable to agree the draft Completion Statement:

    (i) an amount equal to the amount in the draft Completion Statement not in dispute within five Working Days of the dispute being referred to the independent firm of accountants;

    (ii) an amount equal to the amount determined by the independent chartered accountant in relation to the disputed matter within five Working Days of such determination being notified to the Purchaser and the Vendor;

(d) five Working Days after the delivery of the Consideration Statement the Net Asset Value if no amounts in the Completion Statement are disputed or, if any are disputed, the amount not in dispute with the balance being paid within five Working Days of being determined pursuant to paragraph 4 of Part III of Schedule 1.

SCHEDULE 2   WARRANTIES

A   THE ASSETS—TITLE AND ADEQUACY

A.1 The Assets are all legally and beneficially owned by the Vendor and none of the Assets is the subject of any

    (a) mortgage, charge (including without limitation floating charge), pledge, lien, or other encumbrance of any nature whatsoever;

    (b) factoring arrangement, lease, rental, hire-purchase, conditional sale or credit sale agreement or any agreement or arrangement under which any third party has or may acquire any rights in any of the Assets or in the proceeds of sale of any of the Assets or the right to possess any of the Assets.

A.2 The Assets comprise all assets necessary to enable the Purchaser to carry on the Business after Completion in the same manner and on the same scale as before and to enable the Purchaser to comply with the obligations it assumes under the Contracts.

A.3   All Plant and Equipment and Motor Vehicles owned or used by the Vendor in connection with the Business are in good repair and working order, fit for the purpose for which they are normally used and have been regularly and properly maintained and none is in need of renewal or replacement.

A.4   Each of the finished goods included in the Stocks is of merchantable quality and fit for the purposes for which it is normally sold, is undamaged and has been the subject of thorough and effective quality control and storage procedures and practices.

A.5   The Stocks do not include any obsolete or slow moving lines, or excessive or inadequate quantities of any line, having regard to the current level of business and likely future requirements of customers.

A.6   Each item of the Stocks is either capable of being used in the ordinary course of the Business or will realise its net book value in the ordinary course of business.

A.7   [Each of the Trade Debts will realise its full amount in the ordinary course of the Business within [   ] Working Days from the Completion Date and none of the Trade Debts is subject to any counterclaim or set-off of any nature.]

B   ACCOUNTS

B.1   The Accounts:

(a)   are true, complete and accurate in all respects and show a true and fair view of the financial position and state of affairs of [the Vendor] [the Business] at the Accounting Date and of profit and losses of the [Vendor] [the Business] for the period to which they relate;

(b)   have been prepared in accordance with the accounting principles, standards and practices generally accepted in the United Kingdom at their date of preparation for companies carrying on a similar business to that of the Vendor and comply with the requirements of the Companies Act 1985 and of all SSAPs;

(c)   have been prepared, unless otherwise expressly stated, on a basis consistent with the basis applied in the statutory accounts for the preceding three financial years and during that period there has been no change in accounting policies;

(d)   are not and the statutory accounts for the preceding three financial years are not affected by any extraordinary or non-recurring items unless so expressly stated;

(e)   contain full provisions for or adequate details of all liabilities and capital commitments of the Vendor at the Accounting Date, whether actual, contingent, or otherwise;

(f)   contain proper and adequate provision for bad and doubtful debts, depreciation, slow moving or damaged stock and any foreseeable losses.

B.2   The valuations in the Accounts are made on the same basis as that adopted in the Vendor's statutory accounts for the three preceding financial years.

B.3   The rates of depreciation in the Accounts are the same as the rates adopted in the Vendor's statutory accounts for the three preceding financial years and are sufficient to ensure that each of the fixed Assets is written down to nil by the end of its useful life.

B.4 All the accounting books and records of the Vendor in relation to the Business are up to date, are complete and accurate in all respects and are not misleading in any material respect.

C THE MANAGEMENT ACCOUNTS

C.1 The Management Accounts have been prepared on a basis consistent with the management accounts prepared in the year preceding the Accounting Date, and listing the same accounting principles, standards and practices applied in the preparation of the Accounts with all reasonable care and attention, reflect with reasonable accuracy the accounting records of the Vendor in relation to the Business and give a reasonably accurate view of the state of affairs, and profit (or loss) of the Vendor as at and for the period in respect of which they have been prepared.

D BUSINESS SINCE THE ACCOUNTING DATE

D.1 Since the Accounting Date:

(a) the Business has been carried on in its ordinary and usual course without any interruption or alteration in its nature, scope or manner so as to maintain the same as a going concern;

(b) there has been no adverse change in the financial or trading position or prospects of the Business;

(c) the Vendor has not entered into any capital transaction with regard to the Business as vendor, purchaser, lessor, lessee or otherwise undertaken any material commitment in relation to the Business;

(d) in connection with the Business there has been no change in the manner or time of payment of creditors or the issue of invoices or collection of debts, or in the quantities of stock bought or agreed to be bought, or manufactured, stored, sold or agreed to be sold by the Vendor, or in the level of borrowing or working capital requirements of the Business.

D.2 No customer or supplier of the Business has ceased, or has informed the Vendor that it will cease, purchasing from or supplying to the Business, or has materially reduced, or has informed the Vendor that it will materially reduce, the level of its purchases from or supplies to the Business and there is no matter or fact in existence which can be reasonably foreseen as likely to give rise to the same.

E LAWFUL CONDUCT OF THE BUSINESS

E.1 The Business has at all times been conducted in compliance with all applicable statutory requirements, bye-laws and regulations from time to time in force.

E.2 The Vendor holds all necessary licences and consents for the proper carrying on of the Business (details of all of which are contained in the Disclosure Letter) and there are no factors that might in any way prejudice the continuance, renewal or obtaining of any of those licences or consents by the Purchaser.

E.3   The Vendor is not restricted from freely carrying on any activity of the Business in any part of the world.

E.4   The Vendor is not a party to any agreement, arrangement or practice in relation to the Business which is:

(a) registrable under or prohibited by or subject to investigation or capable of giving rise to an investigation by the Director General of Fair Trading or a reference to the Monopolies and Mergers Commission pursuant to any one or more provisions of the Treaty of Rome 1957, the Fair Trading Act 1973, the Resale Prices Act 1976, the Restrictive Trade Practices Acts 1976 and 1977, or the Competition Act 1980;

(b) prohibited as incompatible with or subject to investigation under the European Communities legislation (and in particular with Article 85 or 86 of the European Economic Community Treaty) or with any other applicable antitrust legislation; or

(c) registrable under or prohibited by or subject to investigation or capable of giving rise to an investigation by regulatory authorities in any territory outside the United Kingdom in which such agreement, arrangement or practice was made or is to be carried out under applicable competition or antitrust legislation.

F   THE CONTRACTS

F.1   Each of the Contracts is assignable by the Vendor without the consent of any other party.

F.2   The Vendor is not in material breach of any of the Contracts, nor, so far as the Vendor is aware, are any of the other contracting parties to any of the Contracts. All the Contracts are enforceable in accordance with their respective terms and none is voidable.

F.3   There are attached to the Disclosure Letter full accurate and up to date copies of or written particulars of all the Contracts entered into by the Vendor which relate to the Business and which:

(a) are material to the carrying on of the Business; or

(b) contain any unduly onerous term or terms or obligations of an abnormal nature or magnitude; or

(c) involve any distributorship or agency arrangement or agreement; or

(d) require payment other than in sterling; or

(e) cannot be performed or the manner of performance of which will or is likely to result in either the Vendor or the Purchaser being in breach of contract; or

(f) are outside the ordinary course of the Business; or

(g) involve an expenditure of more than £[   ] by the Vendor or which will or are likely to involve the Vendor (until Completion) or the Purchaser (following Completion as successor to the Vendor in relation to the Business) in obligations lasting more than three months from the date of exchange of this Agreement.

G THE EMPLOYEES

G.1 Schedule 3 contains the names of all persons currently employed in the Business and accurate details of their terms of employment including current salary, holiday, holiday pay, bonus entitlement and profit share arrangements both contractual and discretionary indicated as appropriate, life assurance, medical or permanent health insurances, date of commencement of employment, age and description of their function in the Business.

G.2 Except as detailed in Schedule 3 none of the Employees is entitled to any bonus, commission or other form of profit sharing (either contractual or discretionary), holiday pay, pensions, and pension contributions (either contractual or discretionary), annuities, rights under any schemes of the Vendor or any Group Company of the Vendor in respect of the Business in respect of retirement benefits, life assurance, medical, permanent health insurance, share option or share acquisition and there is no contractual or other obligation to increase or otherwise vary any of such matters in respect of any of the Employees.

G.3 A full copy of the standard terms of the employment of the Employees (including staff handbooks) and a copy of the terms of employment of each Employee employed on terms other than the standard terms is attached to the Disclosure Letter.

G.4 There are no loans outstanding from the Vendor or its Group Companies to any of the Employees.

G.5 No industrial action has been taken or threatened in the last three years or is being taken at present or is likely to be taken or has been threatened by any of the Employees or any trade union against the Vendor or any of its Group Companies in relation to the Business.

G.6 The Vendor has not recognised any trade union or other body representing the Employees and has not entered any agreement or arrangement or negotiation with any trade union.

G.7 The Vendor is not in breach of the contract of employment of any of the Employees nor so far as the Vendor is aware is any Employee in breach of his contract of employment.

G.8 Within the six months before the Completion Date none of the Employees has given or received notice of termination of his employment.

G.9 None of the Employees is the subject of any material disciplinary action nor is any Employee engaged in any grievance procedure, and there is no matter or fact in existence which can be reasonably foreseen as likely to give rise to the same.

G.10 Complete copies of the terms on which all consultants and other independent contractors are engaged in the Business are described in or attached to the Disclosure Letter. The Inland Revenue has not notified the Vendor on any of its Group Companies that it considers any such person to be an employee nor is the Vendor or its Group aware of any reason why such persons should be employees.

H LITIGATION AND CLAIMS

H.1 The Vendor is not engaged in connection with the Business in any legal proceedings with any person other than the collection of debts of amounts not exceeding £[   ] in respect of any customer.

H.2 There are no outstanding claims or unsatisfied judgments or orders by or against the Vendor in respect of the Business, and there is no fact or matter in existence nor has the Vendor received notice of any fact or matter which can reasonably be foreseen to be likely to give rise to any such claims.

H.3 No governmental or other investigation or inquiries concerning the Business is currently being undertaken nor are any pending or threatened and the Vendor is not aware of any facts likely to give rise to such investigations or inquiries.

I THE MOTOR VEHICLES

I.1 The Motor Vehicles are roadworthy, regularly maintained and duly licensed.

I.2 All forms of taxation payable in respect of the Motor Vehicles (including VAT and road fund tax) have been fully paid within the applicable time limits.

I.3 If and to the extent required by law, the Motor Vehicles have been annually tested and passed as fit for service by the Department of Transport.

I.4 Since inspection by the Purchaser on [   ] 19[   ] there has been no material change in the condition of the Motor Vehicles except for fair wear and tear since that date.

I.5 Full and accurate details of the Motor Vehicles including their maintenance and mileage records for the period of 12 months preceding the date of this Agreement are annexed to the Disclosure Letter.

J INTELLECTUAL PROPERTY

J.1 The Disclosure Letter describes all Intellectual Property Rights:
(a) which are registered;
(b) in respect of which applications for registration have been made;
(c) which are material to the carrying on of the Business or any part of it.

J.2 The Vendor is the absolute beneficial owner of each of the Intellectual Property Rights [(except for those Intellectual Property Rights full details of which are given in the Disclosure Letter which are held under licence, registered user or other agreements from the third parties therein named)] and there are no subsisting licences or other arrangements under which the Vendor has granted or any third party has acquired any right or interest in connection with any of the Intellectual Property Rights or as a result of which the enforceability of any of the Intellectual Property Rights against any third party may be adversely affected.

J.3 The Vendor has not had notice of any claim by a third party which might affect the validity or enforceability of any of the Intellectual Property Rights:
(a) which are registered;
(b) in respect of which applications for registration have been made;

(c) which are material to the carrying on of the Business or any part of it;

or on the basis of which title to any of the Intellectual Property Rights may be challenged and so far as the Vendor is aware there is no fact or matter which could affect such validity or enforceability or give rise to such a challenge.

J.4 So far as the Vendor is aware there has been no infringement by any third party of any of the Intellectual Property Rights.

J.5 No aspect of the carrying on of the Business infringes any intellectual property rights of any nature of any third party or involves the use of any confidential information of any third party, nor is any royalty or other payment required to be made in respect of the carrying on of the Business as a result of any such right of a third party.

K INSURANCE

K.1 The Assets are and will remain insured by the Vendor up to and including the Transfer Date to the full replacement value against fire and other risks normally insured against by companies carrying on similar business and the Vendor is and up to such date will remain adequately insured against accident, third party, public and product liability and other risks normally covered by insurance by such companies.

K.2 Full details of the insurances held by the Vendor in respect of the Business are contained in the Disclosure Letter.

L PROPERTIES

L.1 The Properties comprise all the land and buildings owned, occupied or used by the Vendor for the purposes of the Business.

L.2 The particulars of the Properties shown in Schedule 5 are true and correct and the Vendor has good and marketable title to and exclusive occupation of each of the Properties, free from any charge or encumbrance, sub-lease, easement, privilege or rights in favour of any third party and there are appurtenant to each Property all rights and easements necessary for its use and enjoyment for the purposes of the Business in the manner it is now carried on.

L.3 Save as mentioned in Schedule 5 the Vendor is in actual occupation of the whole of each of the Properties and no lease, tenancy or licence has been granted or agreed to be granted to any third party in respect of the Properties or any part thereof.

L.4 None of the Properties or any part thereof is affected by any of the following matters or is to the knowledge of the Vendor likely to become so affected:

(a) any outstanding dispute, notice or complaint or any exception, reservation, right, covenant, restriction or condition which is of an unusual nature or which affects or might in the future affect the use and enjoyment of any of the Properties for the purpose of the Business in the manner in which it is now carried on; or

(b) any notice, order, proposal (of which the Vendor has notice or of which the Vendor is aware) made or issued by or on behalf of any government or statutory authority, department or body for acquisition, clearance, demolition or closing, the carrying out of any work upon any building, the modification or revocation of any planning permission, the discontinuance of any use or the imposition of any building or improvement line;

(c) any compensation received as a result of any refusal of any application for planning consent or the imposing of any restrictions in relation to any planning consent; or

(d) any commutation or agreement for the commutation of rent or payment of rent in advance of the date of payment hereof.

L.5 Each of the Properties is in a good and substantial state of repair and condition and fit for the purpose for which it is presently used and no high alumina cement, woodwool, calcium chloride, sea dredged aggregates or asbestos material was used in the construction thereof or alterations thereto and there are no development works, redevelopment works or fitting out works outstanding in respect of any of the Properties nor any obligation to reinstate any alterations made to any of the Properties.

L.6 All restrictions, conditions and covenants (including any imposed by or pursuant to any lease) affecting any of the Properties have been observed and performed and no notice of any breach of any of the same has been received or is to the Vendor's knowledge likely to be received nor has any such notice been given by the Vendor to any sub-tenant or licensee of the Vendor.

L.7 The use of the Properties and all machinery and equipment therein and the conduct of any business therein complies in all respects with all relevant statutes and regulations including, without prejudice to the generality of the foregoing, the Factories Act 1961, the Offices, Shops and Railway Premises Act 1963, the Fire Precautions Act 1971, the Health and Safety at Work etc Act 1974 and the Public Health Acts and with all rules, regulations and delegated legislation thereunder and all necessary licences and consents required thereunder have been obtained.

L.8 There are no restrictive covenants, statutory provisions or orders, charges, restrictions, agreements, conditions or other matters which preclude the use of any of the Properties for the purposes for which the Properties are now used and each such user is the permitted user under the provisions of the Town and Country Planning Acts 1971 to 1984 and regulations made thereunder and is in accordance with the requirements of any relevant local or public authorities and all restrictions, conditions and covenants imposed by or pursuant to the Town and Country Planning Acts 1971 to 1984.

M ENVIRONMENTAL MATTERS

M.1 The Vendor and all other relevant Vendor's Group Companies have complied with the Control of Pollution Act 1974 in relation to disposal of any waste at or on the Properties.

M.2 Except in accordance with a valid consent, licence, or other authorisation issued pursuant to any applicable environmental statutes:

    (a) there has been no discharge of waste from the Properties;

    (b) there have been no emissions, spills, releases or discharges from the Properties into the surface water, ground water or the sewers, waste treatment, or disposal systems servicing the Properties; and

    (c) there have been no emissions or discharges from the Properties into the atmosphere.

M.3 To the best of the Vendor's knowledge, all wastes sent from the Properties off site for disposal have been properly disposed of.

M.4 The Vendor has complied with the Clean Air Acts 1956 and 1968 and all other applicable environmental laws relating to emissions to the atmosphere from the Properties.

N   PENSIONS

N.1 The Vendor's Scheme constitutes the only obligations, moral or legal, of the Vendor or any Vendor's Group Company to provide any pension, retirement, death or disability benefits or otherwise to provide 'relevant benefits' within the meaning of section 612 of the Income and Corporation Taxes Act 1988 to or in respect of any person who is now or has been an officer or employee of the Vendor in relation to the Business (or the widow, widower or dependant of such person).

N.2 The Vendor's Scheme was set up under a definitive trust deed dated [   ] and is approved as an exempt approved scheme (within the meaning of Chapter I of Part XIV of the Income and Corporation Taxes Act 1988). The employments to which the Scheme relates are contracted out.

N.3 The Vendor's Scheme has assets sufficient to meet its current liabilities to its beneficiaries at the date of this Agreement on the basis used in the last actuarial valuation.

N.4 All amounts due to the trustees of the Vendor's Scheme and to any insurance company in connection with the Vendor's Scheme have been paid.

N.5 There are no claims against the Vendor, any other company in the Vendor's Group or the trustees or administrators of the Vendor's Scheme arising out of or in connection with the Vendor's Scheme.

N.6 Full and accurate particulars of the Vendor's Scheme are set out in the Disclosure Letter, including (without limitation) true copies of the trust deeds and latest actuarial report and full and accurate details of the assets, funding arrangements and current membership.

N.7 There have not been any contributions holidays for the Vendor or any participating company or in respect of the Employees or any group of them for the past six years in respect of any contributions payable to the Vendor's Scheme.

O   GRANTS

O.1 The Vendor has not received any grants from any national or supranational body or any governmental or public authority which would or might become repayable by virtue of the entering into or Completion of this Agreement.

P   TAX MATTERS
PAYE and related matters
P.1   The Vendor has duly deducted all amounts from any payments from
      which tax falls to be deducted at source under the PAYE system and
      national insurance contributions and any other sums required by law to
      be deducted from wages, salaries or other benefits and the Vendor has
      duly paid or accounted for such amounts and all other sums due in
      respect of any benefits that are subject to taxation under Schedule E for
      which the Vendor is liable and in respect of National Insurance or other
      similar contributions to the Inland Revenue or any other relevant
      taxation or other authorities (whether of the United Kingdom or
      elsewhere). The Disclosure Letter sets out details of any investigations
      made by the Inland Revenue within three years prior to the date hereof
      into or affecting the payment of tax on benefits in cash or otherwise paid
      by the Vendor to its Employees, and details of all notifications made or
      notices received by the Vendor or any Group Company of the Vendor
      under section 166 of the Income and Corporation Taxes Act 1988
      (benefits in kind; notices of nil liability) in connection with the
      Employees.
      Stamp Duty
P.2   All documents which are in the possession of the Vendor or under its
      control to which the Vendor is a party or under which the Vendor
      derives title to any of the Assets and which attract stamp duty have been
      properly stamped, and the Vendor has duly paid all stamp duty to which
      it is, has been or may be made liable and there is no liability to any
      penalty in respect of such duty.
      Value Added Tax
P.3   (a) In respect of the Business the Vendor has complied with the
          provisions of the VATA and with all statutory requirements,
          regulations, orders, provisions, directions or conditions relating to
          value added tax, including the terms of any agreement reached with
          the Commissioners of Customs and Excise in respect of the Business
          and has maintained full, complete, correct and up to date records,
          invoices and other documents (as the case may be) appropriate or
          requisite for the purposes thereof and has preserved such records,
          invoices and other documents in such form and for such periods as
          are required by the relevant legislation.
      (b) The Disclosure Letter contains full details of all current agreements
          or arrangements between the Vendor and the Commissioners of
          Customs and Excise.
      (c) The Vendor is not liable to any abnormal or any non-routine
          payment, or any forfeiture, penalty, interest or surcharge, or to the
          operation of any penal provision, in relation to VAT.
      (d) The Vendor has not been required by the Commissioners of
          Customs and Excise to give security for payment of VAT.
      (e) The Disclosure Letter sets out details of any investigation (includ-
          ing the consequences thereof) by the Commissioners of Customs
          and Excise within three years prior to the date hereof into or
          affecting the payment of VAT in respect of the Business.

(f) The Disclosure Letter contains details (including the cost and percentage of input tax claimed on the item in the first interval as defined in regulation 37C of the VAT Regulations) of all land and other capital items which are used in the course or furtherance of the Business to which regulation 37B of the Regulations could apply. No such adjustment as is referred to in regulations 37A to 37E of the Regulations has been made or should have been made and no such adjustment is likely to have to be made in respect of the current interval in relation to any such capital items.

(g) No election under paragraph 2 of Schedule 6A to the VATA to waive exemption from VAT in respect of the grant of any interest in or right over land owned or occupied by the Vendor which is to be transferred to the Purchaser under the terms of this Agreement has been made by the Vendor or by any person making such a grant to the Vendor.

(h) The Vendor has not made exempt supplies such or of such amount that it is unable to obtain full credit for input tax paid or suffered by it.

[*Note*: Additional provisions may be required if the Vendor is selling part of its business and/or is a member of a VAT group].

Industrial buildings and capital allowances

P.4 (a) The Disclosure Letter identifies such of the Properties on which works have been carried out in respect of which industrial buildings allowances have been claimed and in respect of each such Property contains details of:

(i) the amount of capital expenditure concerned;

(ii) the aggregate of initial and writing down allowances claimed;

(iii) the residue of expenditure available;

(iv) the period of years over which writing down allowances may be available to the Purchaser.

(b) The Disclosure Letter contains details in respect of:

(i) the Leasehold Properties, of all fixtures, within the meaning of section 51(1) of the Capital Allowances Act 1990, which are treated pursuant to that section as belonging to the Vendor;

(ii) the Freehold Properties, of all fixtures, as aforesaid, that are treated pursuant to the said Section 51 as belonging to a person other than the Vendor.

Capital transfer and inheritance tax

P.5 (a) The Assets hereby agreed to be sold are not subject to an Inland Revenue charge as is mentioned in section 237 of the IHTA nor is any unsatisfied liability to capital transfer tax or inheritance tax attached to or attributable to any of the Assets.

(b) No person is liable to capital transfer tax or inheritance tax attributable to the value of the Assets hereby agreed to be sold in such circumstances that such person has the power under section 212 of the IHTA to raise the amount of such tax by the sale or mortgage or by a terminable charge on the said assets.

Q   GENERAL

Q.1   All facts and information set out in the Recitals and Schedules to this Agreement and in the Disclosure Letter are true, complete and accurate in all [material] respects and all other information given [in writing] by or on behalf of the Vendor to the Purchaser or any of its directors, officers or professional advisers in the course of the negotiations leading to this Agreement was when given and remains true, complete and accurate in all [material] respects and the Vendor is not aware of any fact or matter not publicly known which would render any such information untrue, incomplete, inaccurate or misleading [or the disclosure of which might reasonably affect the willingness of the Purchaser to purchase the Business for the Consideration and on the terms set out in this Agreement].

[Q.2   The information disclosed by or on behalf of the Vendor to the Purchaser or any of its directors, officers or professional advisers in writing in relation to the current financial and trading position [and prospects] of the Business comprises all information known to the Vendor which is material for the reasonable assessment by the Purchaser of the financial and trading position and prospects of the Business.]

Q.3   The Vendor is duly incorporated, validly existing and in good standing under the laws of England with full power and authority and the legal right and title to sell the Business and the Assets and to enter into this Agreement.

Q.4   All corporate or other action required to authorise the entering into of this Agreement by the Vendor and the performance by it of its obligations has been duly taken.

Q.5   The execution or completion of this Agreement or performance of its terms will not result in a breach of any agreement to which the Vendor is a party or of any court order.

Q.6   In order to enter into and complete this Agreement and perform its terms the Vendor does not [nor does any other member of the Vendor's Group] need the consent of any person other than those consents specified in Clause 4.1.

Q.7   No resolutions have been passed nor has any other step been taken or legal proceedings been started or threatened against the Vendor for its winding-up or dissolution or for the appointment of a liquidator, receiver, administrator, administrative receiver or similar officer over any or all of its assets which would prevent, inhibit or otherwise have a material adverse effect on the ability of the Vendor to fulfil its obligations under this Agreement.

Appendix III

SCHEDULE 3   THE EMPLOYEES

Name	Age	Job Description	Salary	Bonus	Car	Pension	Holiday	Commencement Employment

SCHEDULE 4   THE CONTRACTS

Contract	*Parties*	*Description*	*Current State of Performance*	*Consent for Assignment Needed*

SCHEDULE 5   THE PROPERTIES

PART I   FREEHOLD PROPERTIES

[minimum details to be given for each property]
(1) Description:
(2) Root of Title or Title No:
(3) Matters to which the Property is subject (including any lease tenancy or licence or agreement for such):

PART II   LEASEHOLD PROPERTIES

[details to be given for each property]
(1) Description:
(2) Details of Lease under which it is held:
    (a) date
    (b) parties
    (c) term
    (d) initial rent
    (e) current rent
    (f) next review
    (g) present reversioner.
(3) Matters to which Property is subject (including lease tenancy licence or agreement for such):

PART III   TERMS APPLICABLE TO THE PROPERTIES
(1) The Vendor shall sell:
    (a) the Properties as beneficial owner with vacant possession subject to:
        (i) all matters registered or capable of registration in the appropriate Register of Local Land Charges;
        (ii) the provisions of the Town and Country Planning Acts 1990 and all orders, directions and notices whatsoever made thereunder;
        (iii) all outgoings affecting the same as from the Transfer Date insofar as they are properly the responsibility of the Vendor;
        (iv) all rights and other easements now subsisting in respect thereof for the benefit of property which is not in the ownership of the Vendor; and
    (b) the Freehold Properties subject to (but with the benefit of) the

exceptions, reservations, covenants, restrictions, agreements and other matters specified or referred to in Part I of this Schedule 5;

(c) the Leasehold Properties subject to the rent reserved by and the exceptions, reservations, covenants, restrictions, agreements and other matters contained or referred to in the leases under which the Leasehold Properties are held or otherwise specified or referred to in Part II of this Schedule.

(2) The Purchaser's Solicitors having investigated the Vendor's title to the Properties prior to the date of this Agreement and having made all necessary searches, the Purchaser shall be deemed to have accepted the same and to purchase with full knowledge of all covenants, conditions and matters affecting the same and shall not be entitled to raise any requisitions or enquiries in respect thereof (save those written requisitions outstanding at the date of this Agreement) and save for requisitions or enquiries arising from any results of pre-completion searches in the registers at HM Land Registry, the Land Charges Registry and the Companies Registration Office which differ from the results of any such searches made immediately prior to the date of this Agreement.

(3) The assignments and/or transfers to the Purchaser in respect of the Leasehold Properties shall contain a declaration that the covenants for title implied by virtue of the Vendor conveying and being expressed to convey as beneficial owner and, where the lease is registered, the covenants implied by section 24(1)(a) of the Land Registration Act 1925 shall not extend to any breach of the tenant's covenants in the lease relating to the repair and decoration of the Property.

(4) If the title is unregistered the title to any of the Freehold Properties shall commence with the conveyance or other document specified in Part I of this Schedule as being its root of title and to any of the Leasehold Properties with the Lease under which such Property is held and indicated in Part II of this Schedule and title shall be deduced in accordance with section 110 of the Land Registration Act 1925 if the title to any of the Properties is registered.

(5) Nothing in this Agreement shall affect or diminish the liability of the Vendor in respect of any written reply given by the Vendor's Solicitors on its behalf to the Purchaser's Solicitors in respect of written enquiries regarding the Properties.

(6) The Properties are sold subject to the National Conditions of Sale (20th Edition) insofar as the latter are not inconsistent with or varied by the terms and conditions of this Agreement and are applicable to a sale by private treaty.

(7) If any necessary licence in terms satisfactory to the Purchaser has not been obtained in respect of any of the Properties from a relevant reversioner prior to the Completion Date the Purchaser may (but shall not be obliged to) complete the sale and purchase contemplated by this Agreement excluding the sale of the relevant Property and in respect of any of such Property or Properties the following provisions shall apply:

(a) the Vendor shall use all reasonable endeavours to obtain any such licences as soon as practicable following Completion and if reasonably required by the Purchaser (and at the Vendor's expense) will make an application:

(i) to the relevant reversioner for a licence to underlet the Property on terms as near as possible to those contained in the relevant existing lease (but in any event so that the rents reserved shall be at the same rate in so far as permitted by the terms of such lease); or

(ii) to the relevant Court for a declaration that the reversioner is unreasonably withholding consent to any such assignment;

the Purchaser shall supply such information and references [and such security (whether by way of guarantee or otherwise)] as may reasonably be required of it to satisfy any reversioner that licence to assign or underlet should be granted;

(b) Unless and until the Property shall have been assigned, the Vendor shall hold its interest therein upon trust for the Purchaser and the Purchaser shall have occupation of the same and on behalf of the Vendor (at the Purchaser's expense) perform all the obligations of the Vendor thereunder arising after Completion and indemnify the Vendor against all liability (and all costs reasonably incurred by the Vendor in connection therewith) which may be incurred by the Vendor as a result of any failure by the Purchaser after Completion to perform or comply with any such obligation of the Vendor;

(c) If a reversioner's licence is not granted within six months after Completion either to an assignment (or where requested by the Purchaser) an underlease then the Purchaser shall be entitled (but not obliged) by written notice to rescind this Agreement so far only as it concerns the sale of the Property affected;

(d) If rescission occurs pursuant to paragraph (c) above the Purchaser shall vacate the relevant Property as soon as reasonably practicable but in any event no later than 90 days of the Vendor serving written notice on the Purchaser to vacate whereupon the remainder of the provisions of this Agreement as far as they relate to the assignment or underletting of such Property shall cease to be of effect and the Vendor shall on the date that the Purchaser vacates the Property repay to the Purchaser that part of the consideration attributed to the Property (with interest calculated from the Completion Date to the date of payment both dates inclusive) and shall compensate the Purchaser for all damage and loss incurred by the failure of the Vendor successfully to assign or underlet such property.

SCHEDULE 6   PENSION PROVISIONS

1   DEFINITIONS
In this Schedule the following words and expressions shall have the following meanings respectively:

'Actuary's Letter'	the letter dated [ ] from the Vendor's Actuary to the Purchaser's Actuary a copy of which is attached to this Schedule;
'Adjusted Transfer Value'	an amount equal to the Transfer Value as adjusted from time to time in accordance with

'Adjusted Transfer Value'—*contd*	the Actuary's Letter in respect of all periods from Completion to the date of last payment of any monies due under this Schedule;
'Interim Period'	the period between the Completion Date and the Separation Date;
'Payment Date'	such date as shall be agreed between the Vendor and the Purchaser falling on or after the Separation Date or, in default of agreement, the date which is one month after the Transfer Value is agreed by the Purchaser's Actuary in accordance with paragraph 4 of this Schedule;
'Purchaser's Actuary'	[ ] or such other actuary as the Purchaser may from time to time appoint for the purpose of this Schedule;
'Purchaser's Scheme'	the retirement benefits scheme nominated or to be established by or at the instance of the Purchaser in accordance with paragraph 3 of this Schedule;
'Relevant Employees'	those employees of the Company who are active members of the Vendor's Scheme on the Completion Date;
'Separation Date'	[ ] 199[ ] or such other date as the Purchaser and the Vendor shall agree in writing or the Inland Revenue shall require for the cessation of the Purchaser's participation in the Vendor's Scheme;
'Transferring Employees'	those of the Relevant Employees who join the Purchaser's Scheme with effect from the Separation Date by accepting the offer of membership referred to in paragraph 3 of this Schedule and consent in writing to a payment or transfer from the Vendor's Scheme to the Purchaser's Scheme in respect of their benefits under the Vendor's Scheme;
'Transfer Value'	such amount as the Vendor's Actuary shall calculate in accordance with the actuarial methods and assumptions set out in the Actuary's Letter as representing the values of the interests of the Transferring Employees in the Vendor's Scheme at the Separation Date and as is agreed by the Purchaser's Actuary in accordance with paragraph 4 of this Schedule;
'Vendor's Actuary'	[ ] or such other actuary as the Vendor may from time to time appoint for the purpose of this Schedule;
'Vendor's Schemes'	the [ ] pensions schemes operated by the Vendor and in which the Transferring Employees participate.

2 INTERIM PERIOD

2.1 The Vendor undertakes to the Purchaser to procure that throughout the Interim Period:

    (a) subject to the approval of the Inland Revenue and if appropriate the Occupational Board (which the Vendor hereby undertakes to procure) and to the trustees of the Vendor's Scheme and the Purchaser executing a deed of adherence in agreed terms, the Purchaser shall participate in the Vendor's Scheme in respect of the Relevant Employees;

    (b) without the prior written approval of the Purchaser the Vendor will not amend or terminate or consent to the amendment or termination of any of the provisions of the Vendor's Scheme in respect of the Relevant Employees and shall procure that no power or discretion is exercised under the Vendor's Scheme which affects any of the benefits payable to or in respect of the Transferring Employees;

    (c) the Purchaser is not required to make any payment to or in respect of the Vendor's Scheme except that specified in paragraph 2.2 of this Schedule.

2.2 The Purchaser shall pay to the trustees of the Vendor's Scheme the contributions due under the rules of the Vendor's Scheme during the Interim Period by and in respect of the Relevant Employees who have not opted out of the Vendor's Scheme and who remain in the Purchaser's employment and at the annual rate of [   ].

2.3 The Vendor and the Purchaser undertake to each other to use all reasonable endeavours to procure that such of the Relevant Employees as are in contracted-out employment (within the meaning of the Social Security Pensions Act 1975) by reference to the Vendor's Scheme at the Completion Date shall continue to be in contracted-out employment by reference to the Vendor's Scheme during the Interim Period.

2.4 The Vendor and the Purchaser shall give all such consents and execute all such documents in their power as may be required to give effect to this paragraph 2.

3 PURCHASER'S SCHEME

3.1 On or before the Separation Date the Purchaser shall nominate or procure the nomination of a retirement benefits scheme which is or is capable of being an exempt approved scheme under Chapter I of Part XIV of the Income and Corporation Taxes Act 1988 [and which is a contracted-out scheme (as defined in the Social Security Pensions Act 1975)].

3.2 The Purchaser shall procure that such of the Relevant Employees as have not ceased to be in the employment of the Purchaser or opted out of the Vendor's Scheme or attained the normal pension age under either the Purchaser's Scheme or the Vendor's Scheme at the Separation Date will be offered membership of the Purchaser's Scheme with effect from that date on terms substantially no less favourable than those currently applicable to the Relevant Employees under the Vendor's Scheme.

4 DETERMINATION OF TRANSFER AMOUNT

4.1 Immediately after the Separation Date, the Vendor shall procure that the Vendor's Actuary calculates the Transfer Amount and submits his findings in writing to the Purchaser's Actuary for verification and agreement. If within 30 Working Days from the submission by the Vendor's Actuary of its findings the Purchaser's Actuary is unable to agree the Transfer Amount as determined by the Vendor's Actuary the matter shall be referred to an independent actuary pursuant to paragraph 7 of this Schedule.

4.2 The Vendor shall use its best endeavours to procure that all such information as the Purchaser's Actuary may reasonably request for the purpose of verifying and agreeing the Transfer Amount shall be made available to the Purchaser's Actuary and that all such information shall to the best of the Vendor's knowledge and belief be true and complete.

5 PAYMENT OF TRANSFER AMOUNT AND ADJUSTED TRANSFER AMOUNT

5.1 The Vendor shall use its best endeavours to procure that the trustees of the Vendor's Scheme make a payment to the trustees of the Purchaser's Scheme equal to the Adjusted Transfer Value on the Payment Date.

5.2 If on the Payment Date the sum actually transferred from the Vendor's Scheme to the Purchaser's Scheme in respect of the Transferring Employees is less than the Adjusted Transfer Value (including the possibility that no payment whatsoever is made by the trustees of the Vendor's Scheme), the Vendor shall pay to the Purchaser forthwith as an adjustment to the Consideration the difference in cash between the amount actually paid and the Adjusted Transfer Value.

5.3 All payments under this paragraph shall be made in cash unless the trustees of the Purchaser's Scheme shall agree otherwise.

6 ADDITIONAL VOLUNTARY CONTRIBUTIONS

6.1 For the purpose of determining the Transfer Value any additional voluntary contributions made by the Transferring Employees to the Vendor's Scheme together with the accrued investment return thereon shall be disregarded.

6.2 The Vendor shall use its best endeavours to procure that on the Payment Date the trustees of the Vendor's Scheme shall pay or transfer to the trustees of the Purchaser's Scheme in addition to the Transfer Value any sums or policies which the Vendor's Actuary determines as at the Payment Date to relate to the additional voluntary contributions paid by the Transferring Employees to the Vendor's Scheme.

7 DISPUTES

Any dispute between the Vendor and the Purchaser or the Vendor's Actuary and the Purchaser's Actuary concerning the calculation of the Transfer Value in accordance with the Actuary's Letter or any other matter of an actuarial nature shall, in the absence of agreement between them, be referred to an independent actuary agreed by the Vendor and the Purchaser or, failing such agreement within ten Working Days of one party calling upon the other in writing so to agree, appointed by the President for the time being of the Institute of Actuaries. Any such independent actuary shall reach his decision on the basis of the provisions of this Schedule and the Actuary's Letter and shall act as an expert and not as an arbitrator and his decision shall (in the absence of manifest error) be final and binding upon the Vendor and the Purchaser. The charges and expenses of the independent actuary in respect of any such reference shall be borne equally by the Vendor and the Purchaser.

SCHEDULE 7   MOTOR VEHICLES

Vehicle Manufacturer   Model   Registration No   Year of Purchase   User

Appendix IV

STANDARD DISCLOSURE LETTER

[letterhead of the Vendor or Vendor's solicitor]

Dated [   ] 19[   ]

The Directors
[Purchaser]
[Registered Office of the Purchaser]

Dear Sirs
Disclosure Letter

1   Introduction
1.1   This letter together with all the documents annexed hereto or delivered
herewith and which are deemed to be incorporated herein, is the
Disclosure Letter as referred to in clauses 1.1 and 13.4 of the asset sale
agreement (the 'Sale Agreement') entered into today between [us] [you
and our client [the 'Vendor']] relating to the sale and purchase of
[   ].
1.2   Unless the context otherwise requires, the words and expressions used
in this Disclosure Letter shall bear the same meanings as are assigned to
them in the Sale Agreement and the interpretation provisions in clause 1
of the Sale Agreement shall apply to this Disclosure Letter in the same
manner as they apply to the Sale Agreement.
1.3   [This Disclosure Letter is written by the Vendor's solicitors on behalf of
and under the instructions of the Vendor and no liability is accepted by
the Vendor's solicitors as to the accuracy of any information contained
in or referred to in this Disclosure Letter.]

2   General disclosures
2.1   This Disclosure Letter shall be deemed to include, and there are hereby
incorporated into it by reference and as being generally disclosed, the
following:

(a) the contents of and all facts ascertainable from all documents delivered with this Disclosure Letter;

(b) all matters contained or referred to in the Sale Agreement and any documents expressed in the Sale Agreement to be in agreed terms;

(c) all information and all documents available from a search of the public files maintained by the Registrar of Companies in respect of the Vendor on [   ] 19 [   ];

(d) the statutory registers and books and records of the Vendor;

(e) all matters which are or would be revealed by a physical inspection of the properties;

(f) all information and all documents available to public inspection at the Trade Marks Registry;

(g) all information and all documents available from a search of HM Land Registry, the Land Charges Registry and all local authorities in relation to the properties;

(h) the contents of all correspondence passing between the Vendor's solicitors and Purchaser's solicitors in connection with the negotiation and completion of the Sale Agreement. [NB Consider extending to correspondence between actuaries, accountants, surveyors etc]; and

(i) [Consider including any relevant reports by surveyors, accountants, actuaries, etc]

3 Special disclosures

3.1 Without prejudice to the generality of the foregoing we disclose the matters set out below. For ease of reference only the paragraph numbers below refer to the paragraphs so numbered in Schedule 2 to the Standard Sale Agreement. Each paragraph below shall be deemed to have been disclosed in relation to every provision in the Sale Agreement to which they relate.

A [   ]
B [   ]
C [   ]

Yours faithfully

_____

For and on behalf of
[Vendor]

Endorsement to be printed on copy

We acknowledge receipt of the Disclosure Letter and the documents referred to in it, a copy of which is set out above.

_____

For and on behalf of
[Purchaser]

Appendix V

5.—(1) Subject to paragraph (2) below there shall be treated as neither a supply of goods nor a supply of services the following supplies by a person of assets of his business:

   (a) their supply to a person to whom he transfers his business as a going concern where:
      (i) the assets are to be used by the transferee in carrying on the same kind of business, whether or not as part of any existing business, as carried on by the transferor, and
      (ii) in a case where the transferor is a taxable person, the transferee is already, or immediately becomes as a result of the transfer, a taxable person or a person defined as such in section 2(2) of the Manx Act;

   (b) their supply to a person to whom he transfers part of his business as a going concern where:
      (i) that part is capable of separate operation;
      (ii) the assets are to be used by the transferee in carrying on the same kind of business, whether or not as part of any existing business, as carried on by the transferor in relation to that part, and
      (iii) in a case where the transferor is a taxable person, the transferee is already, or immediately becomes as a result of the transfer, a taxable person or a person defined as such in section 2(2) of the Manx Act.

   (2) A supply of assets shall not be treated as neither a supply of goods nor a supply of services by virtue of paragraph (1) above to the extent that it consists of:

   (a) a grant which would, but for an election which the transferor has made, fall within item 1 of Group 1 of Schedule 6 to the Value Added Tax Act 1983; or

   (b) a grant of a fee simple which falls within (a) of item 1 of Group 1 of Schedule 6 to the Value Added Tax Act 1983,

unless the transferee has made an election in relation to the land concerned which has effect on the relevant date and has given any written notification of the election required by paragraph 3(6) of the Schedule 6A to the Value Added Tax Act 1983 no later than the relevant date.

(3) In paragraph (2) in this article—

'election' means an election having effect under paragraph 2 of Schedule 6A to the Value Added Tax Act 1983;

'relevant date' means the date upon which the grant would have been treated as having been made or, if there is more than one such date, the earliest of them;

'transferor' and 'transferee' include a relevant associate of either respectively as defined in paragraph 3(8) of Schedule 6A to the Value Added Tax Act 1983.

(4) There shall be treated as neither a supply of goods nor a supply of services the assignment by an owner of goods comprised in a hire-purchase or conditional sale agreement of his rights and interests thereunder, and the goods comprised therein, to a bank or other financial institution.

Appendix VI

REGULATION 5 OF THE TRANSFER OF UNDERTAKINGS (PROTECTION OF EMPLOYMENT) REGULATIONS 1981

5.—(1) A relevant transfer shall not operate so as to terminate the contract of employment of any person employed by the transferor in the undertaking or part transferred but any such contract which would otherwise have been terminated by the transfer shall have effect after the transfer as if originally made between the person so employed and the transferee.

(2) Without prejudice to paragraph (1) above, on the completion of a relevant transfer:

    (a) all the transferor's rights, powers, duties and liabilities under or in connection with any such contract, shall be transferred by virture of this regulation to the transferee; and

    (b) anything done before the transfer is completed by or in relation to the transferor in respect of that contract or a person employed in that undertaking or part shall be deemed to have been done by or in relation to the transferee.

(3) Any reference in paragraph (1) or (2) above to a person employed in an undertaking or part of one transferred by a relevant transfer is a reference to a person so employed immediately before the transfer, including, where the transfer is effected by a series of two or more transactions, a person so employed immediately before any of those transactions.

(4) Paragraph (2) above shall not transfer or otherwise affect the liability of any person to be prosecuted for, convicted of and sentenced for any offence.

(5) Paragraph (1) above is without prejudice to any right of an employee arising apart from these regulations to terminate his contract of employment without notice if a substantial change is made in his working conditions to his detriment; but no right shall arise by reason only that, under that paragraph, the identity of his employer changes unless the employee shows that, in all the circumstances, the change is a significant change and is to his detriment.

Index